The City at Its Limits

The City at Its Limits

Taboo, Transgression, and Urban Renewal in Lima

DANIELLA GANDOLFO

The University of Chicago Press   Chicago and London

DANIELLA GANDOLFO is assistant professor of anthropology at Wesleyan University.

The University of Chicago Press, Chicago 60637
The University of Chicago Press, Ltd., London
© 2009 by The University of Chicago
All rights reserved. Published 2009
Printed in the United States of America

18 17 16 15 14 13 12 11 10 09   1 2 3 4 5

ISBN-13: 978-0-226-28097-4 (cloth)
ISBN-10: 0-226-28097-7 (cloth)
ISBN-13: 978-0-226-28098-1 (paper)
ISBN-10: 0-226-28098-5 (paper)

Library of Congress Cataloging-in-Publication Data
Gandolfo, Daniella.
       The city at its limits: taboo, transgression, and urban renewal
   in Lima / Daniella Gandolfo.
          p.   cm.
       Includes bibliographical references and index.
       ISBN-13: 978-0-226-28097-4 (cloth: alk. paper)
       ISBN-10: 0-226-28097-7 (cloth: alk. paper)
       ISBN-13: 978-0-226-28098-1 (pbk.: alk. paper)
       ISBN-10: 0-226-28098-5 (pbk.: alk. paper)   1. Lima (Peru)—
       Social conditions—20th century.   2. Lima (Peru)—Social
       life and customs—20th century.   3. Urban renewal—Peru—
       Lima.   I. Title.
   HN350.L5G36   2009
   306.0985′2509049—dc22   2008034276

♾ The paper used in this publication meets the minimum require-
ments of the American National Standard for Information Sciences—
Permanence of Paper for Printed Library Materials, ANSI Z39.48-1992.

A thing is what it is, only in and by reason of its limit. We cannot therefore regard the limit as only external to being which is then and there. It rather goes through and through the whole of such existence. GEORG HEGEL, *ENCYCLOPEDIA OF PHILOSOPHICAL SCIENCES*

Contents

Preface

In June 1996, during a research stay in Lima, an anthropologist friend of mine and I met one morning for breakfast at El Haití in Miraflores. I was sitting at my usual table in the back, the first coils of cigarette smoke rising and beginning to cloud the air, when he walked into the café. As he put down his backpack to join me, he casually tossed over the table that day's issue of *La República*—a Lima newspaper of left-leaning politics and one of the very few that hadn't buckled under the threats of Alberto Fujimori's autocratic regime. The front page carried the picture of an old woman, her hair disheveled and her torso naked, as she trod the Plaza de Armas protesting the dissolution of the city's cleaning agency with which she and about seven hundred other women had held jobs as street sweepers.[1] Surrounding her were other women and several young men with wooden sticks and fists up in the air. Since most workers' unions had been decimated during the early Fujimori years, the street sweepers' protest was one of only a handful of labor demonstrations that year and the first one (in a string of protests that continues to this day) to demand the reversal of the government's privatization program, which had been in full swing since 1993.

The woman's act of stripping—shocking in a social environment where public nudity of the breasts, particularly by older women, is unusual in the extreme—had a subtle but steady ripple effect, the latest wave of which could be said to be this book. From what I knew then, no one in Peru had ever protested in this fashion. Her nudity didn't evoke some customary form of dissent or an established "technique" of protest intended to produce a result that would instill some obvious sense to it. She disrobed abruptly and wandered half-naked in the crowd, in the fine but relentless cold winter drizzle, drawing glances and vehemently repelling them, pulling the crowd toward her and then brusquely warding it off, as the space around her seemed to fill with a force both magnetic and impenetrable that, transmuted onto the morning's front page, even I could feel.

As I held the newspaper in my hands, I uselessly sought the terms with which to explain her actions to myself. From the article and the images that came with it, I attempted to *ex-plain*, which is to say, to unfold and make plain, flat, clear of wrinkles or obscurities the event of her nudity, which included my reaction to it at that very moment. Her thin and naked arms dangled to the sides, her breasts hung heavily, her abdomen was round and soft, in striking contrast to the rigidity of the riot police, which in one of the images appear to have retreated to the side streets. But I had no way to know what she thought or felt as she moved through the plaza, no way to unravel from the images or the text the being or the character of an intention, of a directing force behind the one wielded by her naked body, at once saturated with and precluding meaning.

Across the street from El Haití, a thick spout of water shot up from the fountain at the center of the Rotunda of Miraflores, rising in a liquid parabola above the scattered heads in the café's outdoor space. After more than a decade collecting dry leaves and dust, the ornamental water jet was working again. On the other side of it and straight down Avenida Arequipa was Lima's old city center; the narrow, decaying streets adjacent to the Plaza de Armas were loud and made impassable by the same street sweepers, as hundreds of them converged there for the third consecutive day to protest the privatization of the city's cleaning services.

The research goals I had set for myself at the time were, in a way, very simple. Six months earlier, in January 1996, Alberto Andrade, a *criollo* small-business impresario, had taken office as mayor of Metropolitan Lima and launched an aggressive campaign of urban renewal of the city center, the impoverished, densely populated cluster of colonial-era districts known today as El Cercado.[2] I had become intrigued by the mayor's aesthetic vision for that part of the city, which was expressed in publicity ads and official documents as the "recuperation" of Lima's lost splendor, and so had spent my first days back walking around the center, taking stock of several dramatic signs of change: Entire "informal" markets were gone, such as the one that, almost from sidewalk to sidewalk, had occupied Jirón Lampa for decades. La Cachina, an intersection of streets that, for as long as I could remember, had been a vibrant market for stolen goods, was also gone, as was the legion of pickpockets, beggars, prostitutes, and *pirañitas* (street children) that used to hover about the market's steady stream of shoppers. The transit of microbuses and *combis* ("informal" public transportation minivans) had been prohibited within the Damero de Pizarro, the city's sixteenth-century grid of streets, whose names, in turn, had reverted to those used in pre-Independence times.[3] And in block after block, groups of police officers in riot gear stood guard against the ambulant vendors who had threatened to return and take over the streets again. Bright yellow billboards and banners announced the new mayor's renewal efforts with the enigmatic phrase: *Lima, como era antes* (Lima, the way it once was).

As I walked along the worn, awkwardly quiet, gutted-out streets, I wondered what the exact historical referent to the mayor's express wish was. What specific point in time in the relatively short history of the city did Andrade's wistful motto refer to? "Lima, the way it once was." But once when? Was it in the 1960s, before General Juan Velasco's nationalist project ultimately failed to vindicate indigenous peasants as a class, paving the way for increased migration and the consolidation of today's urban "informal" economy? Was it during the so-called golden 1920s and '30s, before the first waves of city-ward migration led to the exodus of the *criollo* bourgeoisie from the city center? Was it before the Pacific War (1879–83) and the violent devastation of the city by Chilean troops? Or perhaps during the guano boom of the 1850s and '60s? Was it Lima before Independence (1821), the vice-regal, courtly City of Kings? Or during the Hapsburg days, before the Bourbon's fragmentation of Spain's possessions in South America in the eighteenth century led to Lima's relegation as imperial head city? Or was it in the 1600s, at the summit of the city's baroque refinement, before the earthquake of 1687 razed it to the ground? Or was it Lima after the 1571 construction of the walled-off *pueblo de indios* of Santiago to separately house the city's indigenous servants and map onto the urban landscape Lima's ideal of social hierarchy, whose apex was physically denoted at the city center by the main square?

I had been keenly considering these questions, getting ready to spend some long hours studying the history of Lima at the old municipal library, when *La República*'s front page came to rest on my table that morning at El Haití. Then, it was as if the entire course of Lima's 460-year history had been abruptly arrested in the street sweeper's image, turned inside out and eviscerated into a moment of the city's prehistory. When the old woman bared herself in the main plaza, right at the center of the city center, she tapped into and upset a deeply embedded regime of law lurking beyond the law, breaking through the real limits: the social, racial, and sexual boundaries that ground the order and the hierarchy that Andrade was so invested in "recuperating." These limits are the measure and the content of what I will here call "taboo" to refer to the complex regimen of prohibitions that human beings and societies put in place to create a sense of propriety and order by imposing a distance between themselves and the things and behaviors that they deem to be less than human, the violence and the excess they associate with the dark, abyssal world of their own renounced animality. "The truth of taboos," writes Georges Bataille, "is the key to our human attitude."[4] It is the limit and the link between the realm of what is "properly human" and the realm of what Bataille calls "social heterogeneity" to designate those objects, persons, and behaviors that proper humanity struggles to ward off and exclude from social life but is never able to completely do away with.

On the days following the street sweepers' protests, the only government official that publicly remarked on the nudity noted with indignation that the protesters were "mothers," insinuating, it seems to me, that the woman's transgression had made the entire group of workers lapse from their mere condition of old women, of discharged street sweepers and rag-pickers, down across forbidden limits toward something even lower, more debasing, more violent and disturbing as is an old mother exposing herself publicly.[5] By the same token, to my knowledge *La República* was the only newspaper to ever report on the nudity, which in itself was an eloquent indicator of the complex relation between transgression and language, whereby even to report on such an event as the woman's nakedness was, in a sense, to partake of its indecency, to share in the horror and the shame that had coursed through the main plaza that day, wrenching Andrade's colonialist dream-image of the city out of itself.

In retrospect, the moment I laid my eyes on the image of the street sweeper, the still forming idea I had for an ethnography of Lima took a drastic and irrevocable turn. The mayor's Arcadian vision of the city ceased to be the direct or the exclusive object of my research. Instead, his measures of beautification, of social cleansing and containment, became a magnifying glass through which I could see in action the impetuous, dialectical play of taboo and transgression as a constitutive element of social life. In my subsequent visits to Lima, while I furthered my inquiry into Andrade's urban renewal project, I often felt compelled to direct my attention to similar rupture events. Rather than dismiss them as irrelevant or merely disruptive, I was driven to focus on and immerse myself in those unexpected happenings that threw up for grabs much of what I thought I understood of the culture, the politics, and the history of my native Lima and that, in contradistinction, offered me a glimpse of the city's culture, politics, and history *at their limits*.

The essays and diaries that make up this book are a rendering of that fleeting glimpse. The introduction, called "Taboo," situates its contents in the very unique social and political context of late 1990s and early 2000s Lima, the period before and after the downfall of Fujimori's regime, when Andrade's impulse to order and cleanse the city center coexisted with unprecedented central government corruption. The introduction also aims to position this text within what could be called the anthropology of home, a form of inquiry that, as I have learned from the work of José María Arguedas, brings us closest to what is socially and culturally most familiar, most intimate and real, by critically estranging it from us, by treating it as "other," as fiction. "To describe the life of those villages," Arguedas wrote of the labor of rendering his early home life, "to describe it in such a way that its pulse . . . would beat against the readers' conscience like a river," we must rely on "the possibility, the necessity of an absolute act of creation."[6]

This process of estrangement began for me with my return to Lima after some years of absence when, as I encountered the city anew, I became aware that the distance had radically altered my perception of it. It was as though my leaving Lima and my coming back to it years later had broken the spell of habit and made what should have seemed familiar and intelligible about life in the city take on complex and unsettling new meanings. In a cognitive reversal that resembled Brecht's V-effect, the physical and social environment into which I was born, the geographic limits and markers that regimented social relations in Lima and that I had grown up to perceive as natural, as simply "given," now struck me as anything but natural or given and only the product of a history of oppression, of racial and class conflict, of which Lima had been the center for over two hundred years. The quality of my knowing of the city would be altered forever. Only, unlike Brecht's dramatic technique, my new awareness of the contingent character of those social boundaries would in no way make the hold they had on me any less mystifying, any less formidable or overpowering.

The three essay sections called "Beauty," "Filth," and "Nakedness" deal with the content and the wildly varied forms assumed by those limits, which I examine through the lens of taboo because of their power to structure social relations by separating individuals and groups and at the same time by keeping them in constant interaction, in a perpetual relation of mutual (self-)definition. In these essays, the concept of taboo is traced theoretically and historically to show that social interdictions are so tightly and invisibly woven into prevalent ideas of class, race, gender, and sex that they have become themselves the justification for their own existence. In contrast to structuralism's emphasis on taboo as merely separation, as the expulsion of what doesn't neatly fit into our idea of social order, these essays aim to show that the boundaries we create to structure our social worlds into genders, classes, and races as well as into hierarchies of appropriate behaviors also ensure that we maintain an interest in their de-structuring, so to speak, by keeping an active relationship with what we reject or expel from our lives because of its "lowly" character. As with Andrade's attempts at repressing what did not conform to his understanding of beauty, order, and efficiency, Lima's history teaches us that, even in its allegedly glorious past, the exclusion of the socially heterogeneous was never total, despite great efforts and appearances. The transgression of limits is not something society seeks to avoid by imposing and enforcing taboos; being dialectically inextricable from taboo, transgression, or at least the threat of it, ensures that we remain engaged with what lies beyond the prohibition, exceeding it but not destroying it. Bataille writes, "Transgression does not deny the taboo but transcends it and completes it."[7]

In the four interlocking diary sections, the regular unfolding of the everyday in Lima, the *durée* of my fieldwork experience during my various stays, is taken out of its anticipated course by actions or events that are heterogeneous to what seem to be the conventions and values that sustain Lima's society. Because I had no solid or clearly identifiable object on which I could ground my thoughts on taboo, much of my attention in these diaries is placed on the effects produced by these irruptions of heterogeneous being, whose momentary reality Bataille describes as a force or shock, as "a charge [or] a value passing from one object to another in a more or less abstract fashion, *almost* as if the change were taking place not in the world of objects but only in the judgments of the subject."[8] This "abstractness" is at the heart of what most intrigued Bataille about taboo and transgression: The paradoxical fact that while we often become conscious of a taboo only at the moment of its transgression, the impact of this breach is wholly dependent on its ability to bypass language and thought. The diary narratives in this book thus seek not to capture (which we could never) but to perform a sense of immediacy, of closeness to the moment, of raw experience—in other words, they seek to perform the everyday rigidities, risks, and volatilities of the experience of social difference in a place like Lima.

These diaries are therefore a fiction, in Arguedas's sense, which is also the Geertzian sense of "'something made,' 'something fashioned'—the original meaning of *fictiō*,"[9] an attempt at acknowledging and subverting the limits imposed on us by language and at drawing attention to the creative process of ethnographic writing and critical thought. As such, they expound an important aspect of my fieldwork method since my interest in the dialectic of taboo and transgression required that in the course of a regular day I remain attentive to those unpredictable instances in which I could witness the liberation of a momentary "force" or "charge." But since this yielded no concrete and lasting entity on which to focus or to systematically examine, the subject of my research was, in itself, also the undermining of all method. For in dealing with the character and social power of heterogeneous being, as Bataille explains, there is nothing beyond those special and ungraspable moments that appear to contain it all. There is no obvious beginning or end. There is no infallible conceptual apparatus or language and no comprehensive or immutable set of rules.

There is only a broken taboo.

ONE

Introduction: Taboo

The month I graduated from college, counting only on a rough command of English and a Ford Foundation one-year fellowship to study at the University of Texas, I left Lima. I couldn't have known it then, since that's not what I had intended, but I would not set foot back there for several years. When I did, on the day before the last possible extension of my student visa expired, Alberto Fujimori was already in power. The city I had left, surrounded on all sides by a rapidly advancing Sendero Luminoso (Shining Path), was radically transformed. In September 1992, a small intelligence unit of the national antiterrorism police had caught the rebel group's enigmatic leader, Abimael Guzmán, in one of his Lima hideouts. While news of the capture had prompted a furious burst of retaliatory attacks, this was short-lived and followed by weeks and months of dwindling violence that eventually gave way to days of restored stillness. To everyone's astonished disbelief, even the government's, with that one blow the twelve-year-old insurgent movement appeared to have irreparably crumbled like a flimsy house of cards.

When I arrived in Lima, in May 1994, the general mood was of euphoria. Imported vehicles had flooded the streets, high-rise buildings rose at breakneck speed, and while weekly bombings of electric towers in the outskirts of the city had for years kept entire neighborhoods in a recurrent state of darkness, the streets now seemed to glitter in a continual parade of light. Businesses had opened or reopened their doors, invigorated by foreign capital that poured into the country with Peru's reinsertion in the international financial community after a long period of national debt repayments default. New shopping malls had sprouted all over the city, displaying fancy neon signs and windows full of colorful and unusual merchandise. Old and new squatter settlements on the hills surrounding the Rímac River valley, some of which had existed for decades without the most basic services, were now dotted with huge public school buildings and crisscrossed with new sewer systems, networks of paved roads, and electric cabling. Throughout the city, even the air, stubbornly wet and gray, had been brought alive with advertisement billboards from which the glamorous fair-skinned faces of expensive Chilean or Argentine models looked down with seductive smiles. For a whole generation of *Limeños*, those who like me were coming of age in 1980—the year of democratic elections after twelve years of military rule and, incidentally, the year of Sendero's first attack in Ayacucho—this unexpected interlude of peace and relative bonanza was unprecedented.

The days that led to my departure from Texas were, inexplicably to me then, mired in anxiety. I was only going back home, the place I had known best before, having scarcely traveled abroad as a young person. On the plane I cried myself to sleep and woke up six hours later to a bright sliver of sunlight filtering through a narrow opening in the window screen and suffusing the air around me with a golden glow. The flight attendants were rushing to pick up the used breakfast trays and ordering everyone to straighten up their seats for landing. The belly of the plane soon dipped into the dense bed of cloud that perennially hangs over Peru's central coast, reemerging some moments later inside Lima's dismal skies. Flying under this canopy of dark-gray vapor, it was as if we had gone from sunrise to nightfall in a matter of seconds.

I remember stepping out of the plane and feeling Lima's air, wet and heavy, quickly engulfing me in its slightly constricting solidity. As the passengers walked down the stairs, I stopped for a second and took in the setting in a single stroke: The stagnant layer of cloud, always overburdened but rainless; the cool, almost changeless temperature; the faintly saline taste of the air; the diffused white light of a clouded sun; the dry, lunar landscape framing the view in the horizon; and the voices of the airport workers down on the tarmac directing the passengers toward the arrival gate with an unmistakably *Limeño* inflexion. For that second it was as though the particles of colors and shapes, the familiar noises, textures, and smells were each moving toward me in linear projections that converged in me, as though I stood at or were myself their point of intersection. I hadn't realized until then to what extent Lima's landscape was a part of my memory of this city: Much more than just the setting against which my childhood had unfolded, it was the stuff of which I am myself made, the substance that connected me to this place. Walking around the plane to the arrival gate, I felt more sensitive than ever to those surroundings, aware of myself almost to the point of pain. I was back home, but somehow the flurry of sensorial impressions wasn't only bringing about the sparks of recognition that usually follow the reencounter with familiar things but also sharp and alienating pangs of strangeness.

Outside the airport building, a large waiting crowd had gathered. Through a glass window they watched alertly as their relatives inside tried their luck with a new, beefed-up customs police. In the multitude I recognized the thin, slightly hunched figure of my father, whom I had not seen since the day I left. Numbed by the emotion, we rode silently in his car on Avenida Faucett, headed south through stretches that seemed unchanged and through others that I hardly recognized. We went over the dry and spoiled bed of the Rímac River and drove along the western side of Carmen de la Legua, a small district created in the 1960s out of Lima's first slum, which dated back to the mid- and late 1800s when an early wave of highland immigrants and a group of refugees from the war-torn border with Chile settled on the south bank of the river along the railroad that linked the city with the sea port of El Callao.

The district limit of Carmen de la Legua was marked by a new stone sculpture of the Virgin and child and a new ornamental arch of cement that opened onto the district's lattice of narrow dirt roads and rough or unfinished brick structures. From the slightly elevated road, I could see the low buildings and streets stretch from the flood-prone slopes of the river, where newer immigrants live in *pueblos jóvenes* (shanty or "young" towns, also called *barriadas*) all the way to the now-abandoned railroad, on the other side of which the landscape turns into a bleak compound of fenced-in, run-down, polluting manufacturing plants. I had driven along that section of Avenida Faucett and seen the district's borders from that same road countless times. But on that morning, Carmen de la Legua leapt out to me with a strange newness as I realized that it was one of those sections of the city that had tacitly been off-limits to me in the early part of my life, cloaked in a veil that spoke of poverty, crime, and even death. I had only a vague idea of what the district looked like inside, in its more impoverished northern section, from reports I had seen years ago on TV and in the newspapers deploring the construction of homes on the rims of the low canyon walls, which are periodically swept away by the swelled and muddy waters of the river during the rain season up in the Andes Mountains. The images in these reports were of shacks of thin wooden sticks and plywood overhanging the scarp, losing their foundations to erosion and tumbling down the slope—and the slope was covered with garbage and lush bushes that grew around makeshift sewer outlets, from which liquid waste trickled down to the river.

Of the rest of Carmen de la Legua I did not have a real notion since I had never gone in. And while on the day of my return the district looked unchanged for the most part, just as remote and impenetrable as before, in the bluish light of the early morning, through the gaping distance that separated me from it, Carmen de la Legua also looked startlingly new, brimming with an alluring force.

In time, I would discover that the city was peppered with places, from street corners and plazas to whole districts that, like Carmen de la Legua, would evoke the same mix of emotions in me: fascination and fear, desire and shame. I would realize that these spaces—along with the individuals, practices, and beliefs associated with them—were capable of arousing such uncertainty in me that I had long ago learned to negate them, to ostracize them from my life, to surround them with prohibitions and cast them into the realm of denied experience that is the realm of taboo. The social categories of race, gender, and class would appear to me in a radically different guise, as Lima's social structure, which was physically mapped onto the layout of the city since its foundation, now appeared to rise before me with outright objectivity and renewed authority to demarcate and signal the site of my fears and my desires. It would become obvious to me that what collectively or individually we *Limeños* refer to as our "identity" has in great measure been constructed in relation to these regions of denied experience, and that the process of coming of age in Lima, the very experience of adulthood, depends on our ability to acknowledge these spaces, to accept them, and then to become obdurate about them and oblivious to their subjective nature and their social derivation. My early life in the city would reveal itself as having been orchestrated around these pockets of life imputed with the threatening indeterminacy of radical otherness, because of which they tended to be surrounded with all sorts of limits and prohibitions.

In this and in my later stays in Lima, I decided to let the city reveal itself to me anew through these places and through the dense cosmos of ideas, meanings, and behaviors enshrouding them like a cloud. And it would be in relation to them and to the social character of the limits and prohibitions that constitute them—including the reality that the transgression of these limits brings forth—that the history of the city, as it has been lived, remembered, and forgotten, as it is lived, remembered, and forgotten every day, would become manifest to me, reverberating with a new intensity.

———

After some time visiting with family and friends, I moved to a small one-bedroom apartment I had rented for myself on the top story of a large but modest house right on the edge of the cliff overlooking the sea in the district of Chorrillos. The house belonged to Colonel Contreras, a retired army officer, father of Rafael, a college friend of mine. Colonel Contreras had bought this piece of land by the sea and built the house in stages, according to unpredictable swings in the family's budget, many years before the ocean-view realty fever of the early 1990s turned the waterfront of Miraflores, Barranco, and Chorrillos into a strip of modern and expensive condominium buildings. For years, old, large homes near the water, many of them mud-brick structures, came down to give way to tall cement buildings. Colonel Contreras received continual offers by real estate developers who coveted his well-located piece of land. But the colonel turned them all down.

The section of the house I rented was the most recent addition, and it stood out in the eclectic structure for the wide wood-frame windows, in contrast to the aluminum frames used in other parts of the house. The main entrance gave onto Avenida Chorrillos, but most windows in the house faced the ocean, opposite the street, where beyond a narrow strip of grass and a tall hedge on the border of the cliff the earth plunged down a deep, narrow ravine. Down below, the Circuito de Playas freeway ran north-south along the city's beaches, separating the foot of the cliff from the water by several meters. But somehow, despite the height and the noisy road below, the sound of breaking waves would travel up the gorge, bouncing up the rocky walls, and could be heard, magnified, in every room of the house.

Across the hallway from my apartment, through a door that I rarely used, was the bedroom of the colonel and his wife. Next to them, in Rafael's old bedroom, slept Doña Esperanza, the colonel's mother. His eldest daughter, Carola, shared an attic room with her own six-year-old daughter, Cecilia. And Lily, the family's live-in maid, occupied a room on the first floor next to the kitchen. My apartment also had a separate entrance through the backyard, where there was a *puerta falsa* (or "faux door," a discreet side entry traditionally built for servants). This slender, nondescript door opened up to the patio, where I often found Doña

Esperanza stooping over the cement sink, hand-washing the shirts and pants of her son, as Cecilia roamed about and Lily worked in the kitchen. Behind a curtain of drying clothes that hung across the width of the patio was a spiral stairway that led to my apartment.

Except for the calls I had to make or receive on their kitchen phone, which would bring me to visit with the colonel and his family with certain frequency, I had a fairly independent existence the months I lived in that house. I had a bedroom, a bathroom, and a tiny study, where I kept an electric two-burner stove on which I made simple meals. Often when I cooked or sat at my desk, I was drawn to the voices in the kitchen or patio as they reached my study in fragments of conversations that let me, to varying degrees of awareness on my part, into details of the colonel's personal life. I learned, for instance, that he had been affected by Fujimori's arbitrary handling of the armed forces, which had upset their long-standing system of promotions. When I moved into his house, it hadn't been long since the colonel had been "invited" to retire from his post; he was only in his fifties. But besides those casual visits in the kitchen and the snippets of information occasionally flying in through the window, when I was in the apartment, I worked at my desk mostly in silence, surrounded by windows that opened high onto the west side of the city and that offered a breathtaking view over the Pacific Ocean.

The city of Lima rests on a shelf of alluvial sediment, part of a glacial deposit that once cradled between two cordilleras, the Andes and a parallel Tertiary mountain chain that sunk into the Nazca fault line, off the coast of South America, several thousand years ago. As this old mountain chain slipped in between shifting tectonic plates, it tore and dragged along a portion of this glacial deposit, leaving traces of the fracture in a jagged escarpment along the continent's coastline. Looking at it from the shore in front of Lima, the cliff's bare face rises sharply near the edge of the water, ending on a plateau at about eighty meters above sea level where the city's seaside districts now lie. Lima's eight-kilometer coastland strip, called Costa Verde, follows this jagged wall of compacted sand and boulder rocks, which tend to trickle and collect down at the base of it, often rolling onto the freeway and blocking traffic, occasionally killing someone driving by. On its north end, the wall descends gradually to sea level, tapering off at the peninsula of La Punta ("the tip") in El Callao; on rare cloudless days I could see from my apartment in Chorrillos the pointy neck of land jutting out to the sea. On the south end, the cliff descends abruptly in Chorrillos behind a tall promontory called the Morro Solar, which also sticks out in the sea, forming a wide bay.

The Morro Solar, together with the islands of San Lorenzo and El Frontón, across from El Callao, and the beautiful islet of Peña Horadada (a small rocky formation that high-sea winds shaped into a hollow ring) are some of the few remaining signs of the dramatic geological readjustment that resulted in Lima's bizarre topography.[1]

The city, with its forty-three official districts, is thus sandwiched between the Andes Mountains on the east and the Pacific Ocean on the west. It is located halfway down a 2,000-kilometer strip of arid land that runs, briefly interrupted by narrow coastal valleys, from the desert of Sechura in northern Peru to the desert of Atacama, the driest in the world, in northern Chile. One of these valleys is formed by the Rímac River, which flows from the central Andes into the ocean near La Punta. The original Spanish city was built on the southern bank of the Rímac, twenty kilometers away from the ocean, in the foothills of the Andes, to protect it from pirate incursions. At the time of its foundation in January 1535 as the City of Kings, Lima counted seventy residents. Historians like to remark the fact that, in contrast to the Spanish city of Cuzco, which was built over a populous native urban center, Lima's first streets were laid out over the lands of a rural lord in a region inhabited by scattered, sparsely populated villas. The valley's hinterland, which today is mostly a rugged desert, used to be arable fields and fruit gardens watered by a pre-Hispanic system of canals that linked, through vast stretches of irrigated territory, the adjacent basins of the Chillón, Rímac, and Lurín rivers. Lima's Costa Verde, "green coast," took its name from the vine that grew spontaneously over the cliff's face with overflow water from the canals. In the present, no such green connection between the valleys exists, and the fertile hinterland has shrunk dramatically, as it yielded to fast-spreading desert dunes and the city's urban sprawl.

Lima's initial layout was a grid of 117 square blocks that radiated south out of an empty quadrangle, the Plaza Mayor, or main square, drawn about a hundred paces from the river and planned to be the seat of military, civilian, and religious authority. This grid of streets gradually grew to the south and east until 1687, when a twelve-kilometer wall was erected around it, presumably for military protection; the fortified wall was shaped like a spiked triangle, with the river as its base. For about two hundred years, Lima grew in density primarily within the confines of this stronghold until the last of its bastions came down in 1870 in an assertive modernization impulse that pushed urban life out to the periphery by means of Parisian-style grand avenues and boulevards.

Lima's population surpassed 100,000 inhabitants only in 1876.[2] And in spite of a brief decline in population in the aftermath of the Pacific War

(1879–83), the city grew steadily, though still moderately, through the 1920s. But in the 1930s, Lima underwent a demographic explosion, to the point that in the nine years between the censuses of 1931 and 1940, the city's population more than doubled. Mechanization in the already-ailing hacienda economy of the highlands combined with intensified urban industrialization, a drastic drop in agricultural exports due to the Great Depression, and a growing network of interprovincial roads led to a veritable exodus of peasants toward the mostly "white" or *criollo* coastal cities, most notably Lima.[3] In a little over fifty years, between 1940 and 1993, Lima's population and its territory grew about 1,000 percent, and, today, over 8 million people live in Lima, virtually a third of all Peruvians.[4]

The exponential increase in new, mostly indigenous or peasant, residents in Lima, along with the cultural, political, and aesthetic transformations that resulted from it, impressed the city's *criollo* bourgeoisie as an uncontainable overflow of people—a "desborde popular," as José Matos Mar put it in 1984.[5] Perhaps most critically, the overflow was spatial: first, from the rural highlands into the city center, where immigrants quickly occupied the vacated property of residents who fled en masse to neighborhoods in the south, including the seaside districts of Magdalena, Miraflores, and San Isidro, subdividing their homes into infinitely smaller family units, known as *tugurios* (tenements); then, beginning in the 1940s, from the saturated city center onto the arid slopes of adjacent hills, like the Cerros San Cosme, El Agustino, and San Cristóbal, and by means of land "invasions" onto the riverbanks and desert plains that surround the Rímac River valley, where they formed *barriadas*. Through the 1970s and '80s, waves of "invasions" pushed the city north and south in ever-sprawling shanty towns that reached deep into nearby ravines like the fingers of an outstretched hand.[6] These extensions of the city are known for their shape as *conos* (cones)—*cono norte*, *cono sur*, and, the newest, *cono este*. In 1981, it was estimated that a third of the city was made of *barriada* settlements.[7] Meanwhile, the *criollo* upper and middle classes kept moving south and east, now beyond Magdalena, Miraflores, and San Isidro, to suburban developments on the desert hills of the southeast, where, in recent years, their swimming pools and green lawns have met at the hilltop with the shanties' straw and tin shacks.

For Matos Mar, the massive, de facto land occupation of the *barriadas*, which he referred to as "the most important social phenomenon of the decade," signaled the start of a new era of contestation that brought about an "upsurge of the masses" ("ascenso de masas"), which through the following decades would irrupt with no sense of shame or decency ("sin pudor") to challenge every aspect of the legal and institutional apparatus that had, to one extent or another, regulated life in Lima since the establishment of the republic. Matos Mar's "desborde popular" thus went beyond a spatial overflow to encompass the ascent of unruly urban "masses" across the boundaries of the law and the established order, of that which was considered legitimate, official, or formal, to bring about the revolution in values, beliefs, norms of conduct, and lifestyles that produced what today is commonly referred to as the "culture of informality." This "culture," which for Matos Mar has effected a unique kind of modernization process, is characterized by its reliance on forms of economic behavior that blur the line between what is merely furtive and what is illegal or criminal and for its preference for transactions that are driven by family and personal, rather than institutional, relations.[8]

The ways and means of "informality" irreversibly reconfigured all sectors of the economy, from the manufacturing to the building to the service industries, impacting the areas of commerce and retail, transportation and public utilities (water, electricity, and sewage supplies), health and funeral services, public safety and justice (referred to as "justicia popular")—all these, in addition to the vast sector of domestic service, which predates the "desborde" but which grew into ever-new areas of private and personal service. Informality changed the face of formal education, of religion, and even of institutionalized politics, as all throughout the 1990s the oldest political parties saw their bases seriously eroded. With the rise of this new force, keenly inventive, irreverent, "pregnant with scandal," as Matos Mar put it, the city thus morphed into a thoroughly new entity, as the "formal" and official worlds of Lima recoiled in fear and disgust.

In 1957, at the peak of Lima's peripheral explosion, it was also Matos Mar, then a young researcher, who carried out the first systematic study of the *barriadas* of Lima in an attempt to shed light on what was then the fastest growing but most poorly understood form of urbanization in the city.[9] In this seminal sociological study, Matos Mar traced the development and composition of several *barriadas*, from their layout patterns (which he argued had formal similarities with towns and *caseríos* in the Andes) to the building materials used and the origin and occupation of their inhabitants, as the *barriadas* moved from "invasion" to semi-official barrios to districts. Against the widely held perception that the land seizures happened on impulse, led by frenzied crowds, Matos Mar set out to demonstrate that, as a rule, even in the most violent land occupations, a swath of territory had been identified ahead of time and the settlement's initial layout drafted in advance. Each *barriada*, he noted, was thought of from the outset as an autonomous urban center, with plots set aside for future schools, medical posts, police stations, and churches. But since the planning of these new neighborhoods was done in secrecy, often involving mafias dealing in land, and since they tended to appear overnight in unexpected places, the prevailing impression was of a spontaneous and dangerous onslaught of people. This, along with their constant transformation and their ambiguous legal status, which could go unresolved for decades, led many to think of the *barriadas* as an inscrutable phenomenon, one that posited, in Matos Mar's own words, a "challenge to [scientific] knowledge."[10]

After Matos Mar's work, many other social scientists became interested in the *barriadas*, noticing that one of the consequences of this form of urban expansion is that life in Lima has grown fragmented, increasingly transpiring within well-delimited coordinates of class and race that rarely overlap. Some of them have observed that for Lima's long-standing and better-off residents, the *barriadas* are enclosed by an "aura of mystery . . . , of fear of the unknown, of fetishism and deformation."[11] Speaking from the perspective of psychoanalysis, they have even noted that the city's brusque and steady growth along the periphery, what C. E. Paz Soldán had earlier referred to as Lima's "belt of primitiveness," has kept alive and in a way made real the specter that has haunted Lima since its foundation: the fantasies and anxieties of an "Indian" invasion.[12] But what the source and nature of this aura of fear and mystery are, too few of these social scientists have ventured to suggest, just like too few of them have remarked on the fact that for the residents of these *barriadas*, Lima's newer and most underprivileged inhabitants, a similar aura of mystery and untouchability envelopes the wealthier districts of the city, with their fenced-in houses, their manicured parks, and their fancy, sparkling-clean commercial strips.

An exception to this is a 1994 bachelor's thesis by Eduardo González, a sociology student from the Universidad Católica in Lima, who set out to examine the connections between the ways the city is imagined and talked about and the actual practices of regular *Limeños*.[13] He asked a group of students from the Católica to draw from memory a map of the city and then to label the different areas: beautiful or ugly, clean or dirty, safe or dangerous, fun or boring, dynamic or passive, and high, middle, or lower class. The resulting hand-drawn maps, which were astounding in their graphic eloquence, revealed the city as a place wildly intersected by uncrossable boundaries—a world of "parallel cities," as it were. From the inscriptions on them, it appeared that these boundaries generate an emotionally charged, frontier-like experience that students from all socioeconomic backgrounds seemed to feel relative to unfamiliar, class-distant areas of the city. The maps portrayed the downtown area as one of the city's most contested spaces. From them one can compose a picture of a place split into distinct zones that either brim over with power and beauty (such as the Plaza Mayor, the Presidential Palace, the baroque convents and churches); that allure and terrify with their dense, lively chaos of traffic and commerce (Avenida Tacna, the Central Market); or that are marked off, believed to be derelict or lost to decay, filth, poverty, and crime (the Plaza San Martín, the Rímac River boardwalk, and, for some, the entire center itself). In his analysis of the maps, González remarks that Lima's physical expansion has not translated into an expansion of people's urban experience. Instead, he argues that we *Limeños* "walk the streets . . . led by the hand by ghosts. Our fears and prejudices tell us which routes to take, which zones of the city to visit and which ones to avoid."[14] Life in the city, González states, takes place along separate "circuits of affectivity" that are kept apart from one another by "invisible walls" that, in turn, we each accept and justify through our fears, timidities, preferences, and tastes.

What González's and the other sociological studies hint at, although they never say explicitly, is that lodged at the heart of our social constructions of difference is a basic rule of avoidance, a prohibition of contact, functioning as something like a pivot between our ideas of race, class, and gender and the mass of feelings that underpins all relations defined by difference. At its most basic, I would like to define this prohibition with the same terms James Frazer used in 1898 to render the meaning of *taboo*—that puzzling but oddly practical Polynesian term, which had relatively recently arrived on the shores of England to be quickly adopted by the rule-obsessed Victorians. Breaking it down into its two components, *ta* ("to mark" in various Polynesian dialects) and *bu* (an adverb of intensity), Frazer determined the word to mean "marked thoroughly" or "with intensity." In so doing, he emphasized not just the enforced separation from ordinary existence of beings and things "marked" in such a way but also the strange and elusive power, the force of attraction and repulsion that their very severance from common life appears to charge them with.[15]

In this schematic but thought-provoking piece, Frazer affirmed a model of reality first formulated by W. Robertson Smith and later developed by Durkheim, in which the sacredness of beings and things is treated not as an objective quality but as a condition generated by separation, superadded onto those beings and things by virtue of their having been set apart from the sphere of ordinary, profane life.[16] Frazer refers to the Latin term *sacer*, root of the Romanic *sacré* and its modern derivatives, to remark that it must have meant "exactly 'taboo,'" before prohibition gave way to the more advanced systems of religion, morality, and law.[17]

While Frazer's evolutionist schema led to a dead end, Durkheim's handling of the sacred/profane distinction opened up a world of interpretive possibilities that nourished twentieth-century French sociological thought well beyond the study of religion. In *The Elementary Forms of Religious Life*, Durkheim stresses the social character of the sacred by stating that while the distinctive quality of things sacred is their separation from the profane world, "a pebble, a piece of wood, a house, in a word anything, can be sacred."[18] Perhaps as much as elaborating upon what Robertson Smith had referred to as the "ambiguity" of the sacred—the fact that sacred things can be pure or impure and inspire respect as much as horror—in *Elementary Forms* Durkheim emphasizes the relational quality of it, as sacred beings and things are pure and impure, holy or accursed, not in themselves but in relation to other beings and things, their sacred potential rising and diminishing only in the context of these relations. Durkheim thus alludes to a gradation of sacredness, of which things and beings partake in different degrees, depending on their position in a hierarchy of power and dignity that taboos are there to preserve. "There are relations of disparity and incompatibility among sacred things," he writes. "The more sacred repels the less sacred, but this is because, compared to the first, the second is profane."[19]

These ideas about the sacred—which for Durkheim express society's image of itself—are critical to our collective understandings of what is human. The relationship between the sacred and the profane is one of "absolute heterogeneity"—the sacred and the profane, Durkheim writes, "cannot coexist in the same space [or] the same time."[20] This set-apart, extraordinary quality of the sacred in relation to the profane is what gives power to the norms of thought and prescribed behaviors that socialized individuals must follow, mindful that they cannot free themselves from them without risking to leave human society. "We cannot abandon ourselves to [our own impulses]," he states, "without our thoughts ceasing to be truly human."[21] Yet much of Durkheim's work is devoted to demonstrating that this is an experience human beings actively seek. The separation of the sacred and the profane is the basis for the limits and prohibitions by which we live in human society as well as for the actions and beliefs that allow for transformation and movement, for contact and mixture, for what he calls the "communication" between the two realms. This is the reason for his dedicated attention to ritual, to the mechanisms by which societies enforce the separation between the sacred and the profane and impede their casual mingling (he calls this "negative cult") and at the same time seek and even guarantee the transgression of their boundary ("positive cult").

Later students of taboo reaffirmed the socially constitutive power of prohibition: For Freud taboo is originally a socially imposed prohibition whose rationale, although no longer conscious to individuals, must have been to control the most powerful and base human desires for the survival of the group[22]; for Norbert Elias, taboo and its relation to feelings of shame are functions of the increasing need for self-restraint in what he refers to as the modern, "pacified societies" of the West, where the state has monopoly on the legitimate use of physical violence[23]; for Lévi-Strauss taboo is productive of the social (albeit sexual) order, with the incest taboo being the "fundamental step because of which, by which, [and] in which, the transition from nature to culture is accomplished"[24]; for Mary Douglas the function of taboo is to create and maintain an ideal social order by means of the repression of "dirt," of the ambiguous and anomalous.[25] But it was Georges Bataille's interest, especially in his work with Roger Caillois in the 1930s, to explore the real significance of Durkheim's insight into the role of taboo and transgression (as an inextricable pair) in spurring human sociality, and to place this insight at the center of a critique of the political and social order of Europe, threatened by fascism, weakened by "bourgeois individualism," ruinously devoid of festivals as he thought it to be during the interwar period.

Throughout Bataille's work, taboo figures as some kind of Maussian "total fact." It constitutes a mediating core in all social interaction the way a "church constitutes a sacred place in the center of [a French] village."[26] Through negation, taboo denatures natural phenomena, namely, objects and actions associated with sex, death, and excreta, with the unavoidable reality of our animal bodies, which are expelled from our social lives into "a region that is impossible to penetrate."[27] It is this dark and silent region, the source of what Bataille calls "the sacred," that mediates social intercourse, giving it human meaning. He writes, it "constitute[s] the essential of what is lived by us and, if you like, the heart of existence animating us. . . . Nothing is more important for us than that we recognize that we are bound and sworn to that which horrifies us most, that which provokes our most intense disgust."[28]

By means of the dialectic of taboo and transgression, the split reality of sacred and profane existence reappears in Bataille's work to structure a critical sociology that conceives of the social order of the West, its social, political, and economic organization, as dominated by calculation and utility, that is, by the totalizing rule of "homogeneity" to the exclusion of the "heterogeneous": everything that is inassimilable to the bourgeois order of capital and production[29]—most importantly, individual or collective moments of communication with the sacred, the sovereign exploration through transgression of the limits of human experience. This assessment of the social order of the West became the basis for Bataille's critique of the theory of class structure, including that of Marxism, whose notion of a "classless humanity" is based on a universal human value that cannot account, in Bataille's view, for the class distinctions and discrimination that its own praxis presupposes. It also became the basis for his concern that emerging fascist regimes understood well the power of the experience of collective effervescence and his idea that, within the democratic capitalist order, the social energies no longer expended in moments of collective agitation and communion would from then on fuel the "explosion of class struggle."[30]

For Bataille, if humanity is tied to an anxious rejection of nature, that anxiety that humanizes also produces social distinctions. Humanity's refutation of animality is not just the result of the use of reason, of which animals partake to different degrees, but of the observance of prohibitions, which determine the ways we satisfy our animal needs and give us the feeling that we are not animals.[31] This is the ultimate implication of Bataille's theory of taboo: That in setting us apart from animals, prohibition also sets us apart from other human beings. A more or less anxious, more or less scrupulous observance of prohibitions leads individuals to achieve a greater or lower degree of refinement (that is, a greater or lesser distance from animal nature), the true basis of social differentiation. In relation to social distinctions Bataille writes:

The essential thing is that a punctual observance [of taboos] qualifies socially. The person who protects himself the most anxiously from the various forms of defilement is also the person who enjoys the greatest prestige and who has the advantage over others. . . . It is always a matter of marking between oneself and brutish nature a strange distance, unthinkable at first and so all the greater: the distance between a man eating in a delicate way, according to the aristocratic code, and one who naively drinks the coffee that has fallen into the saucer (it is significant, as I see it, that coffee intentionally spilled into a saucer is called a "foot bath"). The second way is itself human, but not when compared to a more anxious way.[32]

This is what gives rise to social classes and to the division of the human species into different peoples and races, which are distinguished not just by privileges and access to wealth and power but by the fact that they are attributed a higher or lower degree of humanity. "From this point of view," Bataille states, "each man is certainly superior to animals, but only *more or less so*: The way in which he satisfies his animal needs is *more or less human.*"[33] Since wealth and power make the observance of taboos easier, Bataille argues that it is not wealth or power in themselves that make individuals "qualify socially" but the perceived greater distance from animality that these can afford them.

It is in light of taboo that we must therefore deal with Bataille's understanding of social difference—which is how I deal with it in this book. And it is in light of his view of social difference and the unthinking respect for hierarchies that taboo often elicits that we must, conversely, deal with his understanding of class struggle and social revolution. If "respect regulates the humanized world, where violence is forbidden, . . . respect [also] opens up the possibility for violence to erupt in the domain where it is inadmissible."[34] Whereas it was the objective of scholars like Norbert Elias to historicize the emergence of specific prohibitions and prescriptions as part of what he and others call "the civilizing process," it was the objective of Bataille to turn the idea of civilization itself on its head by making so-called primitive or irrational practices and beliefs central to a critique of twentieth-century European political and economic systems, specifically in the context of the rise of fascism and the consolidation of totalitarian communism. Bataille thus pressed for a notion of revolution rooted in the violence of transgression, in social paroxysm and loss, in "the grandest form of social expenditure," the antidote to what he believed was a general complacency in Europe in the face of looming catastrophe.[35]

Spending the long months of winter in Colonel Contreras's home, so close to the sea, was a little like living submerged in it since in Chorrillos the relative humidity of the air is almost at a constant 100 percent. Night after night I would slip under the slightly damp sheets and fall fast asleep, lulled by the roar of the waves. Occasionally, I would wake up at dawn to an eruption of pigeon calls and would be unable to go back to sleep. When I was stirred awake by this daily outburst of bird cries, I would attentively listen to it, feeling a bit mystified by it, as it set off and then slowly stopped. Lying on my back I would watch the wisps of thick white mist flapping in through the cracked window and quickly dissolving in the warmer interior.

The mornings in Chorrillos unfurled to the rhythm of an unvarying succession of sounds: the roaring waves, the birds' cries, then the baker's horn, to which hastily dressed and sleepy-eyed maids rushed out to the street, wrapped in sweaters, empty plastic bags in hand. At this time Lily would come out of her room next to the kitchen buttoning up the shirtdress that she wore as a uniform. She tossed a cardigan over her shoulders, grabbed the house key, and headed out the *puerta falsa*. We would often meet around the bread cart, where she would greet me with a tenuous smile, the skin around her eyes still swelled from sleep, two little openings from which she looked out with a serious or perhaps just timid expression. I greeted her back and tried to engage her in conversation with remarks about something, like the weather, in whose rediscovered monotonous quality I was enticed to seek imperceptible changes: an insignificant drop in temperature, a slightly thinner mist. A few times I asked her personal questions: where she was from, did she have children. With my words I rebelled against or maybe just tried to attenuate the tension provoked by the awkward mix of closeness and distance that defines the relationship between patrons and their live-in maids, where indigenous or mestizo women become privy to the most intimate details of their patrons' lives, familiar with their habits and needs, with the rhythms and functions of their bodies, their textures and smells—all, generally, in the absence of the most basic friendship.

To my questions Lily would offer short, reaffirming responses. But the tone of her voice and her demeanor revealed that my words, no matter how friendly or forthcoming, could not divest themselves from the force of a command, of an order to do something for me, and that she understood my gestures of approach not as attempts to bridge her world and mine but as demands to humor me by talking back. Lily and I behaved toward each other out of reflex, out of the depths of a history that many *Limeños* like to think of as forgotten, as no longer relevant, but that is very much alive and well summed-up in the widespread institution of domestic service. Before too long, Lily would turn around and head back to the house, her increasingly reluctant words pointing to the limits of her servility. As we walked in, she would ask me if I had clothes or sheets for her to wash.

On most days, the colonel and Doña Esperanza would also get up early and come down to the kitchen. He often spent the first part of the morning sitting at the breakfast table in silence, reading the newspaper and smoking cigarettes, while Lily and Doña Esperanza worked around the kitchen and helped Cecilia get ready for school. In the wintry light of the morning, the colonel's tan skin took on a silvery sheen that hardened even more his already austere and stolid expression. His body was short and thin but sturdy and boldly upright. Occasionally I joined him at the kitchen table, where we would share opinions about a piece of news in *La República* or about some unreported political event that had reached our ears in the form of a rumor since, at that time, very little about Fujimori's actions was known with any certainty. Our brief exchanges were followed by long silences when I would turn to talk to Doña Esperanza and, looking tense and restless, the colonel would get up and walk up and down the dining room floor, stopping to gaze out the window and smoke, seemingly deep in thought. Quiet in front of the glass, he looked resigned to the fact of the usurpation of a power from which he had suddenly been cut off, as he contemplated from a distance the unfolding of events in what was probably the most compelling, the most urgent and challenging time in the history of the Peruvian military since the country's return to democracy in 1980. But then I would sometimes see him reach for his felt cap and windbreaker jacket and discreetly leave the house, walking along the boardwalk to Avenida Huaylas probably in search of a taxicab. He would be gone for a few hours, until two or three in the afternoon, when another cab would drop him off in front of the house, where Doña Esperanza waited with lunch ready for him.

Somehow I thought I knew where he went in these morning outings. Maybe I just suspected it; maybe Rafael had mentioned it once. It was surely nothing the colonel had said during our discreet morning exchanges. But from what I thought I knew and what I could distill from those talks, I was able to piece it together: During Fujimori's first term in office, Vladimiro Montesinos, a former army captain who in the 1970s had been dishonorably discharged for spying for the CIA, had become the president's chief advisor, a position he cunningly earned by alternately dispelling and feeding Fujimori's paranoid fears. Montesinos was a master of perfidy and intrigue, and as the Peruvian National Intelligence Service (SIN)'s de facto director, he quickly grew to control the armed forces, all the way to the cupola. He keenly identified corrupt or corruptible officers and then controlled them with simple blackmail tactics; the defiant ones, he reassigned to dead-end posts or pressed into early retirement, in total disregard of the army's internal regulations.[36]

When it became clear that the government's purge of the military would not stop, a number of active and retired military officers, self-described as *institucionalistas* for their defense of the army's institutional traditions and ostensible democratic inclinations, began to meet in

17

secret, working under names such as COMACA (for Comandantes, Mayores, Capitanes) and León Dormido (Sleeping Lion), to coordinate a resistance. After Fujimori's self-coup d'état in April 1992 and a failed countercoup by General Salinas Sedó in November 1992, these groups launched an offensive against the government, filtering information to the press about the army's "excesses" in the war against Sendero. It was their allegations that led to the trial and imprisonment of the Grupo Colina, the death squad responsible for the massacres of La Cantuta and Barrios Altos in Lima.

The months I lived in the colonel's house this phase of underground activity was still going on, but it wouldn't last for long. The Colina members would soon be free once Congress (now under the president's control) passed an amnesty law for the armed forces in June 1995. The rebel, pro-democracy generals Salinas Sedó and Robles Godoy would soon be put in jail or go into exile. And in their place at the head of the army there would be as many as seventeen new generals, an aberration in the history of the military, thirteen of whom were appointed by Montesinos himself from among his buddies in his graduating class of 1966.[37] The mood in the opposition was one of growing confusion and defeat. Yet, every time I saw the colonel withdraw into himself, assuming a look of resignation, every time I saw him slip out of the house with his cap and jacket on, my thoughts unequivocally flew to COMACA and León Dormido even though I never asked him and he never said a word.

———

From the mist-filled, quiet streets of Chorrillos, I thus caught up that year with the extraordinary political developments since Fujimori's fast rise to power in 1990. I soon realized that little or nothing of the social and political life in Lima in the following decade could be treated independently of this unexpected and mystifying electoral event: Two weeks before the elections of April 5, 1990, he had appeared in the political scene, presenting himself as a modest state university professor of mathematics, the hardworking son of immigrant cotton plantation workers, and an outsider to the national political structure, untainted and unbounded by ideology or history. As the political establishment and the minute Peruvian upper and middle classes watched in horror, in the days before the election the name Fujimori spread like wildfire among the urban and rural poor, and the improvised, little-known candidate was catapulted to the presidency with 57 percent of the vote. As a result of this, the Peruvian political party structure, which had been in place for the best part of the twentieth century, was left in ruins.[38]

The urge to name the unnamable, to make what seemed like a volatile social force appear knowable and concrete, led many scholars to turn for explanations for this debacle of institutionalized politics to what Romeo Grompone, soon after the elections, referred to as Peru's "vast universe of informality."[39] His argument was that with Fujimori's rise to power the "informales"—the millions of individuals loosely associated in the eyes of the middle and upper classes with the "informal" sector—had for the first time pronounced themselves politically, demanding formal inclusion and recognition. During the 1980s, the "informales" had more than doubled in size; together with the small-parcel peasants, they now made up about 59 percent of the electorate and thus were, in Grompone's view, "in a position to define the results of an election."[40]

In April 1992, after Fujimori appeared on TV to announce the dissolution of Congress and the annulment of the Constitution, popular support for the president shot up to 80 percent. The next morning, when a group of representatives gathered in front of the shutdown Congress to protest the coup, passersby spat on them. Fujimori's approval on the polls was further strengthened by the police's capture of Abimael Guzmán, although the president had nothing to do with it. Persuaded by Fujimori's IMF-friendly policies, the new Clinton administration turned a blind eye to his undemocratic ways and encouraged the flood of foreign aid and private investment that made viable the public infrastructure spending spree that was the foundation of Fujimori's autocratic regime. With Sendero's leadership down, the runaway inflation of the 1980s under control, the GNP drastically reversed from minus 4 to 13 percent, and Congress and the judiciary more directly controlled by the president than ever, on April 9, 1995, Fujimori was reelected to office in a historical landslide. Whatever was left of the political party structure was nearly finished off in this election.

In public, Fujimori loved to say that he was a "doer, not a talker." He would say, "Philosophizing and speaking pretty does not get anyone anywhere."[41] And the clamor of the opposition for more openness and stronger civil society institutions fell for him under the rubric of "pretty talk." Suggesting a subtle but undeniable coincidence between the president's style of government and the hardworking and ingenious but crassly pragmatic ways of "informality," Fernando Rospigliosi characterized Fujimori as "un presidente combi" (a *combi* president), striking a parallel between his style of rule and the recklessness of Lima's transportation minivans, both of which seek to "impose [their] own law in the country . . . with no respect for rules or institutions."[42]

After his massive win in 1995, Fujimori's much-liked casualness and pragmatism and his laxity toward the law became the basis of his increasingly despotic authority and opportunistic reliance on state and civil institutions. By the end of 1995, he had presided over four different political movements: Cambio 90, Nueva Mayoría, Cambio 95, and Vamos Vecino, none of which was ever intended to evolve into a lasting organization or party, ever celebrated a national congress, or ever called for internal elections.[43] This political reality made it seem that with the tidal-wave elections of 1990 and 1995, the "informales" hadn't actually intended to expand the country's institutional life so as to truly be represented in it. It was as if the opposite had taken place, and, by way of Fujimori, something of the ethos and the values of the "culture of informality" had been infused into the state apparatus. This might explain the tone of uncertainty and the astonishment one senses in the writings of scholars in the left, such as Grompone, who like Marx in *The Eighteenth Brumaire of Louis Bonaparte* cannot hide his surprise and frustration with the course taken by the revolutionary fervor and with the failure of the institutional left to channel it in a more desirable direction. As in Marx's analysis of the dictatorial regime of Napoleon III, supported by France's peasants and urban déclassé, what one can infer from Grompone's writings is that in 1990s Peru the "informales" might not have been driven by a desire for political integration as much as by a feeling of identification with Fujimori; that in the person of the president, the most anti-institutional and inassimilable tendencies of that vast, subproletarian social sector—often regarded by "formal" society to be lower than the low—had surged uncontainable, like some sort of Bataillean pineal eye, to the top.[44]

When Alberto Andrade, the popular mayor of Miraflores, was elected mayor of Metropolitan Lima in January 1996, he stated that his administration of the city would be aligned and supportive of Fujimori's neoliberal policies. Andrade proved his allegiance right away by drastically reducing the city government's personnel, laying off over one thousand municipal workers, and privatizing a number of key services normally provided by the city, such as street cleaning and garbage collection. But feeling threatened more than flattered by the possible peer, Fujimori responded by blocking him every step of the way, arbitrarily changing the law to limit the mayor's access to resources and to curtail his jurisdiction. Fujimori, after spearheading one of the most radical privatization initiatives in the history of the country, all but sided with the laid-off city workers, and when Andrade decided to relocate the center's three thousand street vendors, Fujimori came out publicly in their defense. To Andrade's disbelief, the more agreeable the mayor's policies were to those of the president and the more enthusiastically he expressed his respect for him, the tougher and more vicious were the president's retaliatory attacks.

By the time I left Lima in September 1996 to work on my doctoral degree in New York City, Andrade had begun the center's radical makeover despite Fujimori's obstacles and hostilities. The Plaza de Armas had just been leveled and, like other plazas in the city center, would be rebuilt and rebaptized with its old (colonial) name, Plaza Mayor. The battles to expel the vendors from the city center's streets were well under way, and the street sweepers' protests against the mayor's privatization policies, now backed by the broader city workers' union and, allegedly, instigated by the SIN, would soon become radicalized.

Between 1997 and 2005, I made several research trips to Lima for periods of varied length, during which I witnessed the center's brief renaissance, its stall, and then its inexorable new decline. The diaries and essays in this book garner their content and energy from developments and the accumulation of ideas and experiences in all those visits, but they grow most directly out of a set of events that took place during a three-month stay, starting in October 1999, when the nascent feeling that I would have to find an alternative narrative form for the story I wanted to tell became a pressing necessity.

On that occasion, as soon as I arrived in Lima, I found out that not too long ago, Colonel Contreras had caved in and sold his house to a real estate consortium, which had built in its place a four-story building of luxury condominiums. The colonel and his wife had moved into a small apartment, also in Chorrillos, which had a nice, but only partial view of the ocean. Doña Esperanza, Carola, and little Cecilia had moved into a separate apartment, purchased for them with what was left of the sale of the house, in a building just a few blocks down from the colonel's new residence. Needing a place to stay that would afford me, like the colonel's house once did, proximity to but also independence from my immediate family, I rented a room in the home of a distant relative, who, finding herself alone and in need of an income after the death of her husband, had converted her residence into a boardinghouse.

During the overnight flight that took me from New York to Lima, I traveled on the window seat next to a small, thin man in gabardine pants and leather jacket, who for almost the entire trip did not speak or move. A brief exchange of words came toward the end of the flight when, hurrying to fill out my immigration and customs slips, the man handed me his pen. He asked me if I was a U.S. citizen, to which I shook my head no. He then volunteered that he was, adding that before he left Peru he had been a policeman with the DINCOTE (the police force's head office against terrorism) until 1992. He said that things had turned really ugly then, that he used to live in fear that they would blame it all on them, the ones lower in the ranks. He had fled the country at the first opportunity. After a few months visiting a cousin in Mexico City, he had crossed the border and sought political asylum in the United States.

The man didn't have to say more for me to assume that he had been implicated in some way in the armed forces' "excesses" in their war against Sendero Luminoso, of which the events of La Cantuta and Barrios Altos are only the most salient examples. But he did say more. In the United States, he had settled in New Jersey and married a Puerto Rican woman, with whom he had two children. He had come back as soon as the asylum deal had allowed him to. As the man spoke, I thought that surely he must feel safer now, after the government's sweeping amnesty of the military and the police. I hadn't yet set foot in Lima and had already learned something important about the current political environment of arrogance and impunity.

I really didn't want to hear more or talk more. So when he asked why I was going back to Lima, I said that I was a student and that I had come to do fieldwork research in Lima, turning away from him to look out the window, where a few paltry brick structures were already visible through the haze.

Together the ex-policeman and I looked out in silence. We flew over the northern tip of Lima, over what looked like a never-ending wasteland. One thick layer of trash covered the city's shoreline and went as far down as the mouth of the Rímac River. Thin columns of smoke grew out of the burning mounds, next to which was the dim outline of a straw shack and several pigs. Perhaps prompted by the view, the ex-policeman said that he had heard that the city center was very clean nowadays, very clean and pretty, that it competed in beauty with Santiago and Buenos Aires. I nodded silently, wondering to myself what could be behind the historical compulsion we *Limeños* have to compare Lima with other cities: In the seventeenth and eighteenth centuries, it was Seville or Amsterdam, which Lima's baroque society looked up to and imitated; in the late nineteenth century, it was Haussmann's Paris; and more recently, in the 1980s and early 1990s, with the chaos, the violence, and the poverty of Lima reaching new levels, it was Calcutta, India.

Propped on his elbow, the ex-policeman stretched out toward the window and looked out wide-eyed, seeing Lima from above perhaps for the first time in his life. On one side of the window frame there was the ocean—a lethargic and grayish mass. On the other, all garbage, extending as far as the eye could see—pelicans, seagulls, buzzards circling in the air, landing and feeding off it, and making it seem oddly alive. This sight made me think of Julio Ramón Ribeyro's short story "Los gallinazos sin plumas" about two children who are forced to spend their days in a garbage dump by the sea picking through the refuse, searching for enough food to appease the unquenchable hunger of their grandfather's gigantic pig; the story ends when the sick and exhausted children push the wooden-legged grandfather into the corral, where the pig devours him. Looking on to the pigsty below made me feel a bit queasy, as if I could smell the festering gases, not just see but also smell the smoky, bittersweet stench of the sprawling trash, which from the air made the city appear like an all-devouring garbage dump.

Anticipating the plane's landing, I leaned back in my seat and closed my eyes. As is customary among Peruvians, when the plane touched the ground the cabin erupted in loud applause. The man next to me applauded, too. Then he stood up and brought down a leather bag from the overhead bin, lining up in the aisle and waiting to leave the plane through the rear. Tongues of white mist lashed in when the doors were opened, and I felt Lima's sticky air rushing inside. As the plane began to empty, the ex-policeman grabbed his bag and, before starting down the aisle, turned to me, winked, and said, "Good luck with the research."

First Diary

Thursday morning: The sun had not come up from behind the hills to the east, had not yet burst and risen in slow motion above the hilly skyline to the east when the first ululating cry broke the dawning silence. Sweet but a bit eerie, it was followed by a string of other ul-uls that gradually swelled in intensity and took hold of the hazy atmosphere that cloaks the seaside districts of the city right before its waking hour. Herman Melville referred to Lima's haze when describing the whiteness of the whale and said that it is like a "white veil" that, in swaying over the city, intensifies the "higher horror" one is prone to feel here, making of "tearless Lima," in his own words, "the strangest, saddest city thou can'st see."[1]

Melville, however, didn't mention the birds.

At this hour of the morning, when sea and sky are still a bluish, ill-defined mass and colors have not fully taken hold of things, at this liminal hour begins the birds' singing—if one can call that deep, guttural ul-ul singing as opposed to wailing or howling. The pigeons, known here by the name of *cuculíes*, instinctually reciprocate each other's ul-uls until entire districts along the coast of this very arid and dusty valley are enveloped in thousands of simultaneous cries of lamentation, as if in some kind of sound-aura that seems to bring everything else, the sea, the dogs, other birds, into an awed, reverential silence. Then, gradually, just like they begin, the cries wane one by one until they cease completely.

I know this sound will wake me up at the same hour tomorrow. It always does on the first week I am back home.

Later: At 6:00 a.m. the radio alarm went off. It was set that way when I arrived, and I haven't changed it. *El informativo solar* came on with the news. I lingered in bed, lying on my back, the covers drawn to the chin. The same two voices of years ago, a man and a woman, alternated with the news, filling the airwaves with as many words per minute as they are capable of in a sputtering, monotonic discharge of words, like a machine gun. "*Un especialista norteamericano,*" said the man, "will visit Lima to advise functionaries at the Municipalidad de Lima on their fight against urban crime." His name is William Bratton, and of course I've heard of him: New York City's first police commissioner under Mayor Rudy Giuliani. The news is that he will be hired as a consultant to give Mayor Andrade a hand in strategizing against the waves of assaults, robberies, kidnappings, and rapes that are once again sweeping through the city. The newsman says that they'll elaborate on Bratton's visit at nine o'clock, during *Ampliación de noticias*, before the woman hastily takes over with a related piece of news.

Yesterday morning two hundred undercover and uniformed policemen raided the sixth and seventh blocks of Jirón Renovación in La Victoria, a historically working-class but today a terribly depressed district just south of El Cercado. The newswoman said that, for the past ten years, that narrow little street has been a "no-man's-land." No one (who knows well enough) dares to go in, not even the police. A street reporter doing live interviews in La Victoria talked to a bystander who said that Renovación is a block of robbers—everyone, the women, the children, the old. He said that when some absentminded driver turns the corner onto the *jirón*, a "cripple" who lives on the block and moves around crouched on top of a skateboard—for lack of a wheelchair—rolls down to the middle of the street, forcing the car to stop, at which point other neighbors run out of their homes and plunder the car, unscrewing the windshield wipers, the side mirrors, the headlights, even the tires, in a split second. The reporter said that yesterday, as the police raided the *jirón*, the residents threw rocks at them, and when they broke into some of the homes looking for a few wanted individuals, they were fended off with buckets of boiling water poured out the windows from the top floors.

I eventually got out of bed and went downstairs to the dining room. As always, Eulalia, the house live-in maid, had set the breakfast table last night before turning in. The day's newspapers also spoke of Bratton's possible visit. In this house they buy only *El Comercio*, an awfully dull and conservative newspaper, so I've paid the newspaper delivery lady to also bring *La República*.

La República's section of local news contains some remarks by Mayor Andrade. He says that the rise in criminality rates have largely surpassed the surveillance capacity of the PNP (Peruvian National Police) and the Serenazgo—a district-run neighborhood vigilance system inspired by a colonial practice of nighttime watch that was put in place again (after 150 years) by Andrade himself in 1996. The paper then explains that Bratton was the mastermind of Giuliani's now world-famous "zero tolerance" policies, whereby all minor offenses, such as littering and sleeping or urinating in public places, were severely punished. It also says that Bratton's unorthodox methods were based on principles of economic competition and mass psychology. He presided over a drastic restructuring of the NYPD, which made each of New York's 123 precincts independent from one another and each police chief responsible for what happened in his or her jurisdiction. The idea was that a police precinct should function like a private enterprise, the article states, whose competitors are the criminals. Just like in the private sector, one ought to remain attentive to what the competitors do, and the objective is to always stay one step ahead of the game. To be consistent with this theory, Bratton devised a system in which weekly crime statistics were superimposed onto an electronic map of the five boroughs in order to identify and keep track of trends in crime rates by neighborhood. The precincts would intensify police patrolling and crackdowns in those sections of the city where an increase in the numbers of minor offenses anticipated an imminent hike in other types of crime. This is the policing method that led to the well-known array of police brutality cases during Giuliani's tenure, of which the rain of bullets that killed Amadou Diallo was one of the most notorious.

I wonder what fancy plan Bratton will come up with for the PNP, so hopelessly, so shamefully understaffed and underpaid that they'd rather take a bribe of 5 soles for a beer or Coke (a friend once got away with the spare change, a few cents, she was able to collect from nooks and crannies in the dashboard of her car) than write you a speeding ticket and walk away with nothing; and so unscrupulous that when they're off duty they are the most reliable suppliers of guns for rent on which depend the very criminals they're supposed to protect us from.[2]

Opposite the article on security in Lima there's a full-page advertisement for a banking card company; it shows a middle-class, middle-aged woman, her hair nicely cropped and her face nicely made up, drawing a wide, confident smile as she states, "I was just robbed at the ATM." The ad is for the bank's theft insurance program. I've heard that the latest theft "modality" is the *secuestro al paso*, or express kidnapping, where a band of armed men snatches ordinary people from the street and takes them by an ATM, where they withdraw the maximum daily amount of money from the victim's account; then they wait until just past midnight for another trip to the ATM, after which the victim is let go. Recently it was front-page news that the members of one of the most feared bands of express kidnappers had turned out to be active officers in the PNP's Emergency Squadron.

The "Locales" section of *El Comercio* says pretty much the same thing about Bratton and the crackdown in La Victoria yesterday morning. But in it, there's a picture of the young invalid of Jirón Renovación after the police captured him. He appears alone, crouched in the back of a white station wagon bundled up in a blanket like a mummy, the worn skate-board by his side. One of his atrophied legs sticks out under the cover. In the background, behind the flash-lit forefront and his frightened, bloodshot eyes, is Lima's luminous dawning sky.

At about eight o'clock the doorbell rang. I was told to expect an arrival this morning, Manolo, a distant cousin of my mother's; he is an artist who lives and works in France and whom I had never met. I opened the front door and saw a small, frail man pulling out a large suitcase from the trunk of a beat-up *Tico* (a tiny taxicab) as another man, rather tall, fingered through some bills in his wallet. I introduced myself to the tall man as Marcia's daughter and offered to help him with the bags. I picked up the suitcase, which wasn't too big or heavy for me, but I hadn't taken one step toward the door when I was met by Eulalia, who had rushed out of the house and was now forcing the bag out of my hands.

"Let me, señorita," she said in a whisper.

I hesitated but let it go and watched as Eulalia walked back inside with short, hurried steps.

A wave of feeling rushed through me, a combination of guilt and fear since I suspect that underneath her promptness and servility may be a dormant volcano of anger. As I followed behind her silently and empty-handed, it was as if the weight of the bag she carried was shifting onto me, settling inside me, pressing down heavily. This heavy feeling, I know for a fact, will stay with me until the day I leave.

Friday: Spent the morning downtown. It was past nine o'clock when I got there, but the municipal library hadn't opened yet. At a bodega across the street I ordered their one-sol breakfast: bread & margarine and

27

a cup of anis. My stomach has been hurting again, and I can't really handle coffee. From the bodega I had a view of the northwest corner of the main plaza and the side of Palacio de Gobierno (the Presidential Palace), where twenty or so policemen in riot gear were leaning listlessly against the wall. A strike had been called for today by the CGTP (the Confederación General de Trabajadores del Perú, the national workers' union), and the papers said that the SUTEP (teachers' union), the FNTC (the union of construction workers), and a group of pensioners would also be marching down to the Palacio.

With its gray marble-cement façades and dreary grandiosity, the Palacio looked grim. The front patio was empty, the doors closed and unguarded, all the window curtains drawn. The Peruvian flag raised above the main entrance looked wilted, dingy—the red part discolored, the white one almost gray. The contrast was great with the one on top of the Municipalidad de Lima (the municipal government building), which looked perky and bright.

In fact, next to the Palacio, the entire plaza looked bright, cheerful. The municipal building, the Cathedral's towers, and the arcades on the south side are golden yellow, and the flower beds inside the square are brimming over with red gladiolas. The plaza, which was entirely redone in 1996–97, has been the main focus of Andrade's urban renewal efforts. He has spent over $5 million of the city's meager coffers to return the square to the size it had before it was first paved in 1875 and its perimeter was reduced in the 1970s to make room for parking spaces. He's repaved it with slabs of granite and has dotted it with new marble benches and old-fashioned wrought-iron lampposts. He's torn out the twenty-year-old fig trees from the plaza's outer edge and replaced them with palm trees and thousands of flowers arranged in color patterns that change thematically every three months: red and white in the month of July (for Independence day), purple in October (for the procession of the Lord of the Miracles), and so on. And he's crowned the 1650 bronze water fountain at the center of the square with a replica of the lost statuette of the Angel of Fame, who toots a horn with one hand and holds the escutcheon of the Spanish kingdom in the other.

Since Andrade has forbidden the traffic of buses and *micros* inside the so-called historic center, at this time of the day crowds of office workers walk from one end of the center to the other, crossing the main plaza by foot. They passed in front of the bodega where I was, probably coming from Avenida Tacna, a major point of convergence for *micros* headed to the center from the *cono norte*. Many were young women in office garb. Clutching their purses, they walked determinedly until they reached the square, where their heels went wobbly on the new granite's uneven surface. The men who were sitting on the benches reading the newspaper or looking about idly turned their heads as the young women went by.

As I finished my anis, the first tourist bus of the day circled around the square and pulled over on one side of the plaza. The tourists got off the bus and, with their guide in front, walked in file toward the water fountain. Some of them took out their cameras and, from the center of the square, aimed shots at the surrounding buildings. A candy boy sneaked into a group picture that had the Cathedral as a backdrop and walked away with a few soles. Foreign tourists visiting Peru used to skip the city center and often skip Lima altogether. In 1996 Andrade arrived in office determined to change that. He shut down all pay-by-the-hour motels within the historic center and cleared out the maze of dens along the river and under the bridges, where homeless children hung out and got high on glue. Although many motels on streets close to the plaza have already reopened (aided by rulings of the Fujimori-controlled judiciary) and the riverside dens are back in place, the prostitutes, transvestites, and *pirañitas* steer away from the renovated plaza.

Mr. Ordinola is the man in charge of the municipal library's circulation desk. He has made me a copy of Andrade's "Plan Maestro" for El Cercado. The master plan puts great emphasis on the recuperation of the historic center, which, it says, has been "witness to a meaningful [though unspecified] period in the history of the city." Lima's historic center was declared Cultural Patrimony of Humanity by UNESCO only in 1991— inexplicably almost twenty years after the comparable historic districts of Mexico City, Havana, Santo Domingo, Quito, and Cuzco. Time and again, Andrade's plan states that the buildings, monuments, and public spaces in Lima's historic center ought to be recuperated and conserved because they have "intrinsic value." At what point did such remnants of Lima's past become intrinsically valuable and cease to be obstacles to progress? And what is this form of "intrinsic" worth? On the surface it would seem that he is holding out the possibility of a form of worth that is no longer dependent on use or exchange values, one that would make the recuperation and conservation of these buildings and spaces inherently desirable, desirable beyond utility or gain. But in a world with ever fewer acceptable forms of profitless expenditure, isn't this, in a way, what the booming of the leisure industries, like tourism, is all about, creating marketable and consumable objects out of unquantifiable values such as history and culture? This is, without a doubt, what motivates Andrade to make of Lima an attractive destination for travelers. Writing in 1940, Roger Caillois argued that the fast-spreading custom of taking time off from work to go on vacation was taking the place of society's festivals. In an increasingly fragmented society, Caillois wrote, where "a general ferment is no longer possible . . . the period of turbulence [of festivals] has become individualized": vacation, literally "empty space," has replaced paroxysm with relaxation, exuberance and jubilation with distraction and distance from others, social communication with a desire for further isolation.[3] Is that what tourism is, then, a prepackaged, controlled search for the experience of wasteful consumption, a socially tolerable and tamed reservoir of unproductive activity (one ultimately compatible with capitalism) into which the bourgeoisie of the world pours its amassed wealth?

The security guard on the side door of the municipal building eventually waved to let me know that Mr. Ordinola had arrived. The tourists and the guide were still bunched up around the fountain as if too scared to leave the square. As I paid for my breakfast at the counter, I saw them walking across the street to get back on the bus, which would probably shuttle the tourists from site to historical site for the rest of the day, in a prearranged and efficient order before returning them to their hotel in San Isidro or Miraflores.

———

Saturday morning: A note on yesterday's demonstrations: When I left the library at about 1:30 p.m., I had to walk down to Jirón Huancavelica to catch a cab since the main plaza had been completely blocked to cars. The demonstrators were already there. In two small groups, they circled around the square. One group was of the SUTEP, twenty people or so in all, carrying a red banner with their acronym in yellow letters and a handwritten sign that read: "Sueldos de Hambre" ("Starvation Wages"). The other group was of construction workers, all men, chanting against the elimination of paid overtime with Fujimori's new "pro-labor" laws meant to make the previous labor regime more flexible. I was struck by how tiny the groups of demonstrators were. Since 1992, when Pedro Huilca, CGTP's popular secretary general, was murdered, probably by the Colina death squad, unions have been severely weakened. In the last several months there have been a handful of mobilizations against Fujimori, like the general strike of April 1999, but it's likely that not even this manifestation would have amounted to much had it not been for the backing of university students' federations and parties of the opposition expressing themselves against Fujimori's reelection intentions. Yesterday

I was dismayed to see that those two scrawny groups of demonstrators were all the once-powerful CGTP was able to muster on its own.

———

Saturday night, 9:00 p.m.: At about noon I left the house to go have lunch at my mother's. I walked toward a grassy, manicured rotunda on the edge of the cliff, over which tower several new buildings. From the sidewalk, I watched out for a cab or a *micro*. Not one came by so I kept walking south, thinking maybe farther down.

Short, unruly waves break against pebble beaches down below forming garlands of white foam since the water here is, to a great extent, clean and uncontaminated, becoming even cleaner as one gets deeper into the districts of Miraflores and Barranco. From the boardwalk I watched the waves break, dwarfed by the height but still audible, along the stretch of little beaches that runs north and south. I could see up-close the cliff's wall of loose gravel, rising vertiginously so many meters from the Circuito de Playas right to where I stood looking. (A young man died a day or two ago down in the freeway when a thirty-pound rock rolled down the cliff and went right through the windshield on the driver's side.)

The boardwalk swerves along the edge of the cliff, parallel to the freeway, to the string of beaches, to the garland of white foam. A rosary of towers, many of them newly built, stretches from San Isidro all the way to Chorrillos, separating the city from the ocean like a curtain of cement. Tall, glassy, and of deep, bright colors, the new buildings stand in stark contrast to the few disgruntled homes that remain on the oceanfront, many with their backs or sides to the water, sinking into their neglected, overgrown surrounding gardens. One would think that the ways in which the city has transformed in the last few years should make it seem foreign and remote, but somehow against the glassy towers, the manicured parks, and the strident neon business signs, the rest stands out as strikingly intimate and familiar—intimate and familiar in that inward and unknowing sort of way, as when on coming back to the place where I grew up, and only on coming back, I can take notice of things that once passed inadvertently since they were already there when I was born, like the sea was already there, and I cannot say I ever truly saw it or noticed it for the first time.

My mother, who grew up in the highlands, remembers the time when she first saw the sea. She was driven by her father when she was eight years old three hours down a steep, winding road expressly to see the ocean

for the first time, she and her father alone. After an abrupt turn in the road the car came to a stop and her father said, his voice filled with expectation, "Look!"

The ocean—

She says she will never forget seeing it from the road a few hundred meters above the sea level, dark blue and swollen, enthralling, and its pungent but delicious smell for which she could find no words later to describe it to her younger siblings.

Against all that's changed, the rest has a new objectivity and concreteness, has become observable, graspable in ways that habit had made impossible before and only years of distance and forgetfulness, of unhabituation, can bestow to things at the expense of that intimate and unknowing understanding I had of them, of this ocean, this cliff, this boardwalk, which have suddenly become observable, describable, although with words that could never be perfectly fitting or adequately expressible.

Most of the new towers along this boardwalk sprang up during the construction boom of the mid-1990s when hundreds of condo apartments—especially those with a "sea front view," as it was advertised in English—sold like bread right out of the oven. But today, it is obvious that some of these rising structures have arrived too late to the feast because of the slower or uncertain pace at which they grow or because their construction has entirely come to a stop. Around the city, you can see many half-built structures that have been sitting there for months, empty, silent, no more than a hollow shell of concrete. On any given afternoon you may see little men atop a rising structure hammering away, piling up bricks, pouring cement, and then the next day sheer silence—the builder has run out of money or his credit has gone dry. Thus the structures become ruins before they have a chance to be anything else, unwitting memorials to Fujimori's failed neoliberal policies and today's economic recession.

I have never seen so much empty space in Lima. On every block there seems to be at least one unfinished structure. Occasionally, some of the owners have moved in anyway and are finishing their apartments themselves, with the style, color, and materials they please, leaving the rest of the building empty and dark. And on every block there are one or two, sometimes several signs saying: "Se Vende" or "Se Alquila" ("For Sale" or "For Rent"), advertising empty apartments, commercial spaces, and large and small single-family homes. This is one of the visible ways economic recessions hit the *Limeño* middle classes. As employment rates stall or slump, family members begin to move in together, pulling in resources to wait the crisis out together. As economic recovery translates into more or better-paid jobs, rental spaces and spaces for sale begin to fill in once again since economic independence and the physical independence this can afford are values held dear by the middle classes. It seems to me that this is an important aspect of the desire for distance, the "search for separation from others" that according to Gonzalo Portocarrero is a typical attitude of the *criollo* middle classes of Lima. "Middle-class people," he writes, "define themselves by putting a distance, by re-creating boundaries, thus feeding a narcissistic feeling of superiority, of confidence in their own worth."[4] Portocarrero explains that middle-class individuals justify that distance by regarding those who are below them as impulsive, irrational, and vulgar; and those who are above them as lazy, frivolous, and, worst of all, disdainful of Lima's *criollo* tradition, with which the city's middle classes tend to identify even today—as with the rhetoric deployed by Andrade's campaign of "recuperation" of the city center—despite its questionable colonialist whiff.

Thinking about all this vacant space, I realize that this is exactly what I'm after: the definition and regulation of social distance through our relationship to and management of space. In particular, I am interested in what today appears to be a norm-setting, *criollo* sensibility driving the most aggressive effort since the urban population explosion of the 1930s and '40s to redefine *Limeños'* relationship to their city and its history through ideas of cleanliness, order, and beauty to which, it is assumed, everyone should aspire. The neat, uncluttered sidewalks and refurbished façades of the city center are signs of its restored "decency," a term loaded with class and racial assumptions through reference to the material and moral purity of Lima's middle classes, after too many years of chaos and filth.[5] That Lima needs to be "recuperated" in this way seems to be an uncontroversial fact here—although it is not without its ambivalences since the value placed on the distance obtained through the separation of bodies and the demarcation of boundaries is mired in contradictions. Portocarrero argues that this physical separation, while critical to the self-image of the troubled Peruvian bourgeoisie, threatened as it constantly is by the fear of class and racial displacement, is achieved through "a pained distance" ("una distancia dolida") that is filled with longing for what has been repressed: a desire for spontaneity and physical closeness, which in the middle-class imaginary is an attribute of the lower classes, and a craving for excess and profligacy, which is imagined as an exclusive attribute of the upper ones.[6]

The tower where my mother lives is also new. It's been finished, but signs of "Se Vende" and "Se Alquila" pepper the façade and a weathered signboard near the garage door lists the apartment numbers of the as-yet unsold flats, which someone crosses out by hand with a black marker as they sell. My mother opened the door of the elevator to let me in. Through her oversized white cotton blouse, I could see the bandaging around her chest, from the waist up her torso tightly wound all the way to her armpits. She had made *cau cau* for lunch because of me. I mean, Betty had—because she knows I love *cau cau*. I said, "Thanks, Mother." "A fabulous cook Betty is," my mother said. "She is," I said. "Isn't she?" I said, "Thanks, Betty."

Betty looked in from the kitchen, grinning widely, happily, two orderly rows of teeth showing. I thought, *Happily?* I thought of the days when, needing to work and lacking a proper work authorization, I got a job as a nanny in New York City—the closest I ever got to experiencing domestic service from the other side. A few times, after picking up the girl from school and helping her with homework, I cooked dinner for the whole family. They politely asked me if it was all right to cook for them if I was cooking for the girl anyway. I said it was fine and meant it. They were very nice and fair people. Like with Betty, they praised my cooking and thanked me. I would peek in from the kitchen and smile—but I can't say I felt happy.

Betty yelled in from the kitchen, "Too thin the señorita is!" My mother and a cousin of mine who was lunching with us turned to me and smiled. "You should eat more! Too thin you are, señorita!"

Suppose I'd asked her to come and sit with us, to eat not after we're done but at the same time we ate the food she herself had made? Suppose I'd said, "Come, Betty, eat with us at the table." It would be a harmless thing to do if race and class relations weren't interlaced with prohibitions, if her social position didn't make her categorically separate from us, as Portocarrero would say, we, the table, and the food she herself had made off-limits to her until we're done.

It was as if we were stuck in a frozen instant of unreciprocated giving, like that instant of unequal recognition in Hegel's dialectic of the master and the slave in which the master and the slave exist side by side but as radically opposed forms, as extremes unable to achieve unity. We the masters, Betty the slave, we "pure and essential," she "impure and unessential"—the dialectic rigidly, impossibly, suspended in this frozen instant, and Betty smiling and me smiling back, as if it were possible, conceivable to keep it forever that way; as if this relationship of inequality were Transcendent Nature; as if the tension in this sorely distended instant weren't explosive and her servility weren't the very truth of our "independent consciousness." I thought, *What the master does to the slave he also does to himself.* But suppose I dared and suggested that she come out and join us. I'm not sure I have the courage to unleash and then deal with the disturbance this transgression would set off, to confront and force everyone else to confront the ultimate horror: Hegel's dictum "to stare death in the face." But suppose I had dared and suggested that she come and join us.

After lunch I couldn't keep my eyes open, so I took a nap on my mother's bed. Something more than the rich food sat heavy on my stomach. "Tearless Lima," I thought of Melville's words: the strangest, saddest city. I felt it pressing from inside me like an old, aborted scream—although I wonder if this is at all what Melville meant. The view from my mother's bedroom includes a wedge of ocean. Open and magnetic, it pulls your eyes towards it, making you feel you're seeing it for the first time. On a clear evening like today's, the islands of San Lorenzo and El Frontón (the old prison island) were faintly visible in the horizon. When I woke up an hour or so later, the sunset filtered through the blinds in yellow and purple streaks. Two small fishing boats rocked near the shore to the tide's ups and downs and slowly faded in the dusk. The piles of debris and smoky garbage along the shore are a few kilometers farther north and cannot be seen from here.

———

Monday, 5:00 p.m.: Woke up at the break of day, another spring morning with its cool, white sun. Eulalia hadn't yet drawn open the curtains in the dining room. So I opened them and squinted as the light poured in. A while later, Manolo came down to the dining room and sat down, flattening the hairs behind his receding line with his hand. This is the second time he has been to Lima in twenty-five years. He visited last year with Elie, his French wife. They spent two weeks in the city, visiting old friends and old, familiar places. Like a parent holding the hand of her child as they inspect the bedroom for ghosts, Elie went with him everywhere, having promised never to leave his side. But he didn't see any family.

Manolo said hello, on his face an expression that was calm, open in stark contrast to the low-pitched force of his voice, which filled the room like a roar. From the kitchen, Eulalia stuck her head in through the revolving door, pulling back her undone mane as soon as she realized we were already in there. Manolo leafed through the newspapers as he told me about the upcoming opening of an exhibit of his paintings, his first in Lima since he left. We talked until the old clock in the living room struck the hour, tolling hoarsely eight times. I decided to call Hugo Morales earlier rather than later. A youngish voice answered and told me that Mr. Morales was already out on assignment. I left a message to please call me back. I also called Channel 4, the only TV station that got images of the protests on videotape and, I've been told, aired them uncensored. There was no one in the archives yet.

Back upstairs, I got back in bed with one of my folders, labeled "Nakedness," and shuffled through my notes and newspaper clips, stopping to look at Mr. Morales's 1996 photograph of the street sweepers' protests, which first sparked my interest in their demonstrations. I looked at it and read the caption to myself: "Challenging the drizzle, low temperatures, and the pressured water from the riot tanks, this street cleaner did not find a better way to express her protest and to call attention to her problem than by partially undressing."[7] "Protest Cicciolina-style" was the headline to the note, striking a bizarre analogy with Ilona Staller, the blonde porn star who in 1987 won a seat in the Italian Congress by standing in front of the parliament building and uncovering one of her breasts. The headline also alluded to Susy Díaz, the so-called Peruvian Cicciolina, a cabaret dancer (here called *vedette*) and since 1995 a congresswoman, who collected votes by lifting her skirt during public appearances to expose a naked buttock on which she had painted the number *13* to publicize her location in the paper ballot.

"Cicciolina-style." I remember when I saw this picture and read the headline for the first time, thinking to myself, "They didn't get it." With my head shaking and my eyes stuck to the page, I said out loud, "They just didn't get it."

But, did I? Did *I* get it? I certainly could not articulate an explanation of my own reaction to the image—not to myself, not to the friend I was with that morning, not less than I can articulate one now. It was as if her transgression had disrupted not only the course of things but also the course of thought, of *my* thought, and I was caught in what Bataille would describe as a chain of reactions extending in time and space, moving from one subject to another—from the street sweeper, to the photographer, to me—in a string of mediations that did not seem to make the sight of the woman's naked body any less forceful or shocking.

The looming figure of Manolo just outside my bedroom door brought me out of my absorption. His hair was wet, slickly combed to the back, and he was sliding into a jacket, getting ready to go out. He asked what I was doing, if I was in the mood to go bookstore hopping with him. He said, "What are you looking at?" having already caught a glimpse, his slightly slanted eyes looking round with surprise.

He waited while I showered, and we walked to Avenida Armendariz to get a cab. We got into a *Tico* where he barely fit in the front seat.

Oblivious to the warm, spring breeze, the driver wore a woolen sweater and still carried Lima's winter, this year the longest and gloomiest, in his facial expression. At the bookstore I met Lorena, the owner and Manolo's longtime friend, and since in Lima there is always time for a *cafecito*, that is what we did. Once back at the bookstore I was annoyed at the seemingly whimsical way the books were priced. Aside from the national editions, which are always cheaper, there was no clear logic in the pricing of the rest, as some luxury volumes are sold at bargain prices while books of coarse paper and poor binding are simply unaffordable. The cashier told me that Fujimori opposes the so-called law of the book, which would support local book printing and book importation, and that the uneven prices reflect the tariff policies of the books' country of origin. Of course I had set my eyes on one of the expensive ones, a seemingly well-translated but shabbily put-together Spanish edition of Sartre's *La náusea*, the diaries of Antoine Roquentin. I put it down, determined not to condone such capriciousness with my business, and walked out with only a cheap copy of Ribeyro's short stories, including "Los gallinazos sin plumas," which features the anthropophagous pig. Since I arrived in Lima, I have not been able to get Pascual, that insatiable monster, off my mind.

As for the rest, it was an uneventful afternoon. I took a nap, went for a short run, and talked to Héctor, who is now back from the Huallaga Valley where he does his fieldwork. We have plans to get together on Thursday. I will now reread "Los gallinazos sin plumas," and then, for the rest of the evening, Bataille's *The Accursed Share*, volume 2.

———

Later: From volume 2 of *The Accursed Share*, it is possible to distill a list of forms of behavior and attitudes that, according to Bataille, mark the transition from animal to human being. These are

1. The prohibition of incest
2. The respect for the dead
3. The repulsion of excreta (waste matter, filth)
4. Work—and
5. The meaning we attach to nudity

To be sure, these are not meant to be understood as discrete but as inextricable aspects of the human specificity since they are all equally and foremost the result of our act of negation, of our denial, both in terms of destruction and in terms of prohibition, of the animal that we ourselves were, or are. To that which for the animal is the object of an irresistible but fleeting impulse, destitute of all meaning, humans attach a "value" by negating it through labor and prohibiting it through rules: In the tool, a stone acquires the value of usefulness; in the corpse, a lifeless body turns into a fearsome object; in kin, the women or men closest to us become the receptacle of forbidden desires; and, in decency, the sexual organs are "something" whose name and whose sight both horrify and seduce us.[8]

This, for Bataille, is the process that grounds humanity, a process in which the horror and negation of nature anticipated a nearly simultaneous countermovement, so that what "was denied to the point of nausea ... is remembered as desirable." This basic duplicity can be intelligible only if grasped as a whole, as a twofold movement in which prohibition—which is nature's antithesis—is then regarded as the given and is negated in its turn.

Bataille is intrigued by the associations and judgments, what he calls "the cerebral activity of man," that tends to qualify as, say, sexual or filthy, objects, beings, places, and moments that by themselves have nothing sexual or filthy about them, or anything contrary to sexuality or filth. Yet for him what is worthy of investigation is not whether these judgments and associations are the result of an instinctive repugnance of incest or excrement, or, conversely, of an instinctive attraction to kin and filth (the psychoanalytic argument). For Bataille, what is worthy of investigation is the meaning of a series of prohibitions that do not appear to exist among animals and that manifest in countless rules so culturally specific and seemingly so arbitrary that they appear to be a provocation. These rules, the outward expression of that phenomenon we call taboo, we must understand as having been given historically, not as merely belonging to the order of things. Bataille writes, "We can grasp being only in history." And in history we must attempt to grasp the changes and transitions, the detours and "ceaseless overturnings" undergone by the rules and the taboos that they express.

In speaking of the movement from nature to culture, from animal being to human being, Bataille is not interested in the formal stages of the transition, in their function or progression—which is what distinguishes Bataille's approach from historicist ones like that of Norbert Elias, who explores the internalization of self-restraint, of feelings of repugnance and shame in the "civilizing process," while overlooking the fact that the things banned from "proper life" by civilization retain a strong hold on us. Bataille, rather, is interested in what he refers to as the "drama" in which the boundary between those seemingly abstract terms—animal, human; nature, culture—is established, transgressed, and reestablished every day.

It is in the "drama" that I am interested, too.

———

Tuesday: Spent the day downtown. On Jirón Camaná, at around ten in the morning, I crossed paths with a large group of street boys, *pirañitas*, walking south on both the sidewalk and the street. Their hair was dirty and clumped, their clothes ragged, and their eyes glazed. High on glue? Maybe just sleepy. They moved recklessly as if there was no one else around and no cars in the street, protected by a self-emitting aura of danger. People going up the block, including me, crossed over to the other side to avoid them.

All the expensive cafés in Pasaje Santa Rosa, which opened with much fanfare in 1996 and 1997, now have limited hours. Next to a swanky art gallery (also new), there's the Café Café and the Café Bohemia, both high-end restaurants that were first successful in San Isidro or Miraflores. On looking up close, a thin film of soot is already building on the yellow walls of the passage. Mostly empty even around lunchtime, these fancy cafés now compete with hundreds of cheap eateries around the center by serving lunchtime "menú," an inexpensive, prix-fixe three-course meal, which is loudly advertised by a waiter at the door charged with luring in customers. It hardly looks like a booming area anymore. As in other parts of the center, the metal trash bins that Andrade had placed along the passage have either been yanked out or have bottomed out with rust. Little mounds of trash piled up under the hollow barrels.

When Andrade took office in January 1996, the city center was so dirty that there was talk that Lima was on the verge of an "ecological collapse." Rumors were, and a *Caretas* article confirmed, that the Empresa de Servicios Municipales de Limpieza de Lima (ESMLL, pronounced "Esmil") was bankrupt and working at 40 percent of its capacity.[9] With circulating reports that ESMLL would be disbanded and its services privatized, the cleaning agency's employees went on strike in March 1996, and no garbage was collected for weeks. Every day, 1,400 tons of garbage ended up in the streets and plazas of Lima and along the banks of the Rímac River, where it accumulated in mounds that reached a few meters. But Andrade's government did not yield. The mayor and the city held up until the early hours of July 1, ten days after the street sweepers had stripped in the main plaza, when a new contingent of seven hundred young women was deployed in the streets of El Cercado, brooms in hand

and decked in loud uniforms: trousers, sweaters, and caps bright orange; dust masks; gloves; bright white sneakers; and fluorescent orange vests. They belonged to the new company, called Relima, a Peruvian-Brazilian private consortium that had received in concession the cleaning of the center's streets and the city's sanitation services. Working around the clock in three shifts, for little over half the salary once paid to workers by ESMLL, and with no union affiliation or job security, these street sweepers, the "ladies in orange," as another article in *Caretas* called them, collected on their first week 1,460 tons of garbage, 415 tons of debris, in an area within El Cercado of 2,756.8 kilometers and in 728,983 square meters of plazas and parks.[10]

That same week another cleaning service also began its labors, the Serenazgo de Lima. Dressed in shiny blue fatigues and riot helmet and armed only with shields and leather-covered batons, eighty or so of these sentries also carried out a series of sweep-ups around the center, although to collect "garbage" of another sort. They raided brothels and by-the-hour motels, massage parlors, and illegal discotheques, famous for the graphic live-sex shows they used to put on. They also picked up *pirañitas*, pickpockets, and petty drug dealers from the streets, and forced the ambulant hardware dealers of Jirón Lampa and the sidewalk food vendors of Avenidas Tacna and Emancipación to close up shop and go. The same issue of *Caretas* that reported on the "ladies in orange" showed a full-page photo of two *serenos*, tall, corpulent, and with thick moustaches, as they forced a transvestite out of a hiding shack as she looks into the camera with a terrified grimace.

This marked the beginning of the city center's renaissance. The cleanup, which the street vendors fought against with tooth and nail, was followed by the renovation and inauguration of the new Plaza Mayor, celebrated with a mass in the Cathedral and an all-out production of Calderón de la Barca's baroque play, *The Great Theatre of the World*, on the steps of the Cathedral's atrium; many residents of Lima's wealthiest districts came to the center for the first time in years expressly to see the play. But President Fujimori, the mayor's guest of honor in these celebrations, did not show up to any of them, in what became the first of several public rebuffs by the president to discredit the increasingly popular mayor. After the main plaza came the beautification of the Plaza San Martín, the National Congress building, the Parque Universitario, the Municipal Theatre, and the Museum of Art of Lima. At the same time, all seventeenth-century church-monastery compounds were repainted in vivid colors, their stone-carved porticos restored and placed at the center of an officially endorsed downtown tourist circuit. Three old horse-drawn carriages were made available for nostalgia rides passing in front of these churches and the few other colonial buildings that still exist in downtown Lima and that were also renovated by Andrade. A pamphlet given out by the city government in January 1997 detailing these recuperation efforts was titled "Lima . . . ensueño" ("Lima . . . a dream [fantasy or illusion]").[11]

Around that time, Andrade also launched a campaign called Adopt a Balcony, directed at private businesses that, in exchange for tax breaks, committed to restore whatever was left of Lima's signature Moorish balconies. A number of expensive bars opened in the center, and old and downgraded ones, like the bars at the Grand Hotel Bolívar and the Hotel Mauri, were revamped to cater to affluent visitors from other districts, who now included El Cercado in their weekend nighttime plans. Members of the exclusive Club Nacional on the Plaza San Martín once again felt safe to go there on the weekends for drinks or for elegant dinners. And it became fashionable, among those of means, to get married at the restored baroque churches or at the Cathedral. With all this, the center of Lima saw displays of wealth it hadn't seen in decades, made all the more shocking by the seriously impoverished surroundings and by the dilapidated state of the structures and streets that fell outside mayor Andrade's recuperation plan.

It was clear to me today that the center's renaissance is quickly waning. For one, Fujimori has made it a priority to destroy Andrade as a viable future presidential candidate. If in 1996 Fujimori's disgust toward the mayor was obvious, today it is open war. Building on Decree 776, a law that cut down the city's general budget by 60 percent and the budget for infrastructure by 80 percent, Fujimori has attempted to transfer the administration of Lima's parks and highway tolls, an important source of revenue for the city, to individual districts and the Transportation Ministry, respectively.[12] He has also created a number of new entities within the Ministry of the Presidency to replace or take over functions customarily carried out by the city, such as the issuance of land property titles. Furthermore, Fujimori has blocked two loans requested by Andrade, one to Peru's Banco Nacional and one to the World Bank, which are crucial to his project of renewal of the center. Without them, only a minute portion of the Plan Maestro will be executed, mainly ordering and beautifying works that will have, at best, an ephemeral impact. By the time Andrade's Plan Maestro was made public in the official daily *El Peruano* in April 1999, not only had most of his renewal efforts already stalled, but the high point of the center's renaissance had already passed and many of the "recovered" spaces were spiraling down back to their former, derelict states.

What a better sign of this regression than Andrade's own frustrated effort to move back to the center. In 1996, to demonstrate his commitment to and faith on the future of downtown Lima, Andrade moved his residence into the Casona Gildemeister, a beautiful mid-nineteenth-century mansion on Jirón Ucayali that once belonged to the prominent Gildemeister family. He seemed convinced that other middle- and upper-class families would follow, purchasing or repurchasing property in the center, from where many of them had fled in panic some decades ago. But with the economy entering a recessive stage and the center's repressed problems of prostitution and street crime resurfacing again, this crucial aspect of the recuperation of the center never took place. Instead, his new house (allegedly) became a favorite target of demonstrators of SITRA-MUN (Sindicato de Trabajadores Municipales), the relentless municipal workers' union, who have protested for the last three years Andrade's massive layoffs by defacing the bright mustard-yellow walls of his house with grotesque graffiti and by hurling rocks at the beveled glass of the house's elegant balconies. Because of this and what they feared was an escalating level of aggression, Andrade and his family recently left the *casona* and moved back to Miraflores.

––––––

Later: Something needs to be said here about the undefinability of things political. Or, is it just that everyone is lying? Mr. Ordinola, at the municipal library, gave me copies of two full-page newspaper political ads, one published in *La República* on June 19 by the city government and the other in *Expreso* on June 24 by the secretary general of SITRAMUN, Alejandro Hinostroza, clearly in response to the first ad. The conflict between the city and the laid-off workers is mired in confusion, in legalisms fought back with other legalisms. Also on June 24, the editorial page of *El Comercio* came to Andrade's defense.[13]

In his ad, Andrade says that the workers of SITRAMUN premise their acts on the idea of "class struggle" and calls them "an elite of politicized ex-directives." (One of the most salient consequences of the Fujimori phenomenon is that common Marxist terms have suddenly fallen in total disrepute, and the words "politics" and "politicization" have become insulting terms). The mayor claims to have laid off, in full conformity with the law, a number of city employees based on the results of an official personnel evaluation test that these employees either failed or refused to take. The great majority of dismissed workers, the ad claimed, have accepted and cashed in the severance package offered by the government, thus breaking all links with the municipality. Andrade openly accuses the central government and the judiciary (which is under the president's control) of inciting these "politicized ex-directives" to vandalizing attacks in the Plaza Mayor, against the mayor's house, and elsewhere in the center.

As for Hinostroza, he states in his ad that Andrade is blatantly lying—lying, first, about the number of employees laid off by the city since 1996 (Hinostroza's claim: 1,100 out of 1,400) and, second, about the amount of the severance package paid by the city, not 1,300 soles per year of service (about $377), which is what the workers are entitled to by law, but the rather absurd sum of 12 soles per year of service (about $3.50). What's more, he claims that these payments were conditioned upon the workers' agreement to forfeit several months of back pay. Hinostroza says that the mayor is the only one who is politicizing matters, suggesting, on the one hand, that the workers are terrorists and, on the other, that they are agents of the SIN, both contradictory claims aimed at boosting his numbers in the polls toward a future presidential candidacy.

When I asked Mr. Ordinola, himself a city employee, if he could explain the incongruities of the claims, if he could say who here is in the right, he shrugged. Later, as I walked to take a *micro* back to Miraflores, I saw a Relima street sweeper working nearby in a tarnished orange uniform. I walked up to her and asked her if it was true, as Andrade's government says, that a third of the workers of Relima are former ESMLL employees. She looked at me over her dust mask with surprised eyes. Pulling the mask down and shaking her head, she said, "I don't know anything, anything." What begins to become apparent is that it would be pointless to spend much time trying to tease out the facts, to pursue the "truth," whatever that means in this context, since both sides seem to thrive on confusion, to make use of it, and even to depend on it to further their cause.

Yesterday I went by my father's office to talk to Carmela, the office assistant and my father's longtime friend. Carmela has offered to help me get an interview with Germán Aparicio, Andrade's lieutenant mayor. Their parents were friends from Barrios Altos, so it's no problem to call "Germancito," she said. I asked her to set up a meeting for next week if possible. Maybe I'm wrong and Aparicio will be able to clarify things?

———

Wednesday noon: Got up early and browsed the newspapers. At 9:00, before setting out for the center again, I went for a run along the boardwalk, past the Barranco Bridge to Chorrillos, where I lived at the Contreras's home before moving to New York in 1996. As always, I ran with no wristwatch or cassette player that could draw any attention, and wore sweatpants instead of my usual running shorts.

Once I was back in front of the house, I stopped and stretched on the sidewalk before going in, cooling off in the mild spring breeze and using for support the short wall in front of a new building next to the house. One of my legs was up on the wall, and I was leaning forward, touching the tip of my shoe with my hand, as I tried to bring to mind the house that had stood there before. Next to that building is a construction site, where another tower, fifteen, maybe twenty flights high, is being erected. Several men were sitting on a plank on the third or fourth floor, taking a break. I was stretching and staring at the building when I saw them and they saw me. I was already looking at them, when I realized it was too late.

"Great tits!" one of the men said.

The rest of them laughed.

"Come up here, come keep us company here, *mamacita*!" he said.

Startled, I looked away. Then, almost against myself I turned back to them and found myself saying, "Shut up, you asshole!"

The men laughed harder.

I turned away again and pretended not to care. Now with my back to them I went on stretching, repressing the urge to cross my arms tightly over my chest and run inside. I tried to distract myself by thinking of something else: *What house was there before?* I pretended not to care, but as they laughed and hissed, my limbs tensed up, a hot, dizzying sensation rushed to my head, as if it had not been just words that the man had hurled at me but poisoned arrows. I read once that in the Amazon when men go hunting for monkeys they sometimes dip the tips of their arrows in poison extracted from the skin of certain frogs. Like when a struck monkey tries to escape but falls paralyzed by the poison—it was as if the words the men had hurled at me had a poisoned tip. I felt like a monkey just hunted down, clumsy, stiff. A hot feeling shot from my belly out to my limbs and face, and I felt as though the blood in my body was boiling, bubbling up like water boiling under pressure.

My blood boiled. I wanted to shoot darts back.

"Shut up, you idiot," I wanted to yell again and suspected the men were expecting, perhaps wishing that I yell again, as if this whole exchange had been scripted, just like one expects to hear the punch line in a joke or a story one knows well. I thought of a thousand possible insults, awful, hateful. "Shut up, you *cholo, maricón!*" I yelled in my head, tried against myself to yell, but my jaw was clenched, my throat lumped. I boiled. They laughed. I was a monkey. We all awaited the scripted line, but this time it didn't happen. I felt at a loss. I finally crossed my arms over my chest and walked back into the house.

I know that for a few more days I will be shocked by the men in Lima; like with the birds' cries, I'll be startled when I hear them hissing, catcalling, yelling, as they frequently do with women in the streets. For a few more days I will be shocked at my anger, at my blood boiling, angrily and fearfully as I am humiliated, as thoughts flood to me, hateful thoughts, racist thoughts, and I feel both victimized and hungry for a victim. Then, I will get used to the men. Like with the birds, I'll be deaf to them.

———

Thursday, 4:00 p.m.: Hugo Morales from *La República* finally called back. I have been advised many times that, in doing fieldwork, one ought to be persistent. Being persistent does not come easy to me. Mortified, I must have called Mr. Morales and Channel 4 about ten times since I arrived. On the phone Mr. Morales sounded curt, apprehensive. "Who are you? How can I help you?" From his voice I couldn't gauge if he was younger or older than me, so during the conversation I nervously switched from the informal *tú* to the formal *usted* back to *tú*, afraid, first, of seeming presumptuous or disrespectful, then of appearing aloof and over-deferential, for the use of *usted*, ordinarily a gesture of politeness, can turn, all too quickly, into its opposite, and function as an emphatic marker of social distance. It took me months and not a small amount of anxiety to get used to addressing everybody in the United States, indiscriminately, as *you*. Now, back in Peru, the social convention eludes me. What are the rules?

The rules. I think of Bataille.

I told Mr. Morales that I would like to talk about his memories of the protests of the ex-employees of ESMLL. I said, "You might remember," and mentioned the images of the street sweepers in that June issue of *La República*. I also said that I would like to know if he had other pictures of that day, maybe get copies of them. He reluctantly or perhaps just timidly agreed to meet me. He's expecting me tomorrow at noon at *La República*'s headquarters on Jirón Camaná downtown.

———

12:30 a.m.: Something terrible has happened. It had been a slow and monotonous afternoon of reading when some Uncle Antonio called to inform of the death of Manolo's younger brother, Paco, apparently of a drug overdose. His body, the uncle said, was found two days ago, already in a state of decomposition, inside the family home in Miraflores. That house is a run-down piece of property, which I believe has for years been at the center of a family dispute. Paco is the third of five siblings to die before the age of forty-five. First was Linda, the only sister, who died young of untreated diabetes. Then was Darío, the eldest brother, whom I never met personally but of whom I nevertheless have vivid memories. I saw Darío several times, but all my memories of him converge in one: There is me, looking out the car window and spotting a man, his face, hands, and feet covered in a crust of dirt from roaming the streets. He wears several layers of clothes, all dark and ragged, and a blanket stringed to his neck like a cape, which is fluttering in the wind. Once he traveled, people say, from Lima to Arequipa on foot. In my memory, my mother points at him, as if he needed to be pointed at—a tall, fair-skinned man roaming the streets of San Isidro—and she says, "Look, there goes my cousin Darío," her voice quivering.

When Manolo got off the phone he was livid, his facial features out of joint. His little brother is dead. He was overwhelmed with grief, but rage seemed to bubble up to the surface faster and more easily. He mumbled a few words to me, visibly damming his emotion, while I lay frozen on the couch, gaping at him, with my book still propped up. It has been twenty-five years, he remarked again, since he last saw Paco or anyone in his family, and thirty-five years since he packed up a few things and ran away. He left to forget them all, he said, so why are they calling him now? He said, "Surely for money, surely for money for the burial." Well, they will not get a thing from him. Paco can rot in the morgue, for all he cares.

Manolo went to his room upstairs. A few minutes later, he came back down looking ready to go out, saying he had some last-minute things to do at the gallery before the opening tonight. I tried to go back to reading, but couldn't. I didn't see Manolo until later in the evening at the gallery.

Since it was still early, I decided to walk to El Haití, rather than take a cab or a *micro*, where I had to meet Héctor at six o'clock. With a perfectly round setting sun and blood-red skies, I set out in the direction of Avenida Larco, stepping into Parque Salazar for the first time since it was remodeled. The last time I saw the park, the entire perimeter of it was boarded up while a new shopping mall was built under the very old park on the edge of the cliff. In 1995, while Andrade was still mayor of

Miraflores, the project of building a mall on this site had stirred many residents of the district, among them my father, into action, as they put a long and painful fight against Andrade's idea. But the project involved too much money, a lot of which had already exchanged hands when the neighborhood protests erupted, and it simply could not be called off. So on his last week in office as mayor of Miraflores (he had already been elected mayor of Metropolitan Lima), Andrade modified the zoning of the area, from residential to commercial, and quietly finalized the contract whereby the park's subsoil was leased to a real estate developer to build an underground maze of boutiques, ice cream parlors and restaurants, video arcades, movie theaters, and a huge parking lot.

Approaching the new park from the north, the first thing you see is a two-way cement ramp and a set of escalators that lead into the Larco Mar mall and its underground parking lot. Today I decided not to go in. Instead I stood in the observation deck for a little while to watch the sun go down. Behind me, the huge disk's fiery reflection looked even more magnificent, more dramatic, on the mirror façade of the new Marriot Hotel skyscraper that towers over the park. From this spot I could see a Hard Rock Café on the mall's first level whose front wall sports yellow neon letters that command: SAVE THE PLANET (in English) over a glassed-in dining area where there wasn't a single empty table. I simultaneously had a perfect view of three enormous chimneys in the middle of the park that let out the combustion exhaust from the underground parking lot, and I could see them releasing the grayish fumes. Save the planet, indeed.

I strolled down Avenida Larco to El Haití. When I walked in, Héctor was already there, sitting at a table close to the door and sipping from a cup of tea. He seemed to be doing well, although he'd lost some weight and a strange paleness dulled his jungle tan. We were happy to see each other, after so many months. He'd moved back to the city from the Huallaga Valley on the eastern slope of the Central Andes. The adjustment to the city, he said, has not been easy. There, in the valley, the heat is intense, sultry. He said that he thrives in the heat—and flashed for me pictures of himself in better days, wearing blue jeans, a white sleeveless shirt, and dark sunglasses, standing in the blasting sun or leaning against his motorcycle to the side of a muddy road. It is Lima's sullen skies and humid air that he fears will kill him. He said he hasn't felt warm once this past winter, patting the black woolen scarf he still had wrapped around his neck as if to make sure it's still there. In the Huallaga, the only problem is the stomach bugs, he said. For no matter how much care he took to boil the water that he cooked and washed dishes with, no matter how strictly he adhered to the doctor's advice that he should drink only bottled water, he was never able to get rid of them.

I listened to him eagerly waiting for the details, quietly comparing his ailments to mine, as we gradually got into the specifics, alternating description with questions and advice, laughing at the medical euphemisms—"meteorism"—and Latin derivatives—"flatulence"—that literature on our afflictions is filled with, and giggling as we dared to move away from those terms to try and say it as it is.

Here in Lima, everyone has a story of stomach infection, which normally includes a list of symptoms and possible cures, about which laypeople have become experts over the years and on which they love to indulge. As for Héctor and I, these are the basic facts: Héctor's microbe is a parasite, *Giardia*. Mine a bacterium, *Helicobacter pylori*. His resides in the intestines and so his problems are for the most part in the lower abdomen. Mine resides in the walls of the stomach, so my problems, for the most part, are in the upper abdomen. We both have tried to fight them off with high doses of the most potent antibiotics, after which our infections have recurred. What's worse, both our symptoms are perversely similar to symptoms of stress. So half the time, Héctor said, the doctors recommend that he take it easy and find ways to relax, even though he's bending over with pain and feeling faint. The other half, he goes back home with a box full of chalky oval pills that for other reasons also make him feel sick for days.

In the middle of the conversation, Héctor got up to use the bathroom.

My problems began the day I got back to Lima after years of living in the United States. That day, my mother, father, and I celebrated my return with a bottle of wine. I had finally completed my master's degree and had finally come home. A few hours later I felt thirsty from the wine; I grabbed a glass, filled it with tap water, and drank it all, like I had always done before. Thirst quenched, I looked at the empty cup and for a second wondered if I had done right. Exactly one month later, the pains began. I was first diagnosed with gastritis—an inflammation of the walls of the stomach that can be temporarily soothed with over-the-counter milk remedies but that is often, as it eventually became for me, a chronic ailment. After several months, it was determined that the constant irritation of my stomach was produced by bacteria.

Héctor walked back from the bathroom with a hand placed on his abdomen and looking weak. We then took a *micro* downtown to the gallery where Manolo's exhibit opened tonight. We arrived; Héctor took a brisk and despondent look at the works, said that he wasn't feeling well, and left.

The front patio of the gallery was beginning to fill up. Inside, black-and-white paintings of desert landscapes similar to those of the area surrounding Lima hung impeccably from the walls. The sharp and glossy black-and-white contrast lent these unpeopled portraits of Lima a life and intensity, a radiance, that has nothing to do with the barrenness, the poverty, and the desolation of the actual desert, which could nonetheless be recognized behind the gloss.

A butler was going around offering white wine. I followed him back out to the patio, where I saw Manolo walking in from the street. He was wearing the same black pants but had changed into a black, short-sleeve shirt. His eyes looked glazed, vacant, but he put on a smile as soon as people approached him to greet him and congratulate him. He winked at me and whispered not to say anything. Moving through the crowd, wineglass in hand, I ran into Mariano, one of my many Marxist-turned-radical-neoliberal university friends, who would love to see the role of the state reduced to filling up street potholes. I plugged myself into his circle of friends, and he asked me what I was doing in Lima. I told them about my research into the street sweepers' protests and was astonished to see how quickly the conversation adopted a more intimate tone and turned to memories of having or not having seen our own mothers or fathers naked. Everyone in the group (all men but me) seemed to remember rather well, in all detail and intensity of emotion, the time or times when they saw, or almost saw, their mother naked. We all spoke candidly, except Mariano, who approached the subject with the same witty cynicism with which he approaches everything that is not the invisible hand of the market. When someone in the group pressed him to say whether he had seen his mother naked, Mariano assured us that he had never. Noting that she's now in her seventies, he said, "it would probably be the instantaneous cure for my Oedipal longings!" We all laughed, and someone else changed the subject.

When I left the gallery it was close to midnight, and Manolo was still there.

———

Friday morning: Carmela just called to say that she had tentatively set my meeting with Germán Aparicio for Monday when his secretary called her back to call the meeting off, indefinitely. The secretary told Carmela that Andrade is about to officially announce his candidacy for the upcoming presidential elections and, due to the escalating attacks against him, the municipal building is now out of bounds to journalists.

The printed press is consistently attacking Andrade, from the far-right *Expreso* to the (supposedly SIN-financed) 50-cent tabloids *La Chuchi* (a name suggestive of "pussy"), *El Chino* (Fujimori's popular nickname), *El Tío*, and *El Mañanero*, where Andrade is often called a faggot, a thief, a sexual pervert, a drunk, and a *pituco* (an upper-class, arrogant person). But in the last month or so, the attacks have become physical, mostly with rocks hurled at him and at his sympathizers as they walk down the street or hold public events. Pictures of men and women with bleeding foreheads are common these days in *Caretas* and *La República*. Most recently, a suit filed by Andrade against the defamatory newspapers was dismissed by a puppet judge, and another suit was filed in retaliation against Andrade accusing him of corruption.

I told Carmela what she already knew, that I'm not a journalist. "I know! I told her!" she said apologetically. The secretary said that the interview couldn't be rescheduled for now and to call back in a couple of months. "It is like a clam," Carmela said. "Because of the elections, the accusations, and the violence, the entire city apparatus has closed itself to the outside, like a clam."

———

6:40 p.m.: I arrived at the offices of *La República* right at noon. Mr. Morales wasn't back yet from his morning assignment, but he had left instructions with the receptionist to let me into the archival room. Half of the room was filled with piles of bound newspapers with the dates etched on the spine, January 1 to January 15, 1960; May 15 to May 31, 1984; and so on. I was asked to take a seat around a large wooden table, in which three young women chatted and giggled as they leafed, disinterestedly, through tome after tome of old newspapers, writing down the day and page of every piece of news on a particular subject or person on whom they were there doing research. *La República*'s digital database covers only from 1995 onwards.

A young man tossed one of those thick tomes in front of me, June 15 to June 30, 1996. I fingered through it until I found the issue I was looking for: June 20. The young man jotted down the date and some code down, and a few minutes later brought me an envelope with the negatives of the pictures taken at the street sweepers' protest that day. In it, there were about four negatives with images of the protest, but none of them were the ones that appeared on the front page on June 20. I told the young man that those pictures were missing; he said, "What is one to do?" When Mr. Morales finally arrived, the guy was about to run across the street to the Kodak store to get me prints from the negatives. Mr. Morales suggested that we go ourselves and then sit in a café across the street to talk. He seemed hesitant as he readied to leave, looking at me askance, approaching his desk but stopping halfway, then feeling his back pocket for his wallet, turning to me again, and signaling me to the door.

He began to speak as soon as we were on the street. He spoke softly, cautiously, but I got the impression that it was not because of some underlying reluctance but of a desire to be exact. He said that he had known right away that the women's protest was something "special," "rare" (*raro*: rare and strange), that the undressing of the women that day had left him perplexed, that in his thirty years as a photojournalist he had never seen anything quite like it.

Once at Café Copacabana across the street from *La República*, Mr. Morales noted that, next to the women of ESMLL, the ex-employees of SITRAMUN (which officially didn't include ESMLL) had been taking over the streets of downtown Lima on a daily basis that month of June 1996. Seizing the opportunity to hurt Andrade, Mr. Morales said, the SIN had hired thugs to infiltrate the demonstrations, starting brawls and vandalizing the buildings that were being restored, making it seem that Andrade had completely lost control of the city. Fujimori had even ordered a court ruling in favor of the municipal workers, he said, even though the president himself has ruthlessly fought and virtually eradicated all other unions.

On June 20, 1996, Mr. Morales said, it was mostly workers of ESMLL demonstrating, from street sweepers to garbage collectors, the majority middle-aged and older women. The protesters, whom he referred to as "the mothers," had marched since dawn from the outskirts of the city toward the main square, where they were scheduled to meet with the lieutenant mayor, Germán Aparicio. It was cold and rainy, Mr. Morales said, meaning that there was a thick drizzle. The workers wandered in the plaza, he said, amid mounds of uncollected garbage, which had been piling up since the beginning of the strike. At times they chanted slogans; at times they idly talked among themselves, waiting for the lieutenant mayor, he said.

He said that, at about noon, rumors began to circulate that Mr. Aparicio would not receive them. That precipitated the turn of events, quickly transforming what until then had been a peaceful demonstration into a full-blown confrontation with the police. Some of the workers chained themselves to the fence of the Palacio, while others threw bottles and rocks at the municipal building and tried to pry the main door open. The mass of protesters rushed toward the door as the police struggled to disperse them with their batons, fire hoses, and tear gas. The women screamed and fought back. He said that it was then that he saw a group of women form a tight, narrow circle, which in a brusque movement broke up and from the center of which emerged the old woman, her hair loose, naked from the waist up.

Mr. Morales said that no one dared to touch her. He said that the police stopped the beating and looked at each other scared or confused. The woman wandered in the square, screaming, uttering unintelligible words, "as if in a trance," he said. He said that in some crucial way she had altered the atmosphere of the demonstration, even for the protesters. The police recoiled to the sidewalks as more women began to undress and, in their undergarments, got into the fountain in the middle of the square. When a few policemen came back to the square, he said, it was only to timidly grab the women by the arm and lead them away from the plaza. A few minutes later, the square was quiet again, and empty, except for the half-naked woman, whom a riot policeman followed closely but at a careful distance, seemingly intent on grabbing her by the arm and taking her away from the plaza, but not quite daring to do so. For the rest of the day, as in the days to come, the police would limit themselves to observe further strippings from afar.

While we continued to sip from our coffee in Café Copacabana, Mr. Morales reflected, "Yes, they surely planned it beforehand." But then again, "No, it really couldn't have been planned." The transformation he witnessed, he said, was sudden, impulsive. He said, "Only a radical change, a quick and radical change in her mind could have led her to do such a thing." "An impulse, an instant, a split of a second," he said snapping his fingers, "like what happens in the mind of a person right before committing suicide."

I nodded signaling comprehension, but thought, _Suicide?_ "And the fact that the protesters were mothers gave the protest a boost," he said. I asked him to explain why. He said, "Why? Because a mother is a mother, and policemen are sensitive to that. That is why the woman's undressing was an effective technique. None of them touched her," he said. "They tried, but they couldn't."

Mr. Morales said that it had been him who came up with the front-page caption that evoked the Cicciolina. Smiling, he said that the editor thought it was a brilliant idea, to which I simply nodded, reluctant to point out the gross inaccuracy of the analogy he had devised as well as the conflict between his own references to the women as "mothers" and to the power with which their very condition of mothers infuses their actions, and the tacky, jocular sexualization of their nudity that his

analogy with pornography entails. But is this simply a gross inaccuracy? Or is the unease that the sight of the woman's naked body produced in the plaza, leading the policemen to beat a retreat, also what led Mr. Morales and his editor to turn to and find relief in irony, in cheap humor? This raises the important issue of representation and, perhaps more properly, of the politics of looking, since with their act the women seem to have transferred on to us, the more or less immediate spectators, the anxiety and sense of shame that one would have expected *them* to feel as a result of their exposure, as well as made us responsible for how the visual representations of their transgression are to be viewed, experienced, and interpreted. More than the nudity itself, it is this shift of the shame and burden of responsibility, from actor on to spectator, that amazes me and the fact that, upon this reversal, the vulnerability of the human body, specifically of the female, motherly body struggling for survival, ensures that it is we, the viewers of these images, who feel threatened, unsettled in our safer positions, and who as a result must call our own dignity into question—not the women.

I didn't set him straight. Instead, I asked how the mothers' undressing could have been a technique of protest *and* a spontaneous action at the same time. Disregarding my question or misunderstanding it, he said, "Yes, it is a technique" and restated that he had never seen anything quite like it.

After that, we went back to the Kodak store. I paid for my reproductions, and he retrieved his negatives. I walked him back across the street to *La República*. Before going in, he said he'd look for the two missing negatives. I thanked him, and we said good-bye.

———

Saturday, 11:00 a.m.: Planned but impulsive. Like suicide.

The connection between nakedness and death, whether it is murder or suicide, is also explicitly made by Bataille. He writes, "The act of stripping naked, in civilizations where it has full significance, functions as a simulacrum of the act of killing, or at least as an equivalent shorn of gravity."[14]

In Bataille's scheme of things, the deathly energy released with nakedness stems from its posing a threat to our physical and mental boundaries, to our sense of identity, which guarantees our individual existence in a state of "discontinuity" with other individuals and with the rest of the world. In nakedness, bodies are violently wrenched out of this state and opened out to flux and continuity, Bataille says, "through secret channels that give us a feeling of obscenity. [And] obscenity is our name for the uneasiness which upsets the physical state associated with self-possession, with the possession of a recognized and stable individuality."[15]

Bataille's most thorough examination of the relation between nakedness and death takes place in the context of what he calls eroticism. Eroticism, the sexual communion between a man and a woman, is the deliberate, simultaneous enactment of desire and embrace of the horror of losing oneself in another, the radical but momentary fusion of beings into a state of continuity that is critical to the "drama" of transgression. When Bataille explains that "nudity is unlike . . . decently clothed bodies in that it draws one near the repulsive source of eroticism," he is referring specifically to the nude female body as regarded by the male subject. It is the conjoining of repugnant animality and beauty in a woman's body that gives her nudity the meaning "if not of outright obscenity, of a slipping toward it." The distinction here is critical: Outright obscenity is not in itself as disturbing as the slipping toward it. "A naked woman, if she's old and ugly," Bataille asserts to illustrate his point, "leaves most men unmoved."[16]

But does she really leave most men unmoved?

What follows is from journal and newspaper articles I have recently compiled about the political use of female nudity in East and Sub-Saharan Africa.

Uhuru Park: On March 3, 1992, a group of older Kikuyu women, many of them in their sixties and seventies, descended on Nairobi city to demand the release of some of the women's sons, who were being held as political prisoners. The young men had been jailed for advocating a multiparty electoral system in what was then, by law, a one-party state. On the morning these Kikuyu "mamas" (as the *Daily Nation* refers to them) showed up in Uhuru Park in downtown Nairobi, it had been two months since President Moi and his governing party, the Kenyan African National Union, had yielded to domestic and international pressure and repealed the section of the Kenyan constitution that made it illegal to engage in party politics outside the KANU. The men thus awaited trial for what was no longer a crime. When negotiations with Kenya's attorney general broke down, the Kikuyu women set up their tents in the park and went on a hunger strike.

On the third day of the strike, three squadrons of policemen in riot gear arrived in the park and launched what the *Daily Nation* describes as a brutal attack on the women. With their fists and batons, the police beat the women, kicking them on the ground and knocking some of them unconscious. The women writhed in pain and screamed, "Uuii! Uuii! What kind of government is this that beats women! Kill us! Kill us now!"

as they took off their clothes and thrusted them at the policemen along with insults and shouts of "Shoot us if you dare!"[17] The *Daily Nation* says that "the police shielded their faces at the sight of the naked women," as they retreated and repositioned themselves along Kenyatta Avenue, from where they prevented other people from entering Uhuru Park.

In addition to a description of the confrontation between the women and the police, the articles in the *Daily Nation* quote a Catholic priest, Father Ndikaru wa Teresia, who in support of the women said that the policemen "should apologise to [them] 'because it is against our culture for women to strip in front of men. That is a curse!'" A government official, Njenga Mungai, said that "it was a sad day for Kenya to witness mothers stripping naked in indignation *before their sons* in the face of a brutal onslaught." A KANU party official said that the stripping by the mothers was "shameful and insanity of the worst order," echoing the comments of President Moi himself who referred to the mothers of the political prisoners as insane.[18] A member of a pro-government organization, Maendeleo Ya Wanawake, said that "it was very shameful for an elderly woman to strip *in front of her children*," joining an official KANU statement that demanded that the mothers "pray for 'forgiveness to lift the curse they had put on their children.'" Finally, two women from neighboring Kirinyaga are quoted as saying that the act of stripping by the women was for the Kikuyu similar to "chasing children away from home," for "the nakedness of a woman is an abominable sight. Even mad women do not strip."[19]

Ìjà Obìrin: In 1985, a large group of Ondó women of a Nigerian Yorubá town protested en masse against a special sales tax that the Ondó State had imposed on market vendors, who were in the majority women. As the women paraded down the street, they removed their skirts and cursed the Ondó king by using obscene gestures and singing songs threatening to his life: "We kill and eat him / We kill and eat him / Itiade turns into a goat / We kill and eat him." The women's stripping, the threatening songs, and the obscenities directed at the king in this and other such demonstrations, known in the history of Nigeria as the Women's War or *Ìjà Obìrin*, are, according to Elizabeth Eames, "well accepted as expressions of women's resistance."[20] These expressions are considered to be of such deadly potency that the recipient, in this case King Itiade, had by force to counteract them by means of a costly private sacrifice. And the state's mobile police who had been sent out to appease the disturbances had refused to do so. Eames reports that, after venturing some menacing gestures toward the women, flaunting their guns and cans of tear gas, the policemen broke rank and fled.

Anlu: Kom women in Cameroon employ nakedness as a kind of "disciplinary technique," which Kom refer to as *Anlu. Anlu* is deployed to oppose specific offenses against women, like the beating or insulting of a mother with remarks such as "your vagina is rotten." The following is an account of an instance of *Anlu*, provided by Francis Nkwain, a Kom man, in full length:

Anlu is started off by a woman who doubles up in an awful position and gives out a high pitched shrill, breaking it by beating on the lips with the four fingers. Any woman recognizing the sound does the same and leaves whatever she is doing and runs in the direction of the first sound. The crowd quickly swells and soon there is a wild dance to the tune of impromptu stanzas informing the people of what offence has been committed, spelling it out in such a manner as to raise emotions and cause action. The history of the offender is brought out in a telling gossip. Appeal is made to the dead ancestors of the offender, to join in with the "Anlu." Then the team leaves for the bush to return at the appointed time, usually before actual dawn, donned in vines, bits of men's clothing and with painted faces, to carry out the full ritual. All wear and carry the garden-egg type of fruit which is supposed to cause "drying up" in any person who is hit with it. The women pour into the compound of the offender singing and dancing, and, it being early in the morning, there would be enough excreta and urine to turn the compound and houses into a public latrine. No person looks human in that wild crowd, nor do their actions suggest sane thinking. Vulgar parts of the body are exhibited as the chant rises in weird depth. . . . [21]

With this gesture, Nkwain states, a period of ostracism begins in which no one is allowed to talk to the offender and which for that very reason is said to be like death, or worse than death, since death generates links between the living and the dead whereas ostracism "kills and gives no life." Shirley Ardener notes that the word *Anlu* derives from the root *lu*, which means "to drive away" and which makes it a word curiously similar to the Greek *apotropeic*, used in reference to things attributed with the power to avert or turn away evil.

In Latin America, the experience of state terror during the 1970s and '80s gave way to a form of organized political action among women, specifically "mothers" whose lives were affected by the violence, which is important to consider alongside this more established kind of "female militancy" in Africa. Because of their similarity in purpose, methods of action, and forms of organization, feminist scholars in North America tend to view this array of female political engagements across the region as a series of "motherist movements": movements made up of women who organized as mothers to denounce the "disappearance" of family members in the hands of the state. Among the better known groups are the Grupo de Apoyo Mutuo (GAM) and the Coordinadora Nacional de Viudas (CONAVIGUA) in Guatemala, the Madres de la Plaza de Mayo in Argentina, the Agrupación de Familiares de Detenidos-Desaparecidos (AFDD) in Chile, and the Co-Madres of El Salvador.[22] There is no reported nakedness among the political actions of the women involved in these movements. There is primarily—but perhaps just as significantly—the unapologetic making present and noteworthy, in quintessentially political settings like plazas and buildings of historic and national import, of the motherly body, which was sometimes decked in garments like white head scarves and mourning black dresses, whose symbolism of women's domestic worlds and of the private world of the family clashed with the public and institutional tenor of these settings.

Much of the literature on these motherist movements dwells on a fundamental paradox sustaining their activism. On the one hand, the states against which the women rose have historically—if only rhetorically—valorized motherhood and the family and grounded many of their policies directed at women on the Catholic image of Woman as Mother, the symbol of love, submission, vulnerability, and self-sacrifice. On the other hand, it is precisely this image of motherhood that the women used to their advantage, dramatizing powerlessness, appealing to the "natural order" of family and motherhood, protesting exactly within the role assigned to them by the state to demystify power and make their demands heard.[23] Jennifer Schirmer sums it up this way: "These mothers had to behave as *mothers* in search of their sons in order to survive. In transfiguring their intimacy of pain and domesticity of silence into social protest, these women dramatize[d] the contradictions of the repressive state in its feigned valorization and real destruction of family. By openly and defiantly questioning the state, these women help[ed] to demystify its force and methods of control."[24]

The women's transgression, their presence and visibility in places where they must remain invisible, their testing the limits of permissible political action, elicited a double response from state forces: At first, the military, the police, and other state agents appeared to have been confused by the women's actions, thrown aback by their challenge of authority with such display of vulnerability, and to have felt perhaps a certain degree of respect or awe toward the women. Alicia, a Co-Madre from El Salvador, explains: "'Since we first went out into the street dressed like this [in mourning] in 1983 the army has never tried to disrupt our march, because it is not the same to capture someone who is dressed in civilian clothes to whom one can do anything, and one who is dressed in black. . . . '" To the interviewer's question if she considers their dress a form of protection, Alicia responds, "Yes, the very military refer to us this way. . . . 'Here come the women in black.'"[25]

But while motherhood seems to have offered the women a degree of legitimacy and safety from state repression, the "protectiveness of motherhood," as Schirmer calls it, was for the most part temporary. Like a pendulum violently swinging over to the other side, the armed forces' confusion and respect quickly became rage and led to the perpetration of sheer brutality. All the movements have reported harassment by the state and members (mothers) who were tortured, raped, killed, or "disappeared." If all motherist groups were at first stunned by their ability to confront the police, Schirmer notes, they were also stunned by the particularly brutal ways in which they were subsequently treated. It was as if their transgression, the making political of motherhood, had rendered them untouchable—shielded them with the negative force that Bataille liked to refer to as the impure sacred—before provoking brutal retaliation for their despoiling of motherhood by means of the same violence against which they were protesting.

In Peru, state policies directed at women or the family during the 1970s and '80s also emphasized conceptions of femininity that posited maternity as the most important role taken by women. As a rule, governments removed support from programs considered to be "too political"— in other words, too focused on demanding that women be treated as active agents in their own right.[26] Most notable during this time were the Glass of Milk program, which began in Lima in 1984 as a municipal initiative guaranteeing one glass of milk per day per child and per gestating or nursing mother, and the Mothers' Clubs, which promoted local communal work.[27] There were also, as the 1980s and early '90s economic crisis mounted, self-generated Comedores Populares, soup kitchens run by women in Lima's shantytowns, which were critical in staving off hunger during the most critical times of inflation and IMF-inspired structural adjustment. The Glass of Milk program, in particular, which was eventually adopted nationally, turned into a lightning rod for all issues regarding governmental policy toward urban poor families and mothers: Any proposed amendment to the structure of the program, which became deeply corrupted, summoned thousands of protesting women to Lima's main square. I attended some of these demonstrations and remember well the visual impact of that enormous crowd of nursing mothers in front of national landmarks like the Palacio de Gobierno and the Catedral de Lima, flaunting their babies at the breast and, in so doing, exposing the contradiction of the state's simultaneous rhetorical high regard for motherhood and the family and its utter disregard for their physical well-being.

———

Monday p.m.: My father called; he sounded upset. "Where have you been? I left a message last night! Another one this morning!" It turns out that his friend Carmela has kept insisting, bless her heart, and Aparicio is now willing to see me—tomorrow at ten o'clock in the morning. But she said that I have to call his office to confirm.

———

Tuesday, 2:15 p.m.: My conversation with Mr. Aparicio was brief. I asked him to mention the most serious problems Mayor Andrade had encountered in the city in 1996, and he listed (1) cleanliness, (2) ambulatory commerce (informal markets), (3) security, and (4) what he called "the abandonment of the center." He explained that the center had been abandoned because it was never given the importance of a historic center. "We were on the verge of losing it [*a punto de perderlo*]," he said, "but we recuperated it." The problem was the total lack of control over the city, he said. He said that when Ricardo Belmont was mayor (before Andrade), the unions had virtually taken over the city government. "They were not getting paid," he said, in reference to the workers during Belmont's last couple of years in power when the city was undergoing one of its worst financial crises, instigated by Fujimori's efforts to cut the Municipalidad de Lima off from some of its main sources of revenue. "So they would go on strike and [as a form of protest] would throw real estate property and tax records out the window," he said. He said that they would grab the files and simply toss them out to the streets. "When we took office in 1996, there were no property tax registers," he went on. "We had to start from scratch, request new property and tax declarations, and give out new licenses." Once in office, one of their first measures was to relocate to other buildings the most important files, all original birth, death, and marriage records, for example, in case the workers tried to get ahold of them to impair city operations.

I asked him other questions, which he didn't answer directly but by referring a little randomly to initiatives and projects he and Andrade had undertaken. He then interrupted himself and said, "But your questions, Alberto could offer much better answers to them," as he grabbed the phone and dialed Mr. Andrade's direct number. I couldn't believe it—in

61

no time, I had an appointment with Andrade himself for the afternoon. He said he would be at his factory in San Juan de Miraflores, where I am to meet him at five o'clock.

———

Later: Back in Miraflores, at about 4:30, I took one of the yellow cabs that was lined up in front of Parque Salazar. I figured a "formal," registered taxicab stationed next to the popular seaside shopping mall would be the quickest and safest way to get to my appointment on time in the neighboring district of San Juan. Since I was in a hurry, I jumped in and only briefly bargained with the driver, getting him to lower the fare to what still seemed like an exorbitant amount to go to San Juan, much farther from Miraflores in the class- and race-conscious minds of Lima's residents than it is in reality.

The old, ramshackle *Tico* sped down Avenida Armendariz, then Avenida Grau in Barranco and several little streets in Surco to emerge at the Atocongo Bridge near the abandoned skeleton of Lima's elevated train, whose useless cement columns bear witness to one of the most scandalous public works scams of the 1980s.[28] On the south side of San Juan, where roads and naked brick buildings wage a Sisyphean struggle against Lima's desert dunes, is a wide, partially paved avenue where residences and corner bodegas mix with small industrial plants, motor and rubber tire shops, and sandy empty lots.

Driving slowly along a line of nondescript brick walls and metal gates, we looked for number 665. Each wall had a roofed surveillance tower, where at the peak of Sendero Luminoso's violence private sentinels stood guard day and night, machine guns in hand, looking over the factory compounds. Today the towers are empty. I rang the bell of 665 and was let into the grounds of Casa Alda, a medium-sized leather accessory factory. A short, gaunt man directed me to a waiting room on the second floor, where laying on a table were copies of several glossy coffee-table books published by Mayor Andrade in the late 1990s, showcasing the history and architecture of the city of Lima. I sat down as the man humbly clasped his hands and, in a marked highland accent, said that Mr. Andrade had called to say that he was running late.

One of the coffee-table books was about Barrios Altos, the easternmost section of El Cercado, built during colonial times on grounds that were slightly higher than the center proper. Mr. Andrade was born and raised in that district in the 1940s. The book is a collection of photos and interviews with Barrios Altos' oldest residents, a series of wistful, anecdotal reminiscences of a time when, so the lore goes, the district was a hub for the tradition-loving (and tradition-making) *criollo* culture of Lima. I had waited for over an hour when I heard Mr. Andrade's raspy voice coming up the stairwell and through the door, where he appeared dressed in an impeccable blue suit with Anita, his young and energetic assistant, by his side.

He apologized for being late, said that his previous meeting had gone on for too long, and invited me to come into his office, saying, *"Pasa, por favor,"* using the informal *tú* even though we had just met, and thus instantly, as if by magic, defining the terms of our engagement, his slight transgression of a tacit but powerful social rule both leveling the ground between us but also making it less firm, less definite. We sat at one end of a long, slick executive board table, where Mr. Andrade had placed a photo album that he said he wanted to show me. He said that I probably do not remember how things were before he became mayor since most *Limeños* of my generation grew up with our backs to the center, and he opened the photo album to display a series of pictures of Jirón Ucayali, Jirón Camaná, and the Central Market shot from above before and after the displacement of thousands of street vendors. A sea of beach umbrella tops and makeshift roofs filling up sidewalks and streets on the first shot gave way, on the second, to cleared and clean thoroughfares and repainted façades.

He didn't wait for me to ask a question before he began: "The city center was abandoned due to migration from the countryside. Peasants [*la gente campesina*] are used to doing kinds of work they can't do here in the city, so they went out to the streets to sell things. No one had the authority to say 'not here.' You should have seen," he said emphatically, the familiar, increasingly intimate tenor of his address—*"Tú hubieras tenido que ver"*—conveying a clear understanding that I, too, would have been horrified. "They had [pirate] phone line connections and electricity [at their outdoor vending posts]. They had broken through the pavement and built sewage installations for their bathrooms."

I do remember walking on recently evacuated streets that looked like they had just been bombed: the asphalt and sidewalks were worn out and peppered with cracks and holes—a condition that was noted by city officials to underscore not just the illicitness of what many here refer to as the "culture of informality" but what is thought to be its parasitic nature.

"People who still lived in the center were very ashamed of this," Mr. Andrade said, going on to suggest that the sense of shame and humiliation extended to those who worked in it and those who governed it.

"If you had to take a foreign visitor to [the Ministry of] Foreign Affairs, you had to drive through Jirón Cuzco, through all the great houses that were squatted [*tugurizadas*]." He said, "It was complete lack of authority, complete chaos and dirt," closing the back cover of his photo album as his demeanor turned grave to say that the situation he was describing, in a way, went beyond politics and policy and affected him at a personal level.

"When I returned to the center after a long time," he said grimly, "they [the migrants] looked upon me as if I were a stranger. My identity had been erased," he said with a look of disbelief, "and it had been occupied by someone who had come from another place. There were cultural values that weren't mine. They throw a banana peel on the sidewalk as if it were nothing [*como si nada*], and while back in the highlands that might make sense, since it biodegrades, here in the city it just rots and dirties the streets. You have to realize," he said leaping from the dimension of his own personal, intimate recollection to a historical and collective one, "that Lima was the capital, the political, cultural, religious center of the viceroyalty. It was a great city," he said, "with very special and characteristic architecture, like the [Moorish] balconies, for example. It was the identity of those balconies that we were concerned with. As *Limeños*, we were concerned with recuperating our identity."

Mr. Andrade then detailed some of the strategies he himself had devised to convince the street vendors to leave their deeply entrenched posts voluntarily. He said he convened dialogues and did lots of publicity that tackled the issue from a "psychosocial" point of view with ads that were forceful but of a dissuasive kind. "We used methods to dissuade the vendors [from the idea] that the street was the appropriate place to sell their merchandise as well as [to convince] the pedestrian that the street belongs to everybody, that they have the right to walk on it. To the vendor we said that the city had lent them the street for many years and that now they had to give it back." He also struck deals with the media, he said, which yielded good results in terms of public opinion and set the stage for the most difficult tasks, like the cleaning of the streets around the Central Market.

To go from what in the mayor's photo album was (before) a shapeless, ever-expanding mass of outdoor posts and labyrinthine corridors to (after) a clean and empty set of street intersections, Mr. Andrade waged war with the vendors. "So as you can imagine," he said, "they at first considered me their enemy, but then they began to make me the godfather [*padrino*] of their new [formal] markets. It all changed and turned into acceptance and a good relationship because their self-esteem changed, from the low self-esteem of the person who is in the street, working on precarious conditions [*en la precariedad*], to that of a person who owns his own establishment."

I asked Mr. Andrade who had conceived the terms of the campaign, specifically the idea of casting it as the "recuperation" of the city, and he said that he himself had come up with it.[29] "As the entrepreneur that I am, I know about advertisement," he said. Many people had assured me that it would be useless to ask officials about what exactly they hoped to recuperate and from whom, or about the concrete historical referent for the Lima they were determined to bring back from the past. But, to my surprise, Mr. Andrade's answer was unequivocal. He knew: "My referent is the Lima in which I lived as a child," he said assuredly. "In the 1950s, Lima had 1 million residents. It's that Lima," he said and added, "as well as the Lima referred to by my parents and my grandparents."

After a pause, he said, "I would like to emphasize that everything we did, we did in spite of the central government, who did not want us to succeed." He said he regretted that his accomplishments had been met with such aggression. "They said, 'Andrade is an insensitive person.' So we started to fix the parks, to beautify them. But the central government opposed us every step of the way. We needed the support of the PNP, and they never paid heed to my requests. To the contrary, they put obstacles, blocking the loans we had secured from the Inter-American Development Bank and the World Bank, for which we worked so hard, and encouraging the protesters who were acting violently." I asked, "Like the ones from ESMLL?"

"That was entirely planned!" he said. "They would get naked and scream. That affected me very much. It is widely known that they are paid by the SIN. Meanwhile, all the workers cashed their severance and their back pay." Looking distressed, he said, "They came up with these special aprons where they depicted me as the devil."

He sighed and said that only now the Inter-American Development Bank and World Bank loans he asked for years ago have finally been approved, which means they will become available when someone else is in office. Smiling resignedly, he said, "But that's the nature of the game," giving a gentle tap on the table and marking, it was clear to me, the end of the interview.

Mr. Andrade asked me if I needed a ride back to Miraflores and if I minded waiting a few minutes for him to put together a package that Mauricio was to dispatch right away. He introduced Mauricio to me, the old man who had let me in earlier, and said that he had worked in the company as a jack of all trades for twenty years. I thanked him and said

I would take a taxi, but giving me no option, he said firmly, "You can't walk around here alone!" and pointed to the waiting hall, where I sat and watched him wrap up a cardboard box containing several fossilized giant oyster shells that an admirer had dug and sent him as a gift. Fearing it would be illegal for him to keep the fossils, he had donated them to a small regional museum in a highland province of Lima, where they will be the main attraction.

We climbed up into a huge, bullet-proof SUV, Mr. Andrade, Anita, and I, and a chauffeur/bodyguard drove us out of San Juan swiftly, barely stopping or slowing down at the intersections. I think I felt more scared with all that frantic, eye-catching security than I would have felt walking alone down San Juan's dusty streets. On a two-way radio, Anita worked to coordinate Mr. Andrade's two stopovers for the evening at public events in the center and in San Isidro.

"We're on our way to the center—over," she spoke into the radio. *Prreeet! Prreeet!* The radio loudly signaled an incoming response. Mr. Andrade was running late to both events, and a worried voice on the other side asked what to do with the guests, who had already arrived at the second event.

"Give us thirty minutes," Anita replied. "Can you keep them there for thirty more minutes?"

We left the section of hilly shantytowns behind, and the scenery slowly morphed into neighborhoods of bigger and sturdier houses, of electrified fences and brighter lampposts, and back again into crammed, darkened clusters of feeble buildings as we drove through the different districts that lay along the Pan-Americana Highway. Mr. Andrade's car dashed down the highway in the opposite direction of the dense stream of headlights traveling south during Lima's rush hour. Seen through the car's tinted windows, the city's arid and austere landscape glowed in a warm, amber light.

THREE

Beauty

Beauty is nothing but the beginning of terror. —RILKE, *DUINO ELEGIES*

Within ten square blocks in the heart of downtown Lima there are about ten baroque churches and chapels. Some of them lost their stone-carved porticos long ago, to the earthquake of 1746 or to the no-less-cataclysmic fury of neoclassical renovation. But the few that retained them have also retained, in the riveting intricacy of their sculpted façades, a very eloquent articulation of the dependency of beauty on effect.

Of all those temples, the Church of La Merced is one of the most enthralling. One has to step back and look up from across the narrow commercial street of Jirón de la Unión to fully see its frontal face. Next to the corner bell tower, whose walls are richly textured with plaster padding, stands the church's altar portico like an outward conflagration of its sacred interior. It is carved out of gray and salmon-pink limestone; its two horizontal levels or "bodies" intersect with three vertical corridors or "streets" to form six loosely overlapping niches separated by broken cornices that effect in the whole a rhythmic, skyward movement. In the center niche, behind a wooden balustrade and under a scalloped roof, is the Virgin of La Merced, looking over. She is flanked by four other figurines standing in between tightly scrolled and leafy columns and carrying objects of meaning to the Mercedaria order. Underneath the Virgin, the church's dark arched doorway is like a huge gaping mouth.

In the sequence of low and boxy storefronts along the *jirón*, with their banal window displays and their roll-down steel doors collected at the top, the more substantial seventeenth-century building looks out of place, more awkward, in a way, than awesome. But when looked at from across the *jirón*, under the church's looming stature, the intricate carvings, the ornamental exuberance, the skillful, dramatic play of shadow and light make the eyes jump helplessly from detail to inexhaustible detail to the point that it suddenly appears as though the Virgin is moving, at once rising and descending, in a *trompe-l'oeil* effect that was originally intended to simulate a mystical vision.[1] Only then is it possible to fully understand what historians of the baroque mean when they say that the architecture of this period was effect-driven, that in its treatment of form and its focus on façades and ornamentation (rather than structure), baroque architecture was theatrical, scenery-like. Contrasting it with the classicism of the Renaissance, Heinrich Wolfflin says that, during the baroque, the beauty of a building was judged by its ability to entice viewers, to intimidate and overwhelm them with the lushness of its walls and a fusion of chiaroscuro that aimed precisely at producing a sense of moving masses and shifting forms. Wolfflin explains that while architecture, as an art medium, usually makes an impression by means of "what it *is*, that is, by its corporeal substance," baroque architecture aimed instead at provoking "an event," acting "through what it *appears* to be, that is, an illusion of movement."[2]

Today, despite the churches' dwindling budgets and languishing congregations, one only has to visit La Merced (or San Francisco, San Pedro, or San Agustín, a couple blocks over) to see the power that these baroque altars still command. On any given morning, before the day's first liturgy, a steady stream of worshippers enters the church. Men and women on their way to work sit in silence on pews facing the main altar, or stand or kneel before a side *retablo* (freestanding wooden altar), lowering their heads and stretching their arms out in a gesture of deliverance, taking on the languid or ecstatic demeanor of the images they revere. What's more, just on entering any of these churches and standing in front of a *retablo*, its ceiling-high, angel-rimmed top arching forward and seeming to close in, or on stepping under the low, richly padded or painted domes of the sacristy rooms in San Pedro or San Francisco, one realizes that it isn't necessary to be a devout Catholic to feel deeply moved. There is something about the beauty of these buildings, about the density and elaborateness of the work that is marvelous and uplifting and at the same time crushingly oppressive, and that suggests that beauty derives its power as much from what it arouses as from what it represses in us.

The Church of La Merced along with the few other seventeenth- and eighteenth-century buildings that are left scattered around downtown

Lima were centerpieces in Mayor Andrade's vigorous, if short-lived, project of beautification of the city center in 1996–2002. In one of the many documents and reports of this urban renewal campaign, Andrade defined his role as mayor as that of an "interpreter of the dreams of [Lima's] residents," which for him expressed the desire to recuperate the center of the city from the chaos and violence, the filth and delinquency to which certain "predatory habits" had subjected it for over a decade, pushing it into a state of decadence and anomie.[3] Time and again in this and other documents Andrade refers to his love for *lo limeño*, a term that evokes what is supposed to be truest, most vital and essential about Lima's *criollo* culture, which encompasses a type of music, a set of dances, a culinary taste, and a way of being urban that was once supposed to set *Limeños* apart from that which is Andean or Spanish. *Lo limeño* also includes a particular relation to physical space, an attitude toward the city's organization and its architecture, and a distinctive mode of writing and representing this relation and this attitude as precisely "typical" of Lima.

For Andrade, *lo limeño* thus inhabited the city's oldest architectural specimens and public spaces, which in 1996 he described as being in need of salvation, in need of a "new great crusade" to restore them to their original beauty and give them back their decency, integrity, and dignity; this was to be a critical step in the recuperation of Lima's identity, lost to the years of war and crisis as the historical center was "invaded," ill-treated, or destroyed. As it was made explicit in his master plan for the project, the aim of the recuperation of the historic center was to reinstate in it a sense of "homogeneity" and physical unity through the restitution of the "original appearance of the streets and façades," which entailed "eliminating the elements that are distorting or out of context."[4] Like the Church of La Merced in the bustling *jirón*, the other refurbished buildings and spaces, including the mayor's own mansion in Jirón Ucayali, seemed a little out of place against the eclectic or decayed setting in which Andrade hoped to bring about a reencounter with "our tradition."

Enthralling as the intricate carvings and gorgeous moldings of these buildings are, it is easy to forget that what Andrade refers to as their "original appearance" was, to a large extent, the result of the forceful and often violent Counterreformation offensive of the Spanish Catholic Church, which during the seventeenth century sought to transform the colonies into a bastion of religious and monarchic devotion. It is impossible to overestimate the role that baroque art and architecture played in the efforts of the flailing Spanish Crown to carry on with the conquest and consolidate its dominions in America. In the aesthetic language of the baroque, the crisis-ridden Spanish monarchy thought to have found the perfect medium to advance its own brand of modernity based on the revitalization of the Catholic faith and on the principles of royal power and caste-based authority (*estamento*) in the face of the rationalist and more independent spirit of the Reformation.[5] But rather than contravening Protestantism or stopping the advance of Enlightenment ideas, the Catholic Church's stress on the need for ecclesiastic mediation with the divine aimed at subsuming and overcoming them with the thrust of the church's imperious necessity. Commended with the philosophical justification and the realization of such a project, the Society of Jesus resorted to the human body's capacity for mystical experience, which it sought to extend, by means of the sensuous images of baroque art and ritual, into everyday, secular life. The Jesuit ideal of modern life could thus be described as one in which, saturated by the religious, even lay existence would be rapt in the experience of the divine as it manifested in the form of earthly, man-made things. Paraphrasing the views of Juan de Espinosa y Medrano, a seventeenth-century Peruvian writer, on the importance of artistic form in the transmission of religious and political ideas, historian Mariano Picón Salas explains that, during the baroque, sacred things were thought to be riddled with mystery and therefore to require no embellishment; but art, on the other hand, as a creation of the human mind, started from little more than nothing at all and thus necessitated elaboration to become a mystery through its form.[6]

There is plenty of evidence that artists and writers of the Spanish Golden Age and their counterparts in America, many of whom were affiliated with the court, were aware of the persuasive and potentially subjugating power of art, of the social and political value of artifice and illusion. What Picón Salas calls the "aesthetic will of the time" (Walter Benjamin also refers to the "artistic will" of the baroque age) had none of the pretension of disinterestedness and transcendence of classical art.[7] Because of this, it is commonly argued, as in Antonio Maravall's ambitious literary and historical study, that the Spanish baroque was, first and foremost, a state production, an absolutist and seigniorial form of "mass culture" and therefore the first form of propaganda. With their propensity toward exaggeration and their appeal to extremes, Maravall explains, baroque cultural artifacts sought to impress astonishment and wonder in the public as a way of manipulating and controlling its movements. He puts it this way: "The seventeenth century was an epoch of masses, undoubtedly the first in modern history, and the baroque was the first culture to make use of expedients to produce mass effects. This is attested to by the character of the theater, in its texts and scenario procedures; by the mechanized and external piety of post-Tridentine religion; [and] by the politics of attraction and repression that the states began to use. . . ."[8] Maravall notes that in the context of mounting political and financial crisis, both in the colonies and the metropolis, these baroque expedients were aimed at distracting the public from their ills and, for those in power, at creating the illusion that wealth and power still remained.[9]

For Walter Benjamin, who thought that baroque cultural forms of expression had reached their highest development in seventeenth-century Spain, it was in great measure the new open channels of communication established during this period between power and art, between politics and aesthetics, that made the study of the baroque necessary to understanding the workings of the modern nation-state. Presumably having his own early work on the German *Trauerspiel* in mind, he affirmed the need for "a book that presents the genesis of the baroque drama (*Trauerspiel*) in straight relation to the emergence of bureaucracy, the unity of time and action in straight relation with the dark office spaces of absolutism, the libidinous erotic poetry with the Inquisition already pregnant with the emerging police state, the final apotheosis of the operatic dramas with the structure of the philosophy of right about sovereignty." He believed that this would demonstrate, in light of the political developments in Europe in the 1930s, the baroque's "greater ascendancy, its electrified contact with the current situation."[10]

Being eminently an urban phenomenon, it wasn't just in art or architecture but in the city itself, as a whole, where baroque culture sought to have its foothold. In Lima, as in other early Spanish American cities, monarchic authority was exercised through the regulation of space, through control over its social distribution and use. When Lima was founded in 1535, its first streets were laid out in the Spanish trademark checkerboard grid, called *damero*, with the streets radiating at right angles out of a main square, called Plaza Mayor. After adjudicating the prime lots to the Cathedral, the Governor's Palace, the Archbishopric, and the Cabildo (city administration), the initial thirteen city blocks were divided into four *solares* (or plots) and assigned to each conquistador in a way that the property's proximity to the main square reflected the possessor's rank and social status, thus imprinting onto the urban landscape a late Renaissance vision of society as orderly, rational, and hierarchical. A set of city planning ordinances issued by King Philip II in 1573 reveals the importance placed on urbanization in Spain's civilizing mission and the almost magical, subduing powers the right sort of urban design and architecture were thought to have over the indigenous population. "While the new settlement is being completed," one of the ordinances reads, "the settlers should as far as possible try to avoid communication and trade with the Indians, and should not . . . let [them] into the confines of the settlement until it is completed and fortified, and the houses built, so that when the Indians do see it they are struck with admiration, and they understand that the Spaniards are settling there permanently and not temporarily, and they will fear them and will not dare offend them. . . ."[11]

These ordinances incorporated and sought to expand previous decrees to address the concerns of the emerging Spanish baroque state, which conceived of the city as a "theater stage" where monarchic authority was exercised through the enactment of power and beauty. Alejandra Osorio, in her study of early attempts at image making and identity building in Lima, explains that together with the city's layout and sumptuous architecture, the staging of elaborate public rituals, in which city officials would enact utopian ideals of urban space and polity, as well as of discipline and punishment, was for the Spanish monarchy and the local elite an important instrument of rule.[12] In 1542, with the official creation of the Viceroyalty of Peru, Lima was chosen as the seat of the viceroy and his court and soon became the most important bureaucratic and mercantile center between Panama and Cape Horn. But fearing that it could still be at a disadvantage in relation to other cities, such as Cuzco or Mexico City, which had been vital native urban centers in pre-Columbian times, throughout the seventeenth century Lima vied to legitimate its status of "most principal" city by developing a particularly ostentatious public ceremonial culture.[13]

Emulating Madrid and Seville, and surpassing them, Lima followed a yearly ceremonial calendar that included over three hundred fiestas, both religious and civic, for which the city embarked on the construction of elaborate and expensive sets, reconfiguring the Plaza Mayor and adjacent streets into classic or faraway, exotic sceneries by means of ephemeral architectural devices, such as triumphal arches, altars, obelisks, drapings and walls, new lights, and special sounds and smells. These theatrical displays included a profusion of emblems, ciphers, apologues, and hieroglyphs carrying complex political messages to be interpreted by the attendees, who were largely illiterate. During these ceremonies, the city itself was turned into a "work of art," complemented by the participants' sumptuous attire and rigid etiquette, which in the baroque culture of public scrutiny spoke to the political and social value of ostentation and appearance as markers of class status and authority.[14] Going to the heart of this complex play of surface and depth, John Beverly states that in the aesthetics of the baroque, "pomp, or the appearance of power [was] not clearly separable from its substance: power [was] in a certain sense ostentation."[15]

Just as important as the role of rituals and celebrations in the crafting of Lima's unique urban identity was that of the *relaciones de fiestas*, written accounts in which an official scribe described each ceremony in vast detail, from the ephemeral arches and façades down to the name, ornate clothes, and jewels of notable participants. These panegyrics about the city, which were intended to be disseminated abroad and in the viceroyalty's interior, were an occasion for the Lima Cabildo to exalt the city, to present it as a beautiful, harmonious, and unitary body, as well as to develop a historical memory of its preeminence over other cities.[16] Looking to represent Lima as the ideal embodiment of courtly life, it was not uncommon for seventeenth-century artists and chroniclers to exaggerate its ceremonial magnificence, to invent all sorts of details, and to embellish or aggrandize its physical appearance.

But if it cultivated an image of opulence and magnificence, Lima also sought to portray itself as deeply pious and decorous. During the seventeenth century, Lima claimed to have in its midst more churches, convents, monasteries, and saints than any other city in America (five of those saints were eventually canonized and the beatification of at least a dozen is still pending in Rome). In 1685, after only the first segments of the city wall had been erected around Lima—which arguably had less of a military than an aesthetic function[17]—a colorful print of a bird's-eye view of the walled-in city was already circulating in Lima and in Europe. The print cleverly combined actual details with ideal urban stereotypes of the time with the intention of placing Lima on a par with Amsterdam and Seville by having its ultimate baroque physiognomy evoke the idea of a monastery-city.[18] And in 1700, around the time the altar-façade of La Merced was completed, almost a fifth of Lima's population lived a secluded life in one of the city's forty-three convents and monasteries; the incessant tolling of bells was said to bring about such an atmosphere of reclusion and mysticism in the city that some chronicles of the time referred to Lima as a "levitative city."[19]

Situated at the point of juncture between the Spanish monarchy's absolutist rule, the moralist repression of the Catholic Church, and the complex, rapidly shifting social and political reality of the seventeenth century, Lima saw the emergence of what Bolívar Echeverría has called a "baroque ethos," in which fiercely conservative and radically modern forces coexisted in teetering tension. One way in which this ethos manifested was in the colonial state's impulse toward order, social control, and

Lima

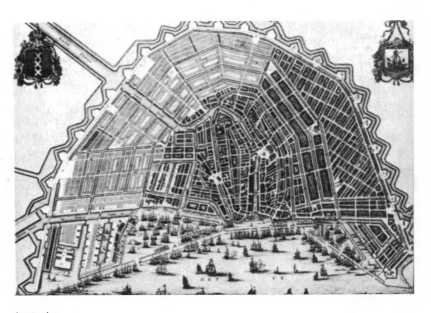

Amsterdam

efficiency—itself expressed in the city's rigid layout, its swelling bureaucracy, and its fixation with the control of flows—which in turn generated an excess of its own, unleashing opposite tendencies toward irrational, extravagant, sensuous, or rebellious forms of political and artistic expression. In a three-pronged definition of the baroque, Echeverría captures most effectively the conundrum posed by this "ethos." For him, the baroque existed in the productive tension generated by its contradictory aesthetic and political tendencies: First it was prescriptive, formalist, and ceremonial, characteristics that stemmed from its *repressive* qualities; it was also false, ornamental, and theatrical, which stemmed from its *unproductive* qualities; and it was extravagant, artificial, and exaggerated, which stemmed from its *transgressive* qualities, themselves made possible by the first, *repressive* ones.[20]

Echeverría's is a Bataillean interpretation of baroque culture, and from that perspective he distinguishes its ethos from other forms of "modern ethos," that is, from other ways of dealing with the contradictions inherent to postcolonial contemporary life in Latin America. These contradictions, he explains, are generated by the loss or the repression of "the qualitative," of the irreducible—at once most sovereign and basest—aspects of our human (and in the last instance, our animal) reality to the advantage of the rationalist, productive, and progress-oriented values of capitalist culture. Echoing claims made by other Latin American intellectuals, such as Ángel Rama, Alejo Carpentier, and Severo Sarduy, Echeverría argues that the baroque was the earliest and most decisively constitutive form of modernity brought to the Spanish colonies and that, as a result, a "baroque way of being modern" is more deeply rooted and current in Latin America than the attitudes toward modern life brought later either by the enlightened colonialism of the eighteenth century, the republicanism of the nineteenth, or the liberal (but still largely dependent) forms of capitalism of the twentieth.[21] As such, while the baroque ethos could be said to be Latin America's heaviest burden, its worst historical encumbrance in its path toward a liberal modernity, it is also held by Echeverría as its most hopeful alternative, the core of its utopian possibility.

For Echeverría, the baroque ethos, which he counterposes to what he calls the "realist" (protestant), the "romantic," and the "classic" (humanist) ethos, doesn't just affirm the contradictions of modernity like the realist does, or deny them like the romantic does, or resign itself to them like the classic does. Instead, it encourages us to see the contradictions of modern life, the repression or destruction of "the qualitative," as a source of energy for the re-creation of a different and more radical

75

dimension of it. In Echeverría's perspective, the extreme moral tension provoked by the baroque ethos is not too far from what, as a contraposition to the calculating rationalism of modern, capitalist society, Bataille calls eroticism and characterizes as "the affirmation of life even in death." This sovereign affirmation of life is not to be conceived of as a return to a former (natural or animal) condition but as something new, as something charged with the power of the aspects of humanity least assimilable by rationality but possible only in light of the limits and prohibitions that rationality imposes.[22]

From the late 1550s on, this colonial baroque ethos radiated from Lima out to the viceroyalty's interior, to other Spanish cities as well as to the countryside, where many new towns were created to be the main locus of political power and cultural production. Osorio describes how the city of Cuzco, for instance, shared and competed with Lima in the baroque process of "inventing traditions" by refashioning its Incan dynastic history and portraying itself as the seat of the Inca empire, still brimming with indigenous vassals ready to serve the king.[23] The countryside, for its part, was reorganized through a vast system of resettlement of the indigenous population, whereby entire rural villages or hamlets were relocated to new, larger, and more uniform towns, called *reducciones*, built according to the Spanish grid pattern. "Reducing" indigenous people into standardized towns was seen as a prerequisite for their conversion to Catholicism and for their attainment of order and justice, which for sixteenth- and seventeenth-century Spaniards were bound up with what they referred to as "*policía*."

As one of the chief benefits that the native population was to derive from these urban resettlement schemes, *policía* referred to a broad range of attributes of civilized life, such as social order, cleanliness, and rationality. Related, on the one hand, to the Greek *politeia*, the term *policía* implied life in a community in which individual desires and interests were subordinated to those of the group by means of ordinances and laws. On the other hand, it entailed, as in the Latin *politia*, aspects of personal comportment and private life, such as morality, refinement, and good manners.[24] In both senses, the Spanish notion of *policía* referred to virtues associated with urban life, the only mode of living conducive to a properly human way of being; those living beyond the confines of the city or independently of it, as the Greeks had long ago defined them, were believed to be barbaric, bestial, or subhuman.[25]

The notion of *policía*, which was central to the empire that the Spanish sought to establish in America, was an interestingly multifaceted concept, riddled with ambiguities. In fifteenth- and early sixteenth-century

Spain, the term was related to *pulidez* (polish or burnish) and used mainly in reference to artistic objects and literary texts to allude to their author's refinement of spirit, delicateness, and elegance of expression. It was used, however, also in reference to manners and deportment, a context in which it could easily turn into a negative quality denoting excess of luxury or ostentation of dress, as with the dolled-up appearance of "a vicious daughter and of public women."[26] With the conquest, the concept of *policía* was brought to America, where its meaning expanded to encompass the natives' way of life and perceived intellectual refinement. It appears in the earliest writings about the New World, where it is employed as a yardstick to measure the degree of "civility" or "urbanity" of indigenous people and their ability to live in reason, agreement, beauty, and order.[27] It referred to life in the city understood both as *urbs*—as an architectural entity, expressed in the design, appearance, and quality of its buildings—and as *civitas*—as a human community—juxtaposing these two historically opposing views of the city into a single notion of urban life, in which the city's physical reality and the social and moral bond of its residents engendered one another.[28]

Some of the earliest instructions concerning the foundation of Spanish towns and indigenous *reducciones*, even earlier than those emitted by King Philip II, showed how close city or town life was believed to be to the acquisition of *policía*, and this to the attainment of a moral and properly human existence. After requesting that indigenous people be gathered and assembled in urban settlements, each with a plaza, a grid of streets, and a church, the instructions emphasized that outside every new town an appointed Spanish administrator should settle in a house of stone (as opposed to mud brick) and be "responsible for seeing to it that the Indians lived in *policía*, that, for example, they wore clothes, that they slept in beds, that each had only one wife, and that they did not eat off the floor but . . . from tables."[29] *Policía*, in short, referred to a town's orderly layout, to the adornment, beauty, and harmony of its buildings as well as to the degree of politeness, civism, and courtesy of its residents, to their sociability and level of instruction in the Christian doctrine, their composure, good upbringing, and refinement of manners, their good sexual habits and industriousness, and their clothing, especially if adorned or elegant.[30]

At the beginning of *Historia del Nuevo Mundo*, the 1653 chronicle by the Jesuit missionary Bernabé Cobo, the supposed lack of *policía* among native peoples upon first contact with the Spaniards is attributed to the way Cobo assumes they were brought up, left by their parents, he writes, "to grow up like little beasts," exposed to their own (their parents')

[handwritten margin, top] The limits are both interior and exterior

[handwritten margin, right] The extravagance of baroque architecture contains beautiful & terrible, subsumption, subordination, oppression of genocide, subordination of beauty

[handwritten margin, right] Simultaneously enthices and terrifies us.

[handwritten margin, bottom right] The feeling of fear brings us to our climate, sublime/beauty

unrepressed unruliness and sensuality. Later in the text, Cobo expresses certainty and relief in noting that the "memory" of the Spanish nation (in the sense of tradition or culture) was already so deeply rooted in American soil that, even if the Spaniards were to leave it for good, it would not be eradicated from it or completely erased from the soul of the natives. Emphasizing the power and importance of orderly cities and of beautiful or magnificent architecture in implanting this lasting "memory," Cobo notes that there already are "so many towns built to our design [*nuestra traza*], so many sumptuous buildings of stone and mortar, so many stones worked with the delicacy and art [*primor y arte*] of Europe, in the shape of columns, bases and all manner of carvings and moldings; so many majestic sepulchers, so many domes, irrigation ditches and bridges of stone and mortar, and of brick, tile, ceramic, and glass, none of which the Indians knew before; and, finally, [so many] temples, castles, walls . . . and other strong works of deep foundations" that there is no reason why Spanish culture and power should not last as long in America as time itself.[31]

It is interesting to think of the effect-driven character of baroque forms of expression, what following Echeverría I am calling the baroque ethos, in light of later European ideas regarding the place of physical beauty in the constitution of social, "civilized" life. Starting with Edmund Burke's 1757 *A Philosophical Enquiry into the Origin of Our Ideas of the Sublime and the Beautiful*, which was inspired by a 1674 translation of Longinus's text on aesthetics, a series of modern reflections developed in Europe as an alternative to the humanistic, "enlightened" idea of art as the expression of full and integrated subjectivity. Stressing the element of fear in the aesthetic experience, as opposed to neoclassicism's emphasis on judgment of form, Burke's ideas about beauty concern the emotions that certain qualities in things are capable of arousing in us. Physical beauty, like sublimity, is for Burke not subject to reason; it bypasses reason and induces us to a state of submission that can lead to a complete loss of self. Because Burke's interest is the aesthetically induced passions—ranging from terror to the erotic, to a blending of terror *with* the erotic—it is perhaps not surprising that much of his discussion of beauty is centered upon the female body. The body of a woman, he writes, is like "a deceitful maze, through which the unsteady eye glides giddily, without knowing where to fix, or whither it is carried."[32] But beauty, unlike the sublime, also leads to love, to "sentiments of tenderness and affection" that stave off our feelings of desire, lust, and fear. The feelings of attachment inspired by love bring about the taming of desire or, in more contemporary language, the sublimation of it. That is why beauty, of which arguably animals are not aware, is for Burke a "social quality." On the one hand, it directs and heightens the sensual appetite that man has in common with other animals; but on the other, it awakens in him a feeling of love, which represses the "violent and tempestuous passions" that we associate with animal desire. Men, who are not "designed like [animals] to live at large," have beauty, which channels desire into forms that are agreeable with human society and morality.[33]

With this, Burke tapped into what would turn out to be (from the romantics to Kant and onwards) a fundamental modern preoccupation in aesthetic theory, namely, the idea of excess as a key element in subjectivity. This excess, which the secular language of Burke's text develops into the source of aesthetic feeling, of the erotic, and even of the sentiments provoked by things considered sacred, both enables the self and, at the same time, terrorizes it and threatens to annihilate it. Beauty is, in other words, the suggestion of limits through reasonableness of size, smoothness of texture, polish, lightness, and grace, which lure us to it by suggesting, too, the transgression of those limits, the enticing possibility of getting lost. Sublimity, conversely, is that which is already in excess of any limit or boundary and which more swiftly and directly arouses fear through greatness of dimension and through the absence of light and sound. But what lurks behind beauty and what excites us in the presence of the sublime is equally disorienting and undermining of reason, involving the risk of madness or death, the total expenditure of the self. "The mind is so entirely filled with its object, that it cannot entertain any other," writes Burke, "nor by consequence reason on that object which employs it." For the overwhelming influence of a beautiful or sublime object "anticipates our reasonings, and hurries us on by an irresistible force."[34]

As Adam Phillips points out in his introduction to the *Enquiry*, these forms of aesthetic experience are closely connected in Burke's thought to his ideas about power and social hierarchy. They are "bound up," Phillips explains, "with the idea of authority as a species of mystification."[35] The power of institutions such as kings and leaders, clergy and churches, arises from their assumed ability to inflict pain and, above all, death so that in the presence of these authorities one is engulfed by fear, which for Burke is the common stock of the sublime. "I know of nothing sublime," Burke states, "which is not some modification of power." Aristocracy and tyranny are sources of sublime feelings, just as is the power of other mysterious social forces, likewise threatening of life, that Burke would later associate with social upheaval and revolt, where the intoxication of the "unsteady eye" is evoked again in relation to the roused mob during the French Revolution.[36]

Burke's idea of beauty and sublimity, in their power to overwhelm with fear and to fold aesthetic feeling, the erotic, and the sacred into one another, strongly evokes what Bataille refers to as the state of "continuity." The search after beauty is, for Bataille, an eminently human effort "to escape from continuity," to set up limits that will bestow an identity to things and interrupt the chaotic, indistinct continuity that we relate to the animal world.[37] As with Burke, Bataille's most complete discussion about beauty concerns female beauty. Beauty, according to Bataille, denies the animal in us, whose presence in the human form we find to be repugnant. In women, the absence of certain attributes, a "heaviness" of the limbs, for instance, associated with physical work, enhances the erotic value we assign to their human form. He writes, "The less clearly [a woman's shapes] depend on animal reality or on a human physiological reality, the better they respond to the fairly widespread image of the desirable woman."[38] Yet for Bataille there would be nothing attractive about a woman if her beauty did not conceal a mysterious, animal aspect: "her private parts, the hairy ones, to be precise, the animal ones."[39] The naked body of a woman thus arouses only to the extent that it is also obscene, that it causes anguish without suffocating, and that its animality is revolting without exceeding "the limits of a horror which beauty makes bearable and fascinating at once."[40]

Andrade's project of beautification of the center of Lima came in the wake of a global trend, which only in Latin America led to the rehabilitation of several city centers, including Havana, San Juan, Mexico City, Quito, Puerto Madero (Buenos Aires), and Salvador de Bahia in Brazil. This trend was supported by UNESCO's World Heritage Program, which since 1972 has promoted the protection and preservation of "historic" cities as sites whose "outstanding universal value" must be considered humanity's cultural heritage; it was also tacitly acknowledged by the second U.N. World Summit on Human Settlements (Habitat II), which took place in June 1996 in Istanbul and in whose platform of action Mayor Andrade found validation for his plans for the center of Lima, specifically its call to governments to contribute to the conservation and rehabilitation of historical and cultural sites as part of their efforts to develop socially and economically sustainable human settlements. Buildings, spaces, places, and landscapes, the platform of action states, are important expressions of the culture, identity, and religious beliefs of societies, "particularly in light of the need for cultural identity and continuity in a rapidly changing world."[41] The platform's recommendations exhibit a great deal of ambivalence regarding, on the one hand, the need for progress and development and, on the other, for conservation and continuity—principles that, arguably, run against progressive change and the U.N.'s goals of democratization, civic participation, and universal human rights.

This ambivalence can also be detected in city government documents outlining the goals for the "recuperation" of Lima. In the late 1990s, when the Plan Maestro was drafted, as the national institutional avenues for democratic and civic participation were becoming scarce and as the first signs of Fujimori's impending political downfall were becoming manifest, Andrade attempted to resolve this ambivalence by presenting the recuperation of the city center, of what he called Lima's "foundational space," as a way of overcoming the tensions between conservation and modernization. In the restitution of the center of Lima as a clean and secure place, as the "ordering nucleus of Lima's urban dynamic," Andrade hoped to redefine the notion of tradition so that it would transcend its opposition with modernity; to recast *Limeños'* understanding of the past so that it would transcend its potential conflict with the future; and to reformulate the terms of *Limeños'* identification with tradition so that it would become compatible with the forces of globalization. Andrade's campaign revealed his strong belief that modernity and Lima's future as a world city could be achieved only through the recuperation of tradition and the past.[42] What's more, both the summit's platform of action and Andrade's campaign of recuperation were premised on the idea that there is an objective and universal understanding of the value and significance of places, landscapes, and buildings as historical sites; but if there is anything Lima's history and its most recent experience of urban renewal have shown, it is that the value and meaning of such places, landscapes, and buildings is historically contingent, that in postcolonial realities like Peru, it can only be the object of brutal contestation.

A critical dimension of the way Andrade succeeded in mobilizing certain notions of beauty, order, and cleanliness as neutral or natural categories, as qualities universally valued and desired, can be best understood through what Bataille calls the "assimilation" of heterogeneous social forces and what, more recently but with the same concern in mind,

Elizabeth Povinelli has referred to as the modern state's "practice of commensuration."[43] In a way that Bataille might have, had he witnessed the onslaught of liberal political self-certainty that followed the end of the Cold War, Povinelli addresses the challenge that the existence of alternative—she calls them "radical"—social, cultural, and moral worlds pose to the norms of liberal civil society. She examines the social practices and forms of social power that are employed to make those radical worlds commensurate with the idea and norms of civil society without the use of repressive force. One of these forms of power, whose emergence Povinelli traces back to seventeenth-century Europe, is the notion of "public reason" and its deployment to effect forms of communication (between "free" and "equal" citizens) and nonviolent judgment that are assumed to give way to a shared cultural and moral community. Finding justification for actions on the existence (or possibility) of this shared community, Povinelli remarks, universalizes historical reason through appeal to consensus as the basis of nonviolent means of commensurating diverging moral and epistemological worlds. But, in practice, democratic regimes often resort to violent means of repression of disparate or diverging—we can call them "heterogeneous"—social and cultural practices. Considering the widespread "real-time violence" that, in the guise of reason, liberal democratic systems commonly employ, Povinelli wonders what it is that makes it possible "to characterize moments of social repression and social violence as moving forward a nonviolent shared horizon, as the peaceful proceduralism of communicative reason, rather than as violent intolerance, i.e., the pragmatic aspects of communication."[44]

In the context of shattered civil society institutions and broken-down channels of communication, as was the reality of Fujimori's last years in power, it seems reasonable to ask how naturalized notions of beauty and order came to take the place of "public reason" as a means of reaching the same kind of consensus and as justification for the violence employed in making disparate social worlds part of a cohesive cultural and moral community. Crucial to this was the use of politically and historically sanitized principles of urban planning and renewal, which relied heavily on aesthetic ideals that, historical evidence would suggest, hearken back to the fantasies of the urban panegyrics of Lima's baroque period, of whose historical and political import baroque artists and intellectuals were, conversely, extremely conscious. Andrade invoked the aesthetics of a time that, contrary to his own understanding, conceived of the relationship between art and power, aesthetics and politics as inextricable. Beverly puts it thus, "The paradox of baroque art is that it [was] a technique of power (aristocratic-absolutist) and, at the same time, the consciousness of that very power's finitude."[45]

In Lima, the ideals that manifested in the complex, highly ornamental, and deeply religious tendencies of baroque cultural life were aggressively fought as obscurantist and irrational by city officials with the arrival in the late 1700s of the more "advanced" and academicist ideas of the Enlightenment. They were further shunned, along with all things colonial, after Peru's independence from Spain in 1821. In 1870, the last vestiges of the city wall were torn down, reflecting a strong urban modernization impulse best expressed in a 1872 law that proscribed the construction of carved-wood balconies and *celosías*, the Moorish-style enclosed galleries that for about three hundred years had been Lima's architectural signature and were now seen as retrograde. Lima's baroque past was thus suppressed until the late 1920s when it reemerged as a group of abstract, formal traits known as neocolonial style. Emptied out of its historical and political significance and reconstituted to reflect the new social and cultural climate in the city, between 1925 and 1955 these neobaroque traits became a dominant feature in constructions, both residential and institutional, erected in the city center and in Lima's expanding neighborhoods. The neocolonial style, which architect Héctor Velarde has characterized as a "reactionary" style,[46] was thus decidedly popular during the decades of heightened city-ward migration from the highlands. This period of urban transformation, whose beginning was perhaps marked by the 1921 publication of a collection of traditionalist vignettes called *Una Lima que se va* (*A Lima That Goes Away*), also saw the revalorization of *criollo* culture as the essence of *lo limeño*, of which neocolonial architecture quickly became and has remained a key component.

Along with those formal traits, twentieth-century architecture also witnessed the resurgence of the baroque concern with "atmosphere," which translated into an approach to architecture that Velarde has described as "*escenográfico*" (scenery-like), as "dynamic, pathetic, 'emotional,' and capricious."[47] Nourished by a short period of architectonic eclecticism in Europe, from 1925 onwards, besides the erection of neocolonial structures, hundreds of houses were built in Lima in a chaotic blend of styles, displaying the oddest, most whimsical and artificial combination of elements copied from all sorts of European illustrations and postcards depicting distant, exotic places. These architectural elements were turned into fanciful, anachronistic styles of Moorish, medieval, Napoleon II, Tudor, Chinese, and Incan inspiration, or into local interpretations of residence types, such as the *petit chateau,* or of modern architecture, such as the art deco *estilo buque* (houses in the shape of steamships).

As a result, within the twelve square kilometers of the city center, today one can see mansions or *petit hotels* (apartment buildings) with seventeenth-century French mansard roofs (such as the Edificio Rímac, built in the 1920s), imposing Greco-Roman colonnades (such as the Palacio de Justicia, built in the 1930s), stone baroque porticos and carved wood balconies (such as the Palacio Arzobispal and the Palacio Municipal, built in the 1920s to 1940s), porticos with Incan or pre-Incan motifs (Escuela de Bellas Artes, built in the 1920s), medieval castles (Casa Rospigliosi, 1920s), and Incan fortresses (Museo del Indio, 1940s). Walking around the center, one is often under the impression of having stepped backstage in an empty or abandoned theater and moving among discarded props and faded backdrops designed to give a feeling of "pastness" or "farawayness." In his cultural history of Spanish America, Picón Salas states that, figuratively speaking, Renaissance art and culture could be described as "a dialogue" because of the way that writers and artists relied on rules that made individual features and pieces of work enter in conversation with one another. In the baroque, he says, forms of expression were more like a series of soliloquies that contradicted each other or cancelled each other out.[48] One is tempted to say something similar about downtown Lima's material culture. In the fanciful eclecticism of the city's architecture, each building, with the atmosphere of mystery, grandiosity, or primitiveness that it gives off, strikes the one who's looking at it as one such soliloquy.

———

That baroque art and architecture tended toward artificiality and effectism; that, in addition, seventeenth-century writers were prone to hyperbolic expression and fond of illusionism are widely known facts. Despite this, the idea that Lima during its long baroque period was a time of abundance and urban splendor has thrived and persisted in some important corners of the modern historiography of Lima. From Ricardo Palma's *Tradiciones peruanas* published in the mid-1800s to José Gálvez's nostalgic *Una Lima que se va* to contemporary historians like José de la Riva Agüero, César Pacheco Vélez, and Juan Manuel Ugarte Eléspuru, Lima's baroque epoch, running roughly from the mid-1500s to the early 1700s is held as a time of plenitude. In the following excerpt, Riva Agüero describes this epoch of baroque plenitude, managing to weave perhaps more seamlessly than any seventeenth-century panegyric Lima's contradictory images of saintliness and voluptuousness:

The capital lived in a continual feast, and its inhabitants, as is known that a certain viceroy said to the monarch, did nothing but toll bells and light fireworks. Any event was a motive for loud and ostentatious ceremonies, secular and of the Church, the kissing of a royal hand, processions, parades, horse-riding events, masquerades, feasts of light and bullfights. On great occasions, as with the crowning or obsequies of kings, the celebration of a victory, the birth or wedding of princes, the public entrance or the death of viceroys and archbishops, the canonization of saints, and the autos-da-fe, the whole of Lima took part of the solemnities; and through the streets replete with crowds, under balconies swelled with women dazzling with lace trimmings, diamonds and pearls, passed in colorful formation the militia companies and their cheerful kettledrum and clarinet players, with crimson bows of silver fringes; the religious communities with their habits of varied colors; the students of all three schools [presumably Universidad de San Marcos, Convictorio de San Carlos, and Escuela de Medicina de San Fernando], with blue, red and brown capes and hoods; the university cloisterers, with their vestments and garlands; the grave cortege of the tribunals [of the Inquisition] and the Audiencia, in horses draped in black trappings; the mayors and councils of the Cabildo dressed in scarlet red; the body of the nobility; the gentlemen with lances and the elegant floats.

The most famous literary men would then dispute the honor of perpetuating in writing the memory of this courtesan magnificence; and the complicated arabesques of style, the embroideries, the precious stones, and the *churriguerismos* [extreme baroque quality] of the phrase, the contorting metaphors and the artificial and sonorous clauses of the printed descriptions were to surpass the ostentation and splendor of the very feasts they evoked.[49]

In this Lima, life is supposed to have transpired to the tumultuous and never-ending pace of carnivals, bullfights, and hundreds of other "traditional" fiestas and, when these subsided, to the melancholy rhythm of the monasteries' bells and their interminable calls for prayer. In these representations of the colonial past, swaying between sumptuary excess and religious fervor, Lima is often peopled by "types"—the *tapada* (or covered woman), the *beata* (or beatific woman), the *faite* (or street fighter), the *huachafo* (or vulgar arriviste), and so on—each of whose character was a crucial ingredient of what, together, made up the essence of *lo limeño*. In the two extremes of Lima's baroque art and culture, past and contemporary historians have seen indisputable signs of the city's apogee. They attribute this cultural climax and grandeur to the economic bonanza produced by mining extraction, especially from the immensely rich silver mine of Potosí, whose trading route forcibly passed through Lima on its way to Europe.[50]

Many other writings of the time, however, such as those based on the letters and reports by the Count of Lemos, viceroy of Perú from 1667 to 1674—a period considered by Pacheco Vélez to be of fervent baroque production—describe a viceroyalty on the verge of collapse: The silver mine of Potosí was bankrupt, its output rapidly decreasing, and its *mita* (mandatory service for indigenous people) experiencing large numbers of defections; the Real Hacienda (fiscal offices) as well as the Audiencia de Lima (administration of justice) were entirely corrupt and ineffective, its posts used as no more than sinecures; the Caja Real de Lima (the city's treasury) was mired in debt and always struggling to finance its most pressing expenses (like the fiestas); crime in the city was rampant and deaths by firearms a daily occurrence; the clergy, according to the viceroy, lived an entirely dissolute life and was given to offbeat mystical and millenarian ideas; and the streets of the city were filled with "licentious women" wearing indecent clothing, which the Count of Lemos attempted to regulate.[51]

In a short article called "El virreinato peruano y la llamada 'crisis general' del siglo XVII," historian Luis Miguel Glave says that at different points in the seventeenth century the viceroyalty was threatened by conflicts between caciques (regional lords) and by various bursts of social rebellion. He shows that the production of silver and mercury, the viceroyalty's fiscal revenues, and its remittances to the metropolis were systematically dropping throughout the century before experiencing a brusque drop and a long period of stagnation after the turn of the eighteenth century. He speaks of a labyrinthine system of administration in which officers of the Crown "bought" their posts and continually backed up fraudulent deals, such as the one by a minor functionary at the mint of Potosí who managed to lure authorities at the highest spheres of government in Lima into a financial scheme that left all currency in the viceroyalty carrying 25 percent less metal than its nominal value, shaking up the colony's entire economic edifice.[52]

The *Libros de Cabildo* of Lima (city's colonial records) also describe a city mired in debt and permanently caught in budgeting problems. María Antonia Durán Montero's study of the *Libros* exposes the city's difficulties keeping up with its *policía* (in the sense of order and beauty), its constant struggle against the traffic of wagons and carriages, and its helplessness with regard to the handling and disposal of refuse, which in more than one occasion sent the city into a sanitation crisis.[53] Likewise, Durán Montero's study of a 1613 census of "Indians" in Lima presents evidence that in the interstices between *solares*, a vast network of *corralones* or "corrals"—modest one- or two-room dwellings lined along a narrow, open-air passage—had already broken up the original model of plot distribution based on rank in order to house the city's laborers and workers. This study also shows that, in 1613, there already was a widespread problem of *tugurización*, or squatting, whereby dozens of family homes in the city had been partitioned and leased or subleased to multiple family groups.[54]

As with Durán Montero's census, Bernabé Cobo's 1639 record, *Fundación de Lima*, draws attention to the undesired transformation that the city's original *traza* had undergone in its first century of existence. The Cabildo's efforts to maintain the uniformity of the grid plan hadn't sufficed to impede its gradual deformation. The cause for this, Cobo explains, is that, as the city expanded beyond the first city blocks, "Indians" and servants built their "vile ranchos" in such a way that "some sections of the city [are] broader than others and have blocks that are uneven and crooked streets and others with a dead end."[55] Thus, despite the colonial state's best efforts to build and represent the city as a racially and hierarchically ordered space, Lima's hybrid plebeian cultures were already thriving in the seventeenth century. In 1689, what should have been the peak of Lima's baroque period, Viceroy Count of Monclova, the last viceroy of the Hapsburg dynasty, entered Lima and felt beleaguered, he wrote in a letter home, by the "pitiful state" of most buildings and churches; his descriptions of the city depict it as overtaken by an atmosphere of "decayed opulence," as one of the editors of his letters puts it, which was compounded by the city's financial shortcomings and inability to rebuild after the earthquake of 1687.[56]

The tension between the extreme and contradictory facets of illusion and reality, beauty and decadence, order and chaos, apotheosis and the looming threat of catastrophe, was thus lodged at the core of Lima's baroque experience and lingers in the social and political culture of the city. At the heart of this grinding tension is what Sebastián Salazar Bondy in 1954 characterized as a "Colonial Arcadia," as a historical mirage that tendentiously attributes an idyllic character to a time in which life, organized as it was around rigid social castes and wealth-based privileges for the few, was rather mired in social and political problems. In his critical essay *Lima la horrible*, Salazar Bondy writes,

The colonial period, idealized as an Arcadia, hasn't yet met its judge, its incorruptible critic. The image of it offered to us in articles, stories, and essays is made up of supposed abundances and serenities without ever figuring in it the conceivable tension that there was between masters and servants, foreigners and natives, the powerful and the miserable, which must have torn society apart at least in its underlying depths. But . . . those of us who suspect the existence of a social fissure in that historical subsoil have only a dim possibility to bring it to light. To belie the Colonial Arcadia will always be a difficult, thankless task, for the multitude has ingested with scarcely any misgivings or suspicion and for more than a century countless pages written by memorable doctors giving them their respective hallucinogenic dose.[57]

During the course of Andrade's project of recuperation of the center, the grim battles against displaced vendors and dismissed workers alternated with flashy, open-air enactments of colonial daily scenes, complete with period dresses and carriages as well as with spectacles of contemporary *criollo* music, theater, and dance financed by the city. With these splendid events *Limeños* of all backgrounds celebrated the inauguration of each "recuperated" space until about 1999 when they began to somberly yield again—in the most baroque of fashions—to the filth, the crime, the corruption, and the political debacle that lay ahead.

FOUR

Second Diary

Saturday, 10:00 a.m.: I woke up to Manolo's cries over the phone. Clearly it was his uncle Antonio at the other end of the line.

"Don't you dare ask me where I've been all these years," I heard Manolo say. He said, "The question I have is where were *you . . .*"

He must have swung the door to the kitchen closed because I couldn't hear anything anymore.

Yesterday I heard him come into the house at around six in the morning. He'd been out all night. He woke up at around noon, and as I got ready to leave for the day, he came into my room, looking weary and sullen, and sat on the bed. He said he hasn't gotten much sleep lately, maybe something having to do with Paco. He said, "You know the story, right?" and proceeded to tell me about his father's frequent violent outbursts against him and his brothers, which eventually tore the family apart. As soon as he could, he moved into a boardinghouse and then to New York City, breaking with the family for good. He did not see any of them until some years later when he flew back to Lima, arriving the day after his father's funeral. That day, he said, he walked straight to the backyard of the house, sat on a patio chair, and stared out to the garden without aim, quietly for more than an hour, swimming in grief but determined not to shed a tear. Then he heard his mother say, "How can you be so coldhearted, Manolo?" He left. He said that before he left the country, Darío and Paco began getting into trouble. He and his other brother Ricardo decided to check on them periodically, meet with them, give them a little money.

Ricardo was in charge of Darío, Manolo of Paco. But on a day that they met, he said, Paco robbed him with a gun, took his wallet and his watch, and never came back.

I walked into the kitchen right when Manolo was telling Uncle Antonio to never, ever try to contact him again and hanging up on him. He was fuming, but seeing me, he turned away and in a softened tone of voice told me, as if to justify his anger, that Uncle Antonio was insisting on getting money from him. But he won't give him any, he said again.

Today, however, Manolo didn't seem so resolute. While I ate breakfast he got on the phone again and called several funeral homes to find out about options and prices. He even called his cousin Javier, Uncle Antonio's son, who appears to have connections in the navy's funeral home, where the body could be cremated for $500. And while he talked with the undertakers, with his cousin, with the morgue, I thought to myself, *What made you change your mind, Manolo?* But I didn't dare to ask. I thought, *Is it fear?* It must be fear shooting through me, the chill I feel when I hear him say that the body of his brother should rot in the morgue. *Is it? Or else, what's keeping you up at night? Grief? Rage? Or, should I ask who? Is it him? Paco? Sneaking into your dreams and startling you awake?* I thought, *Does he speak?* I thought, *What?*—but did not dare to ask.

Instead, I asked him if I could be of any help. "Nothing to help me with," he said with a fake lighthearted tone. He said, "Only, if he calls again, I'm not in." Then, abruptly changing the subject, he asked me if I had plans for next Friday night, if I'd like to go to a small dinner party that a lawyer friend of his is giving for him in his house in San Isidro. I said sure, as he turned around and left the kitchen.

———

Later: At about noon Manolo knocked on my door to tell me that he was going to the morgue to retrieve Paco's body. He said, "I just want to get this over with." I offered to keep him company, maybe borrow my mother's car to get there sooner. "No, no, no. Not your mother's car," he said, motioning with his hands as though trying to keep some invisible force at bay, as though the mere idea of taking something that belongs to my mother's world, the cleaner and more orderly world of Miraflores, into the corrupted one of downtown Lima, the world of bureaucracy, of bribery and prostitution, of lunacy and corpses, could defile it to the point of no restitution. "Let's take a taxi," he said. He said, "Let's make this easy."

The cabdriver got on the Vía Expresa and, once downtown, turned onto Jirón Cangallo, where the morgue is, off of the perennially congested and polluted Avenida Grau. He pulled over in front of the morgue, and Manolo asked him to wait for us right there. "Right here," he said. "This will be quick."

Across the street from the morgue there is a line of funeral parlors, several low-lintel doors crowned with signs that say "La Americana— Agencia Funeraria," and other such names. Manolo and I hadn't reached the morgue's gate yet when a group of funeral employees swarmed to us like flies to honey and offered, first, their condolences, then, their services in an openly fierce competition for our business. Before I could shoo them off, one of them was already grabbing Manolo by the arm and shaking his hand, "Aurelio Ventura, at your service." He wore a silky purple shirt and a golden cross on his chest, and his thinning strands of hair were neatly gelled to the back. Against his dull gray skin and two dark circles of flabby flesh stood out a set of rapacious eyes. I thought, *The eyes of a vulture*. He clenched his hands and bowed his head, adopting an air of solemnity to tell Manolo that he understood his pain, that in the event that he decided to "leave it all to him" he would facilitate the process, simplify the paperwork, retrieve the body, transport it, cremate it, and very soon bring the ashes to him in an urn. He now wrung his hands as he said that he knew everyone inside the morgue, that he, Manolo, would not have to step once again in that building. Exactly what Manolo wanted to hear. Like a hungry vulture flying in circles over an agonizing animal, the man could smell Manolo's closeness to death, his fear, his sense of helplessness. He anticipated Manolo's questions and looked to appease his anxiety by giving him reassuring answers. Manolo had fixed his look on him—again the glazed eyes, the vacant expression. I put my hand on the man's shoulder and began to push him away when, to my dismay, I heard Manolo's faint voice, "All right, you're hired," in a monotone.

Manolo and I walked into the building and up to the receptionist booth. Vulture-man stayed outside, clinging sulkily to the gate but carefully following us inside with his eyes. Without looking away from the paperwork in front of her, the receptionist stretched her hand out and demanded to see Manolo's identity card.

"Manuel Santillana Mendoza?"

"Yes."

"And you are here for... [moving her finger down a list] Francisco Santillana Mendoza?"

"Yes."

"All right, you can take a seat," said the woman pointing to the waiting area to the right. "There are other relatives of the deceased in there, and we can only let in one visitor at a time," implying that we had to wait for them to leave.

As if screwed to the ground, Manolo and I stood there without moving and looked at each other for a second or two, me thinking, *Who in the world could be in there?*, he knowing exactly who. He then turned back to the receptionist enraged and yelled, "I *am* the closest relative. I am the brother. You shouldn't have let anybody else in there!" She finally looked up and let him in.

I was ordered to take a seat and wait. So I did and passed the time looking about myself: The walls inside the building have been repainted recently, hospital green, and there was new white tile on the floors, both of which gave the building an antiseptic look. A bronze commemorative plaque said that the renovated building was inaugurated by Fujimori in 1998. The contrast between the inside and the chaos and filth outside was great, although I'm sure it was only apparent. The waiting area was a small square room with rows of metal chairs fixed to the floor facing a wall, from where, like one would see at a race track, a huge electronic billboard announced the names, the day, and the time of arrival of the deceased in luminous red letters that moved from left to right:

. . . López Montoya, Carmen, 25/11, 11:23AM . . .
. . . Rosas Chuquinca, Tomás, 24/11, 12:35PM . . .

I saw Paco's name. He had been there for five days.

I walked out to the gate to talk to Vulture-man. I asked him what I would never ask in Manolo's presence.

"So, how do we know?" I said. "How do we know you won't just take the money, dump the body somewhere, and then fill up an urn with anything resembling ashes, maybe even dirt?"

"But no, señorita! We would never do that!" He pretended to be offended. "How can you think that? We would never! It has to be official, signed by the authorities here. Never, señorita!"

I nodded and kept nodding even after he had stopped, now beginning to wonder if perhaps I had indeed offended him. Then he went on.

"Before, yes! Before it was possible to do such things, work under the table, as they say. But not today," he said, most likely referring to Fujimori's early attempts at reorganizing the state bureaucracy and stopping corruption.

"But how do we know?" I said again, knowing there's really no way we could possibly know. And as he deployed his unconvincing act again—"But no, señorita!"—I thought to myself, *And why do I care so much?* Yes, I felt indignant, but exactly over what? The truth is, I never met Paco. It surely angers me how much corruption there is in this country, although in the past I have certainly made use of guys like this myself, many times and with no regret. I also find it upsetting that, today, we were the ones who were the object of a scam, and, of course, I feel for Manolo. He looked so desperately anguished, so overwhelmed by feelings of . . . Was it grief? Pity? Fear? He was running around with the compliant attitude of someone seeking to repair a harm done or contain an imminent danger. I did feel for him. His imposing stature, his seemingly unassailable, fortress-like demeanor was slowly reduced to that of a vulnerable child.

Robert Hertz says that the motivation behind providing for the recently deceased is as much to spare the dead person's soul a painful wait as it reaches its final destination as it is to free the living of the corpse's presence. Since a decomposing corpse is an object of dread, the impure object par excellence, the survivors make use of a complex set of prescriptions (in the form of rituals, sacrifices, and prayers) and prohibitions (in the form of avoidance of or closely managed physical contact with the body or the things of the deceased), the transgression of which is thought to bring about serious consequences.[1] But lacking himself any explicit prescriptions, feeling somewhat at a loss, Manolo seemed to be desperately searching for a means to appease his fear and assuage his pain, apparently finding no other way than speeding up the process by putting himself in the hands of someone who promised to take charge and work fast, by spending the money he does not have, just so that he can go home as quickly as possible and . . . What? Pretend that nothing happened? Try to forget it all? Will disposing of the body—now if possible, if not, tomorrow—make his pain go away, his fears dispel—today, tomorrow? I think it is the idea of Paco's body being tossed away on some barren land, buried anonymously on some communal grave by colluding men who will get a share, or merely "disappeared" somewhere, somehow, by someone whose face I cannot even imagine, that strikes me as wrong, as terrible, as something that I ought to prevent, for fear that . . . I don't know. I cannot explain it. But the idea of it, of the body undergoing a fate that we will never know, makes me cringe.

Manolo, Uncle Antonio, and his son, cousin Javier, came back out of the forensic chamber, where they were probably asked to identify the body, but I don't know for sure. Manolo introduced me to them, and they both greeted me with a kiss and a hug charged with emotion, which struck me as a bit contrived, exaggerated perhaps, but they didn't seem to me to be eager to take advantage of Paco's death. To the contrary, they seemed meek and passive before Manolo, maybe even afraid of him and readily let him be in charge.

"They need my authorization for the autopsy," Manolo said to me, huffing. He said, "An autopsy! What an absurdity! Can you imagine? What for?" The introductions and Manolo's comment gave way to an awkward silence, which was opportunely cut short by the receptionist, who called Manolo back inside. And as soon as Manolo was not within earshot, the cousin lit a cigarette and began recounting the circumstances of Paco's death in somewhat of a confessional tone: He had seen Paco just a few weeks ago. For several years now Paco had come by his parents' house every month or so to pick up some money that the family would put together, not much, but enough to hold him over for a few days. But last month Paco did not come to get his money, and he and his father thought that this was odd. Well, last week he was driving near the Santillanas' home in Miraflores where Paco still lived and decided to stop by. He noticed that the small side door, the only usable entrance to the house, was locked from inside. He pried open one of the wooden slabs nailed to the glassless front window and only then came across, first, the smell and, then, the sight of Paco's body, lying on the floor of what used to be the main living room and now looked like a gutted, damp, dark cavern. He climbed inside and walked toward his cousin's corpse but didn't touch it, he said. He said that, coughing, retching, he climbed back out the window and, from his cell phone, called the police.

Then there was a long pause: I looked at Javier, at Uncle Antonio, and stood there cross-armed and motionless, except for my head, which I nodded slightly back and forth, back and forth, in a tense, silent corollary to Javier's account. Javier lit another cigarette and took a long, deep, avid drag, held it in for a while, and blew it out with force as he lowered his eyes and fixed them on some indefinite point on the tile floor. Uncle Antonio pulled his cell phone from his jacket, stared briefly at the glittery screen, and—*beep beep beep*—punched a few keys before putting it away and turning his back to us to face the street.

It was a slow, somnolent Saturday afternoon. The sun was shining pale and thin as if it were shining from farther away than usual. Things everywhere looked discolored like in an overexposed photograph. In the silence I could hear the hissing of palm fronds from the botanical garden next door. I noticed that, except for the receptionist, the security guard (who was dozing off in his shabby booth), and a little man in an oversized white robe who walked by once, it was just us at the morgue. Does death respect the weekend? The electronic billboard kept spitting out names and days and times of arrival before the empty metal chairs, and I wondered to myself, *Why aren't more people reclaiming their dead?*

Vulture-man still clung to the gate with morose eyes that widened when he saw Manolo coming out again. Manolo walked past us straight to him at the gate. They muttered something to each other. Manolo scribbled on a used piece of paper that he pulled out of his pocket, and then, to my horror, handed a large bill to the man. Inside myself I screamed, *No, Manolo!* But it was too late. When Manolo joined us, his uncle announced that he was leaving. He looked tired. Javier decided to stay with us for a while longer, and Manolo offered to drop him off in our cab.

"By the way, they found only a lighter, fifteen soles, and his ID on him..." said Uncle Antonio as he walked away.

"For god's sake," Manolo interrupted, clearly not wanting Paco's belongings anywhere near him, not even in words. "Let them put everything inside the coffin," he said, bitterly.

"Yes, that's exactly what I told them," said Uncle Antonio before turning around again and closing the gate behind him.

Javier lit a cigarette, and Manolo went back to talk to Vulture-man. This time I followed him. The problem was that it was Saturday afternoon, and the only medical examiner that could waive the autopsy requirement and authorize the release of the body would not be coming back until Monday. Manolo made it clear that he did not want to wait until then. From the other side of the gate, Vulture-man offered to pick up the body in his van today and keep it in his funeral home until Monday, when he would come back for the autopsy waiver and take the body to the crematorium. I timidly interjected with questions, "But how do we know...?" Manolo looked at me pleadingly. Complacent, Vulture-man rushed across the street to the funeral home and came back driving an old and dented gray van. He jumped out waving a half-filled form and stuck it in through the bars for Manolo to sign. It all gradually became clear to me: The guard cannot let any funeral service personnel into the morgue unless they have a signed business contract; and the morgue cannot release the body to anyone, not even a family member, except to a licensed undertaker.

Manolo and Vulture-man slowly slipped into a parasitic relationship, the unsigned business contract extending toward Manolo, reaching and sticking to him like the sucker of a leech. I looked over Manolo's shoulder and Javier over mine while he filled in the blanks and signed the form.

Vulture-man looked in from behind the gate. The security guard finally opened the side gate, and Vulture-man pulled in with the van in reverse and drove it around the building to the morgue's loading area. Manolo followed the van, and we followed Manolo as if by force, as if pulled by the gristly organ by which Manolo and Vulture-man were now ineluctably attached to each other.

We turned the corner of the building and encountered the van right in front of us, closer than we had expected, with the doors to the back already open. The little man in the oversized robe was next to it emptying a large black plastic bag into a wooden box. The clunking sounds for an instant made it seem like he was dumping a bundle of loose bones. But I thought, *Impossible.* I then saw a forearm and a hand sticking out from the box. An entire hand! Paco's hand? Fleshless, skeletal, the dry brown skin stuck like leather to the bone. I was startled by the sight and thought of backing off. I thought, *We're not supposed to be seeing this!* I turned around on my feet and bumped against Manolo, who was standing right behind me, pale as death. I looked at him and, this time, unable to remain composed, I threw my arms around him. Standing on the tips of my toes, I placed one hand on the nape of his neck, gently pulling his head down to my shoulder, perhaps hoping that he would finally break down and cry, perhaps comforting him so that he wouldn't, perhaps wanting to be held myself.

"That's not him, it cannot be him," I whispered in Manolo's ear, trying to sound reassuring, not really knowing what else to say. Could he have dried up like that in just five days? I kept saying, "That cannot be him!" but thinking, *Could it be him? Could preservatives do that to a corpse?* Why did he seem to be chopped up into pieces? Did they freeze him? Or burn him? I thought, *Was it with fire? With ice? With acid?* I thought, *Did they?*

But no, he wouldn't shed a tear. His eyes welled up, but he contained the tears once more, and, in an ultimate effort at self-restraint, he dropped his eyelids and lifted his chin up the way an assailed medieval fortress would drop the gates and lift its bridges to cut all flow with the exterior and protect whatever remaining life there is inside. Eyes closed, face up, he took a deep breath. When he opened his eyes again, the van was already going through the gate and crossing the street to the funeral home. Manolo and I walked inertly in the direction of the van, the sucking organ pulling hard, and met Vulture-man in front of the store.

"I'll be there Monday afternoon with the urn," he said, his little, chubby hands rubbing manically.

"All right, Monday afternoon."

Manolo, Javier, and I got back into the taxicab. Javier sat in front; Manolo and I squeezed in the back. I ventured to touch, then to hold Manolo's hand, even though I knew that the most minimal gesture of sympathy from my part could make the fortress tumble. The taxi drove off. Manolo looked out the car window and sighed. Javier tensely and self-consciously cleared his throat before he began:

"You know, I got remarried last year..." as he lit a cigarette.

Sunday morning: It's a little after seven o'clock. Again, alone at the breakfast table. A note on Bataille's ideas on animality from his *Theory of Religion.*

Considered from a narrow viewpoint, says Bataille, meaning from our human viewpoint, animality is the model of life without history. It is the sense of continuity that the animal has with its physical surroundings, the sense of being in the world "like water is in water." Following Hegel (through Kojève), Bataille suggests that the development of the tool is what affirms man's difference from his environment by bringing a sense of exteriority to his world. The tool, therefore, is a nascent form of the non-I. The animal's sense of continuity with the world, which, from the creation of the tool onwards, man has devoted himself to negate, is, according to Bataille, the source of our darkest terrors and our deepest longings, of the most intense feelings we experience in the presence of what we call the sacred. By offering man the fascination produced by sacred things, the denial of continuity also offers him a possibility that the animal does not know: the possibility of transgression.[2]

Later: On a map of Lima that I have stretched out before me, I have retraced my steps through the city yesterday. The morgue on Jirón Cangallo is tucked in between the Escuela de Medicina de San Fernando and the Botanical Garden. After leaving the morgue we drove, for a block or two, on Cangallo, then turned onto Jirón Cuzco and then onto Jirón La Mar in order to get back on Avenida Grau, which on the map is a wide, clear thoroughfare that effortlessly connects the Cementerio El Ángel, on the far east side of the city, with the Plaza Grau, a large rotunda on the far west side.

In reality, it is nothing like that. Yesterday we were stuck in traffic for about forty-five minutes at the intersection of Avenida Grau and

Paseo de la República, where thousands of cars, of all makes and shapes, had formed a tight knot as each of them tried to maneuver in physically incompatible ways. There were those who, like us, wanted to go west, circle around Plaza Grau, and turn south onto Paseo de la República; there were those going north on Paseo de la República, who either wished to circle around Plaza Grau and go west or drive straight into the downtown area; there were also those who were headed east on Paseo Colón, who wished to circle around Plaza Grau and keep going east or go north into downtown; and, finally, there were those headed south on Paseo de la República, needing to turn east onto Avenida Grau or just keep going south on the Paseo.

Right at the center of this mess, of this sea of roaring engines and blasting horns, barely distinguishable on the perimeter of Plaza Grau, was a flimsy metal station from where a policeman tried to direct the traffic, all on his own, he and his whistle, which he blew as hard as his lungs allowed but which was lost in the noise madness. He looked minuscule from where we were; if he only knew how minuscule he looked, how helpless and adrift in this sea of cars. He raised his tiny hand covered in a sooty white glove to signal the cars to stop. He then turned forty-five degrees and signaled the ones coming the opposite way to move forward. One by one, the cars inched forward in stops and starts, completely ignoring lane divisions, gliding in inconceivable contortions into every bit of empty asphalt as if lubricated by a viscous substance. Our driver did the same, pressing the gas, jerking forward and halting until we were fused with other cars into what seemed like a compact mass of tin and rubber. Again—forward—halt—and we solidified into another impossible configuration. Inside the car, we all traveled in silence.

From where we were stuck around the Plaza Grau, I had a full view of the Centro Cívico, the massive, 1970s cement structure in the brutalist style that is emblematic of General Velasco's military government. Its raw cement façades, it was said, were the government's sparing, practical, nationalistic response to Lima's rainless skies, to its inability to periodically wash itself from the dust and soot that, with Lima's high levels of humidity, tend to stick to every surface. These constructions are indeed mimetic of Lima's overcast skies and polluted atmosphere. Across the Centro Cívico was the Palacio de Justicia. The colonnade of Doric columns and the triangular pediment are a small-scale replica of those at the Palais de Justice in Brussels, supposedly the largest neoclassic structure erected in Europe in the nineteenth century. The building here in Lima was commissioned in the 1920s by President Augusto Leguía, a well-traveled merchant who, inspired by Baron Haussmann's redevelopment of Paris, dedicated much of his eleven-year autocratic regime to modernizing the city by making it look like a European capital.

The pedestrian walkway on Paseo de la República, flanked by busts of Peru's naval heroes, was lined with the greenest grass and the most gorgeous flowers I have seen so far: yellow daffodils that looked like trumpets, red gladiolas that towered over thick beds of pink and red geraniums. In the seriously desiccated, rainless valley that is Lima, *this* is useless expenditure. Breaking the silence in the car, I said that with all those beautiful flowers the Palacio de Justicia looks like a real European palace. "Too much palace for so little justice," the driver muttered under his breath. We all fell back in silence.

I remembered the day my friend Aldo and I visited the center late on a Friday night sometime before I left the country at the peak of the Sendero's war. We were hoping that the bar in the old Hotel Mauri would be open. Aldo loved to go to this bar because of its former glory and currently old-fashioned, down-and-out state. Looking for a parking lot where we could leave the car, we drove around and around in his white VW beetle through the dark and narrow streets, many of which had been blocked to traffic to protect bank offices or public buildings from car bombs, which at the time were going off in the city with certain regularity. We turned onto Jirón Miró Quesada, but no parking lot was open. Unable to turn back—four huge cinderblocks obstructed the way on Jirón Puno—we found ourselves having to turn on Avenida Nicolás de Piérola and circling around the totally deserted Plaza San Martín, which we had hoped to avoid.

On each corner of the plaza, dim traffic lights switched to green, to amber, to red, or didn't switch at all, for the handful of vehicles that dared to venture that far, that late into downtown Lima. In the plaza, one or two lightbulbs shone from lampposts; the rest were burnt out or broken. Aldo drove tensely, slowing down at the traffic lights but hesitating to fully stop, thinking better not, then better yes, then coming to a stop but keeping the foot on the gas pedal, ready to step on it and dash through the red light if necessary. In front of us, there was a diffuse cloud of amber light from the car's headlights, which heightened the bleakness of the atmosphere in the plaza. There were mounds of garbage piled everywhere and not a single patch of green, from what we could see, but garbage all around, and it wasn't fresh. From a pile that was burning grew a thin plume of smoke, and from behind it a scrawny dog, the rib cage popping through the skin, came out and crossed the street in front of the car, pausing and turning to us, its eyes flashing in the lights before it scurried into the pitch-black arcade on the north side of the plaza.

As we drove around, we saw faces peeping out from behind the columns, first one, then another and another, three or four figures coming out from behind the arcades, young mestizo faces made up heavily, their thin bodies squeezed into tight and revealing clothing. One of the boys waved at us, motioning toward a side street behind Cine Colón, in whose elegant but decayed art nouveau interiors the most sordid pornographic films were projected at the time. Behind the theater, two cars stood a little ways from each other, their headlights turned off. Aldo and I looked at each other, I don't know if with surprise, fear, or sadness, perhaps all three at once, and we kept driving until we finally reached Carabaya again. We parked in front of the Hotel Mauri and from inside kept an eye on the car. The barman said they were about to close, but we talked him into letting us have one pisco sour. We drank and left. We drove against traffic on Jirón Ucayali in order to avoid the roadblocks on the Plaza de Armas. Driving straight down Jirón Azángaro, we finally reached the Vía Expresa, Lima's first and only highway until Andrade became mayor, which links downtown Lima with Lince, San Isidro, Miraflores, Barranco, and Chorrillos—and which we eventually got on yesterday, too, on our way back from the morgue.

Monday p.m.: No news about Paco: No signs of Vulture-man, no urn of ashes. I asked Eulalia to stay alert while I was gone. She says that no one has called or come asking for Manolo this afternoon.

I've been thinking about the street sweepers' protests, noticing the tension they produced in the media between the compulsion to silence their public stripping and the compulsion to speak of it in order to explain it away as a "technique" of protest or as a government-backed staged performance for political gain, Cicciolina-style. Besides the news article about the street sweepers in *La República* and a TV report on Channel 4, the rest of the media, as far as I know, covered the occurrence of the demonstrations but skipped the nudity, which is surprising given that the images lent themselves to the most sensationalist, and thus profitable, front-page coverage, the type so loved today by the SIN-run, scandal-filled tabloids and dailies. During my interview with him, Mr. Morales mentioned in passing that he thought he'd seen the TV cameras of Frecuencia Latina, Channel 2, on the plaza the day the street sweepers disrobed. But the person in charge of the video archive at Channel 2 has assured me that they never aired a report about those protests and that there isn't any footage of it in their archives. Since the government expropriated the broadcasting company in 1997 (from Baruch Ivcher, under the excuse of his holding a foreign citizenship), the company has been completely overhauled, and it is no longer in the opposition.

Yesterday, it finally dawned on me that to have access to the video archives at Channel 4 I might need an insider's help. I called my friend Verónica, whose youngest daughter, Amanda, reads the headline news on an early-morning variety show (modeled after *Good Morning America*), for which she is also a street reporter. Verónica said to call Amanda at nine o'clock, when she's off the air for a few minutes before heading out to report for the next day's local news. Amanda is really an actor and a singer—that is how she thinks of herself. But last year she was cast on a popular soap opera for a stint as a TV reporter, and a manager at Channel 4 who saw her performance thought she would do great as a real reporter and decided to hire her. Amanda and I agreed to meet at one o'clock, when she'll be back in the studios. She said to ring her up in the editing room.

I borrowed my mother's car. This time I wanted to drive. I took the Vía Expresa and exited in La Victoria, U-turning onto the bridge that ends in Calle Mariano Carranza, where the building of América Televisión, Channel 4, is located. I knew this route by heart. For four years before I left for the United States, I drove through these streets every day to get to the place where I worked as a teacher, maneuvering around the TV station, which was surrounded by streets blocked to traffic for security reasons. From the car I used to watch the military trucks, the barricades, the armed soldiers, standing guard at the building.

There hasn't been a single terrorist attack in Lima since 1993, but to reach the station's main entrance I still had to zigzag around staggered blocks of concrete. Near the door, instead of soldiers, there were a number of *huachimanes* (from the English "watchmen"), young men working as private security guards, dressed in uniform brown slacks and jackets with the word SEGURIDAD written on their backs. From the sidewalk, they kept a watchful eye on the zigzagging cars coming down the road and pointed to possible parking spaces along the block but away from the building's entrance. As I approached, one of the men crouched, looking to see who traveled in the car, and then to my surprise directed me to a parking spot just steps away from the entrance, even removing for me the trestle that was blocking the spot.

I parked the car and got out, thanking him as I locked the door. He eyed me and smiled while another *huachimán* whistled from across the street in complicity. I felt his eyes rubbing on my back; from the top down and up again, I felt him feeling me with the eyes. I sprinted up the stairs and disappeared into the building, noticing to myself, this time without anger or indignation or remorse, just remarking to myself the twisted nature of the privilege afforded by fair skin and class in this city, whereby you grow up to be the unwitting heir of a privilege that you accept as if it were the natural order of things, as if you didn't have to pay a price for it. And for the most part you go about it unawares, oblivious to its repressive violence, insensitive to its devastating effects, and ignorant of the price you've had to pay to feel entitled to a certain kind of respect. And when you're granted that respect and then some more, you take it, but never without a little suspicion, never without a tinge of disbelief, without watching over your shoulder, without twice examining your purchase and twice counting your change, because deep down you know, and you know everybody else knows, there's nothing natural in the order of things, and deep down you're scared and angry just like everyone's scared and angry, because you know it's not just those below but you, too, who loses, who loses even as you gain—although you don't know how to fix the situation or undo it. So you just don't. Because you're in some ways invested in this power to be and do as you please, as if your skin color were some kind of warranty or seal of goodness and trustworthiness, even as you're simultaneously taken to be—because you are—complacent, righteous, and unthinking, and whenever possible are abused in little ways.

The receptionist told me that Amanda was on the fourth floor. I was given a visitor's pass and sent upstairs, where Amanda met me outside the editing room. She greeted me with a broad smile; her smooth, light brown hair curled out right above her shoulders, framing her almond-shaped eyes and beautiful face, perfect for TV. She's very young. She's smart, keen in her words, and eager. She said she remembers the protests as she walked me to the archives, where she introduced me to Roberto, the guy in charge. Amanda asked him to please help me with whatever I needed before kissing me good-bye and leaving the room. I suppose she didn't expect to see me again.

Roberto nodded and turned away, going back to rewinding a tape in silence. Even though he didn't ask, I told him I was looking for the *24 Horas* installment of June 20, 1996, covering the protests of ESMLL. Only then he turned to me. He said he knew what I was after and, looking through the tapes on the shelves, he found it: Tape #V-4873. He popped it in and fast-forwarded until I saw the street sweepers appearing on the screen. It was a three- or four-minute segment of that 1996 evening news show that spoke about the demonstrations as an ongoing event. "The ex-workers of ESMLL were out in the streets again today . . ."

103

the report explained, before the focus switched to the woman, who was already walking half-naked in the plaza, looking frightened and screaming into the microphone of a male reporter, who somewhat timidly but persistently questioned her behavior:

"Señora, what do you expect to accomplish with this? Ah, señora?"

To which only more screams followed. And then again,

"But, what do you expect to accomplish with this, señora?"

In the tape, the reporter looked nervous, confused. He was sweating.

In reference to the young men that appeared in the background, Roberto said that he's heard that they were thugs hired by the SIN to take advantage of the protests and harm Andrade. He also said that rumors were that very early in the morning, even before the protesters had made it to the plaza, these guys drove around the center in trucks filled with garbage collected from other parts of the city and dumped it on or near the Plaza de Armas. Rumors were, too, that it was them who moved stealthily through the night, vandalizing recently restored buildings, breaking windows or defacing them with insulting *pintas* (graffiti), to hurt the mayor, he said. He said, "It's just that 'El Chino' doesn't like to share the spotlight, you know?" by which he meant that Fujimori was intent on destroying Andrade, as he has done with so many other popular public officials. "He wants to annihilate him," Roberto said, "not because they differ in their ideas but because they think too much alike; not because Andrade wants to work against his government, but because he wants to work *with* the government." "You see?" he said, "his best peers are also his contenders."

Roberto then played the *24 Horas* edition of the following night, June 21, where there was another three- or four-minute report in which a dozen or so shirtless women chatted and sang slogans as they bathed in their underwear in the fountain (which has been against the law since the late 1800s). They shouted insults at the police and laughed as they hurled water at each other, soaping and shampooing themselves and one another, then dipping their bodies in the murky water to rinse off. For the first two minutes not a single policeman appeared inside the frame. Then, quietly, a police officer approached the women and, looking a bit self-conscious in front of the camera, gently helped the half-undressed women out of the fountain, ignoring their insults and unlawful behavior.

With his eyes still on the TV screen, Roberto said that all of this could be the work of Luza. "You've heard of Segisfredo Luza, of course . . ." he said.

"Heard of whom?"

What follows is from an article and an interview in *Caretas*:

Segisfredo Luza: the shadow behind the shadow. Everyone knows who he is and what he's done, but no one knows it with any certainty. He is a psychiatrist by training and a self-described specialist in mass psychology. He is now in his seventies and is retired. He lives alone in a luxurious, well-guarded home in a sunny suburb of Lima. Thirty years ago, Luza was at the center of a media scandal caused by what was said to be a crime of passion, for which he eventually pleaded guilty due to insanity and spent the following eight years in a prison-asylum. The victim was a young and beautiful patient of his, who had become his lover. To pressure him into leaving his wife and marrying her, the young woman had led Luza to believe that, if he didn't, she was ready to accept the romantic propositions of another man, who in reality was a gay friend of hers eager to get in on the prank for fun. This drove Luza into such a fit of jealousy that he went after the man and stabbed him to death.

At some point during his incarceration, perhaps seeking insight into his own behavior, he became interested in the workings of persuasion and suggestion, quickly seeing their application in mass psychology. He received a presidential pardon in 1974, when he began a long-term collaboration with the military regimes of General Velasco and General Morales Bermúdez, working in the office of communications to promote governmental policy, and, later on, with Fujimori, for whom he has allegedly orchestrated mass psychology operations to help the government achieve, in his own words, "stability and equilibrium between the government and society."[3]

At the time of the *Caretas* interview, Luza said that, save for a few advising jobs, he was now devoting his entire time to putting the final touches on his upcoming book, *El poder psico-social*. About the subject of the book—the workings of psychosocial power—he said,

It's a subject that interests me and that I've studied for years. . . . To my knowledge, the stability of a regime is grounded on a great system of communication and information. . . . Equilibrium is [attained with] automatic obedience, when all social agents obey certain patterns of discipline. . . . I'm not speaking of manipulation, but of a suggestive control. Here it is that persuasion comes into play. . . . Look, we all have deep, intimate needs; I call them "pulsations." . . . Desire is a potential trigger behind which emerge primitive pulsations. . . . [It] becomes necessary to have real, concrete knowledge in order to reach the being of each individual. Those who don't have an efficient information apparatus . . . must suffer the consequences. . . .

In 1995 I carried out a study on how to win the elections with little [financial] investment. I was asked to analyze the marginal voters and to establish a psychological profile. I observed [that they have] a low or moderate level of education, and that additionally they live emotionally: [They are] gullible, susceptible, manipulable, and [have] a need for hope. They were a group to whom you couldn't talk about abstract things or macroeconomic concepts. There you had to utilize a language that is direct, emotional. . . . That always works. That which is emotional.[4]

Roberto said that he had heard that the woman's stripping had been an *"operativo psico-social,"* a psychosocial operation directed by the SIN but thought out and staged by Luza himself. "Just like with the crying virgins," Roberto said, referring to the commotion provoked in 1991 by rumors that two ceramic statues of the Virgin Mary in the district of Carmen de la Legua were shedding tears, drawing huge crowds to the modest homes where the Virgins were and eliciting several trance and healing episodes among the visitors, which included President Fujimori himself.[5] At around the same time there was a tree along Avenida Javier Prado, one of Lima's main thoroughfares, whose top was said to have grown in the shape of Jesus' head, causing enormous congestions along the already-busy avenue and an onslaught of media coverage that lasted for weeks. Roberto also said the government's public display of Abimael Guzmán, the leader of Sendero Luminoso captured in Lima in 1992, could have been another of Luza's psychosocial operatives, which reminded me where I had heard Luza's name before. It was around the infamous parading of Guzmán before the TV cameras right after his arrest decked in a black-and-white-striped prison suit and inside a metal cage, which was intended to ridicule him just as it made him look like a wild beast. I do remember hearing that it was Segisfredo Luza who had masterminded Guzmán's staging.

But perhaps what I have here referred to as the compulsion to explain away, to attribute an ulterior end and expose the "real" motivation behind acts of transgression like the street sweepers', is not much different from the compulsion to remain silent about them. Here E. E. Evans-Pritchard's 1929 essay on obscenity in Africa comes to mind. The essay opens precisely by drawing attention to the fact that, when faced with the task of reporting on behaviors deemed obscene or indecent to Western sensibilities, most European travelers and observers have historically opted for complete omission or, at most, referred vaguely and condemningly to the acts witnessed, calling them "anti-social," "ultra-bestial," and, more importantly, "too infamous to bear repetition."[6]

This attitude, to which Evans-Pritchard alludes only briefly, points to what seems to be an inherent paradox in prohibitions involving indecency or obscenity, whereby a compulsory silence appears to be built into the prohibition, ensuring that the rules remain tacit or that they're put into the vaguest of terms since any degree of explicitness would risk crossing the line. The same occurs with denunciations of obscenity, let alone with reports or social scientific analyses of obscene acts, which simply cannot be done without falling, even if just slightly, into obscene or indecent language oneself. Or else, how does one legislate against or report on obscenity or indecency without defining it, and how does one define it without spelling out the forbidden acts?[7]

Bataille notes that the silence around some of the most basic prohibitions is in many cases so extreme that the prohibition itself is rarely, if ever, stated explicitly. One is rarely instructed, "You ought not to sleep with your brother" or "You ought not to eat your pet dog." With regard to these prohibitions, one just knows—as when in the Old Testament Adam and Eve just *know* that their nakedness is a sign of their fall; they realize they are naked and feel shame. The negation of our animality, says Bataille, is at times so drastic that the rules concerning the basest aspects of our humanity are seldom the object of our attention, for the mere affirmation of the taboo is deemed or is experienced as a transgression. In the case of the sexual organs, Bataille observes that the shame and attraction we feel toward them are made all the more intense by their closeness to the organs of excretion, the basest organs of all, about which the silence is even more severe. Think of the abundance of names for the genitals and of the fact that, despite their abundance, none of those names are ever fit for use regardless of context. Think, too, of the fact that the only more or less socially acceptable terms to refer to these organs and to their physiological function and sexual application are in Latin: penis, phallus, vagina, anus, coitus, fellatio, cunnilingus, fæces, urine—as if Latin provided some form of protection from defilement, some kind of neutral ground from where to name these body parts and actions, although even these words are never so completely devoid of charge for them to appear in just any conversation—hence the euphemisms of baby talk and the gestures we employ to teach children to relate to their genitals and to their physiological needs: poopoo, pee, pipi, tushi, or in Spanish, popo, caca, pipi, poto.

The fear, prudishness, and silence around our genitals and bodily wastes are, for Bataille, one of the hallmarks of our humanity. He says, "There exists a mode of the transition from animal to man so radically negative that it is not even spoken of.... The negation is so completely successful on this point that merely to note and affirm that something *is there* is deemed less than human."[8]

Tuesday noon: On my way back from an early morning run, I stopped by my mother's apartment. From the boardwalk I could see that she had already opened her curtains. Once up there, by the sound of the kettle whistling in the kitchen, I knew it wasn't too early or too late. I found her sitting up in her bed reading the newspaper. I put her cup of coffee on a tray next to her and sat on the carpet between her bed and the window to stretch my legs, sore after a long jog on cement, and browse the sections she had already read. A few moments later she got up. She undressed and began unwrapping the bandages to shower. She gently unfastened from behind and removed some sort of girdle that she wears around her thorax, then unwound the elastic bandage, skillfully rolling it with both hands into a perfectly even roll. Only in seeing her breasts again, bruised and newly scarred, I realized I had not seen her naked in years.

She said, "What do you think?" fully turning to me. She said, "He did a good job, I think, but I don't know, I thought that maybe..." Then she said again, "What do you think?"

I looked at her, posed my eyes on such a familiar yet such a terrible sight that brusquely exposed me to myself as nothing but a plaything of my intellectual endeavors as I obsessively pursue the study of a subject that seems to have been, all along, pursuing me. In one of my earliest memories linked to my mother's innumerable operations of reconstructive surgery, I am standing next to her while she speaks on the phone. She has just been released from the hospital and is wearing a summer robe with a red and yellow flower pattern. Underneath, she is wrapped in bandages from the waist to the armpits. Suddenly she hangs up the phone and begins to cry out in panic, so she cries without tears. In between sobs, she yells that the bandages are too tight, that something inside them is about to burst. I feel helpless as she unbuttons her robe and begins to tear open the bandages. Then there is a strong odor of rubber and antiseptic lotion, like the smell of Band-Aids but more pungent, and then the image of her cut-up breasts, which she never hid from our view.

Looking at her now, I confronted a myriad of obscured moments of my childhood, densely condensed in a still-life image of scarred flesh and skin as my mind became open to impossible associations. I was struck by a brief moment of clarity and understanding, like I had discovered the key to an enigma, to *my* enigma, which for an instant shed all its mystery or complication and appeared clear and straightforward.

I said to her that she looks great, beautiful, much better than before. She cast a doubtful look on me.

"You do!" I said, as perverse correspondences between my academic pursuits and my personal life, between the public events I'm attempting to describe and analyze and what I always thought of as private matters, between Lima's social history and my own history, became obvious, inescapable, and forced upon me the realization that the choice of my subject of study was anything but fortuitous. This realization adds an entirely new set of meanings to the notion that perception, understanding, and knowledge take place at the interface of subject and object, that perception, understanding, and knowledge are nothing but their mutual, incessant reflections. It happened like in an instant out of time, like an experiential parenthesis: Before me was the image that promised to deliver the answers to all my questions if only I was able to find the right words. But how can I begin to explain the events I'm writing about here if my interest in the events themselves and my need for an explanation of them could be said to explain me? To begin and to end in me? How?

———————

Later: Spent the afternoon at the Universidad Católica going over the master's thesis of Eduardo González, the sociology student who, as part of his senior research project, asked first-year students to draw from memory a map of the city of Lima to determine how different class groups imagine the city they live in. Of all universities in Lima, the Católica is one of the most diverse, attracting students both from the uppermost and the least privileged echelons of society. The results of González's experiment were so revealing that *Caretas* wrote a report on it. They printed composites of the maps, each of which contained a cluster of streets, drawn in more or less detail, in what one can assume are districts familiar to the authors; and from this cluster, an artery or two shot out in some direction, beyond which there would be pockets of empty or fuzzy space—little hearts of darkness—signaling unknown areas in the city that were labeled in some cases as low class, ugly, dirty, contaminated, and dangerous and in others as upper class, beautiful, clean, and rich. These areas, into which presumably the students rarely or never ventured, contained few topographical referents that were as general as "the Pacific Ocean" and "the beach" or were simply demarcated by a line separating it from the areas the students knew. Looking through the thesis, I was disappointed to see that these fabulous drawings were missing from the bounded text, that, in the thesis, they have been interpreted and condensed into a series of tables and percentages that managed to suck out every trace of life contained in them.[9]

After a couple of hours at the social sciences library, I went upstairs to the office of Professor Roberto Mendieta, planning to get his office hours and return at a later point. But luckily he happened to be there, and so mustering all the courage I could, I went in and introduced myself. Last year I applied for a fellowship to spend three months in Lima following up on the ex-municipal workers' strife. The fellowship announcement called for applications for innovative research on authoritarianism and violence from the angle of "culture." It hoped to elicit proposals that addressed the intertwining of social causality and "subjective logics" in the context of Peru's decades-long crisis. It read, "A long-range perspective . . . cannot fail to notice the inertia of old and deep-rooted processes current in the daily life and in the cultural habits [of Peruvians, expressed as much in] massive manifestations [as in] the most private registers of intimacy." I went for it, thought my project was perfect, but I did not get the money.

Mendieta was at his desk. A research assistant typed away on a computer terminal right behind the door. I apologized for the interruption and told him who I was. He remembered my name from the grant competition last year but could not quite recall the topic of my proposal or why they had rejected it. I summed it up for him, but clarified that I wasn't there to talk about the application. I wanted to meet him since I have for many years followed his work.

He said he would be there on Thursday at around two o'clock, that he will have more time to talk to me then before he goes off to teach for the rest of the evening. We said good-bye, and I was already leaving the office, when he said, "I remember now, those guys were '*lumpen*,' criminals, weren't they?" He said, "It was one of those filthy tricks of Fujimori against Andrade, wasn't it? They were just '*lumpen*.'"

Lumpen: I hadn't heard the word used like that in years. It of course refers to Marx's term *lumpen-proletariat*, which in Marxist theory alludes to the most destitute segments of society, made up of individuals of such low and disenfranchised condition that they cannot or will not identify, as a class, with the workers' cause. What I took Mendieta's comment to imply is that the behavior of the street sweepers and their supporters wasn't quite what one could call progressive, anti-authoritarian activism (perhaps of the kind worth doing research on), not quite the kind of actions one would expect of a serious workers' movement, of a commendable fight against the runaway capitalism and corruption that has sustained Fujimori's dictatorial regime for almost a decade. They were rather the apolitical or even antipolitical actions of vandals, each and every one of them an expression of the *anomie* and the disdain for civil society institutions that is believed to have corrupted Peruvian society at its core.

I am not certain to what extent the street sweepers' demonstrations were linked with the actions of former SITRAMUN members, widely known for their belligerency, but I didn't argue with him. The image flit by of passersby, regular men and women, showing their support for Fujimori's coup and their contempt for democratic institutions by spitting on their own elected representatives the day after the president disbanded Congress in 1992; this image was captured by cameras covering the representatives' protests outside the locked doors of Congress. Now Mendieta's comment suggested the need to set apart Fujimori's right-wing authoritarianism, saturated as it is by charges of corruption and underhandedness, from the perhaps more reasonable and inclusive right-wing administration of Andrade, whose market-oriented policies have arguably been just as dismissive of the rights of workers as the central government's. My impression, however, is that it isn't so much the mounting evidence linking Fujimori with the actions of the former workers of SITRAMUN, and by extension of the street sweepers of ESMLL, but the kind of activism that distinguishes these workers, one that involves garbage and nudity, that prompts people to easily, almost naturally associate them with the president.

I didn't dispute Mendieta's observation, didn't even attempt to articulate what for me is still largely a formless idea, a bundle of intuitions, telling me that there is some important political and sociological insight to be gained from the actions of the women of ESMLL. I didn't tell him that it strikes me as a mistake to cast their actions as nothing but a series of despicable incidents whose violence goes contrary to the communicative rationality that must underpin Peru's fledgling democracy, or that rather than seeing them as merely damaging of the left's nascent efforts to support the growth of civil society institutions, the women's actions, even SITRAMUN's alleged involvement, could shed some greatly needed light on the apparent disinterest in and mistrust of civil society institutions, including those of the left, among the majority of Peruvians. So I just stood in the doorway and nodded. Now I am haunted by what he said and what I wanted to say but didn't.

Got back from the Católica at about 7:30. Still no news from Vulture-man. I don't know whether I should bring it up with Manolo.

———

Wednesday, 11:00 p.m.: Following a suggestion by Mr. Morales, I set out to the center this afternoon, straight to the locale of SITRAMUN, where I would try my luck finding someone from ESMLL. Squished in the back of a *colectivo* behind the driver's seat, as the car glided down the ramp in Chorrillos into the Vía Expresa, I thought again and again of Mendieta's comment: "The street sweepers, just *lumpen.*"

Then it hit me: Mendieta is, in a way, right, right in pointing out the difference in the ontological status of a unionized worker, fighting a clear opponent under certain rules and with an obvious sense of direction, and that of a sub-proletarian worker directed by an indefinable authority, hurling garbage, stripping naked, screaming like an animal. That is exactly the point of Jeffrey Mehlman's reinterpretation of Marx's *The Eighteenth Brumaire of Louis Bonaparte*, in which Bonaparte's coup and his two prosperous decades in power, supported by the disenfranchised urban poor and a pauperized peasantry, are rendered as the "pineal eye" of capitalism, as a political and social instance of Bataillean *dépénse*, of profitless expenditure and loss. To do so, Mehlman relies on Bataille's notion of heterogeneity to refer to the inassimilable quality of the sub-proletarian social force that irrupted in France in 1852, disrupting and displacing, to Marx's exasperation, the revolutionary but clean dialectic between two distinct poles, the proletariat and the bourgeoisie, like an unwelcome "third term."[10]

So in dealing with what many refer to as Fujimori's Bonapartist style of rule, the iron-fist brand of populism he has rustled up from Peru's ailing democracy by curtailing civil liberties and at the same time engaging in political and economic libertinage, it might be important to go back to Bataille's earliest formulations of his critique of political economy as in the 1933 articles "The Notion of Expenditure" and "The Psychological Structure of Fascism." In these texts, published a few months after Hitler's rise to power, Bataille set out to rework the relationship between base and superstructure of Marxism in light of Europe's growing fascist forces.[11] In his reconfiguration, the base is expanded to include society's nonproductive elements, its most disenfranchised individuals, and the superstructure is seen as emerging from the interplay between two tendencies in social life: production and loss, whose role in the maintenance of power structures, once neatly discernible in societies ruled by kings, had become obvious again in Europe under the influence of fascism. For Bataille, what democracy glosses over and its crisis and disintegration make evident is the dialectical tension between these two tendencies—the first, generating what he calls social "homogeneity" to refer to society's closed circle of production and consumption, and the second, what, conversely, he characterizes as social "heterogeneity" to denote everything that opposes or is inassimilable to productive organization, including beings and objects of base or ignoble qualities (bodily waste, corpses, deranged or violent individuals, the underclass) and of superior or imperative ones (gods, kings, the aristocracy, charismatic leaders). Often, as in despotic regimes that arise out of crumbling democracies, the latter, higher kind is recruited by homogeneous society to guarantee its stability, which calls for the violent suppression of the former, lower kind.

Writing at a time suffused with skepticism about democracy's viability, and with the tyrannies of fascism and communism appearing to be the only available options, in these essays, Bataille redefines the notion of class struggle—to center on the struggle not so much for control over the means of production as over the means of expenditure—and affirms the value of social revolution on condition that it be taken up by the most indigent and abject segments of society, the *lumpen-proletariat* (as opposed to the organized proletariat or peasantry), characterized by their total, unopposed exclusion from the world of production and the system of social exchange.[12]

This is also the direction in which Matos Mar's argument goes in *Desborde popular y crisis del Estado* as he reinterprets Lima's history as the history of the masses' overflowing ascent, but only up until those moments in the text when he takes an about-face to call for the need to "channel the overflow" toward a socialist project of nation building. What Matos Mar so brilliantly articulated years before the "Fujimori phenomenon" is that, along with the massive embrace of urban life, the conscience-raising campaigns led by General Velasco in the 1970s forever altered the paternalistic terms with which most Peruvians had always engaged national society, giving way not to the enduring nationalistic ideology of Velasco's dreams but to what Matos Mar would suggest is a contestation nonideology. In these new, essentially transgressive terms of action, Peruvians have found a response to their disenfranchisement, an alternative to conventional forms of political activism. Matos Mar even goes as far as to argue that these transformations may amount to "a new style of revolution." But rather than taking this argument to its ultimate consequences, the author stops short and, in brief but determined reversals throughout the book, advocates for dialogue with the masses and for the "true integration of their emerging institutions," which will be critical, in his view, in any work toward the redefinition of a Peruvian national identity, toward the construction of a just social order, and toward the foundation of "the future legitimacy of the State and the authority of the Nation."[13]

These ideas were still fluttering in my head when I got to the headquarters of SITRAMUN in Pasaje Santa Rosa, right behind the municipal building. On the first floor, union workers run a bodega, where they sell candy and soda to raise funds for the union. A group of men and women were hanging out in the bodega, chatting and joking with each other. I asked them for directions to the main office, and one of the men pointed to the union's new president, a serious, plainspoken man, who was leaning against one of the counters. He said what I already knew, that ESMLL was not a part of their union. He also said that where we were was the locale for the union's active members and added that the laid-off municipal workers have formed their own organization that operates out of another building, on the other side of the plaza, across the street from the Church of San Francisco. But he said he wasn't sure I would find anyone from ESMLL there.

By then it was a bit past five o'clock, but somehow it seemed later. The haze and the day's built-up pollution made the thick bed of cloud that always hangs over Lima appear darker and closer to the ground. In that brief slice of time, when it isn't either day or night, the atmosphere in the center begins to change. The tourists are normally gone, as are the bureaucrats and the pairs of lovers from the plaza's benches; there are noticeably fewer women and fewer cops. There's a strain in the air, an edge to the looks everyone casts on everyone else. I crossed the plaza on the sidewalk in front of the Palacio, where a single armed soldier was left to safeguard the entrance. His body was blurry against the dusky light. I walked past him and saw his face, very young, a child. Leaning forward slightly, he whispered, "Hello there."

The Convent and Church of San Francisco are on the last block of Jirón Lampa, a short distance from the river. The street was almost empty, and the last vendors in the church's atrium were packing their foodstuffs and trinkets, getting ready to leave. Across the street from the church, an old man mopped the sidewalk of a little café, which also seemed about to close. I asked him for directions to the locale of SITRAMUN, and he pointed to a building farther down the block in the direction of the river, where two men holding briefcases stood talking. As I got nearer the building, the two men walked inside, and I followed right behind them.

The old and heavy wooden doors opened to an outdoor patio, where another three men ate from bowls of soup and talked at a picnic table. From a room upstairs, a bolero song spilled onto the patio below. I introduced myself to the sitting men as an anthropology student and said that I was interested in talking to someone from ESMLL. The three turned their heads in unison toward one of the briefcase-men lingering by the door who, overhearing my query, turned to look at me. His name is Héctor Gómez, and he is the new representative of former ESMLL employees.

We sat on a bench in the patio, where I was as straightforward as I could be in asking about the 1996 protests, about the women's actions, about their use of nudity. I said I also wanted to know what has happened to the women since. He put his briefcase on his lap and opened it to show me a newspaper clipping that reported that ESMLL has filed a suit before the Inter-American Commission of Human Rights claiming a labor rights violation by the city. He said that the city initially offered a severance package of 40 percent of the twelve salaries the workers were entitled to by law, but that Andrade didn't even pay them that. In 1998, the Constitutional Tribunal (which by then was already controlled by Fujimori) ruled in the workers' favor (and against Andrade), ordering the city to reinstate those workers who hadn't yet claimed their benefits. He said that Andrade has completely ignored the tribunal's resolution.

Mr. Gómez then said that the woman had undressed spontaneously, out of despair. In 1996, more than 80 percent of ESMLL workers and virtually all the street sweepers were women, he said, mostly single mothers older than forty or fifty. They stripped so that the police would stop the beating, he said. It was to draw the attention of the press, he also said, perhaps feeling the need to offer a more sensible or concrete explanation than just "despair." He said that someone he knows has all the newspaper clippings about the women in the plaza, including another undressing that took place in 1998 (I've never heard of it). He couldn't give me an exact date. One of the women who stripped in 1996 is terribly sick with diabetes; another died recently. But one of "las señoras," he said, comes regularly to ESMLL's meetings. He said he could put me in contact with her if I'm interested. Mr. Gómez and I exchanged phone numbers, and he said that he would call me after their meeting next Tuesday so that we could agree on a time when the señora and I can get together to talk.

Thursday night: Met with Mendieta at two this afternoon. He asked me about my thesis, how I hoped to explain the effect of the women's nudity on the police. I talked about taboo, animality, the impure sacred . . . He talked about Freud, the uncanny, the dreadful sight of a mother's naked body. The situation of SITRAMUN did not come up. The conversation was nice, cordial. He listened attentively and was very generous with his time. We made tentative plans for me to participate in a conference on Arguedas that he is organizing.

I had not been back from the Católica for ten minutes when the doorbell rang—three odd little rings. I drew the curtain aside to peer out the window, to see who was calling, and, as if I had not been silently, anxiously waiting for him, my heart leapt in shock and I could not believe my eyes when I saw Vulture-man down below. He had taken a step back from the door and, with his hands on his hips, was looking up at the house, as if expecting someone to look out the window. Another man, tall and thin, leaned with his arms crossed against a ramshackle 1970s Dodge that had been parked sideways, blocking the driveway. I called down, "Yes?"

"Oh! Good afternoon, señorita!" Vulture-man shouted back animatedly, his hands clasping immediately. "Is Mr. Santillana in? I urgently need to talk to him."

Manolo must have heard us in his room because he had already opened his door before I had a chance to knock.

"It's the guy from the morgue," I said. "Do you want me to come down with you?" He shook his head.

I stood by the window and from there I saw the whole exchange, which, to my now endless horror, ended with Manolo handing more money over to Vulture-man. I backed off the window and ran down the stairs, furious, determined to do something, but unclear as to exactly what. Manolo had come back inside and was closing the door behind him. When he saw me, he lowered his head, and without looking at me began to explain.

"They say no one will sign off the body for the cremation without the autopsy," he said with a flat and sorrowful voice. We started up the stairs.

I said, "Did he ask for more money? You didn't give him any, did you?" I said it without knowing why I was saying it, having seen the whole transaction from above. I said it wishing that I weren't, wanting to say something else.

He shrugged and turned away from me, walking back into his room. I nodded, not really wanting to nod but to yell. Then I said I understood, feeling puzzled and frustrated by the utter disconnection between my thoughts and my speech. I said that all would turn out all right, wishing I weren't saying it, my voice thin, my tone unconvincing, scarcely audible over the slamming door.

———

Friday: It is difficult to know what to make of all the warnings about street crime. People say to me, "Be careful!" They say, "It's worse than ever!" They say I must be especially cautious with my camera and recording equipment. The other day I hopped on a *micro* with a bag of books and my laptop computer, and a woman sitting next to me pointed to the case and said, whispering, that I shouldn't leave my house with it. Is it really worse than ever, or is it just the ever-growing paranoia of an ever-shrinking middle class? My sister, Flavia, who is a visual artist, ventures almost everywhere with her camera. But she's been assaulted and robbed of her purse and wallet many times, with each and every one of the in-vogue "modalities" you hear about at different times. My friend Rosario was recently robbed on the doorstep of her building, from where she was thrown back down to the sidewalk by a man on a moving motorcycle who pulled the strap of the purse she had hanging crossways from her shoulder. She was dragged down the block until the purse broke loose, going off with her entire monthly salary, which she had just cashed. Manuela, an anthropologist, the same: robbed and mugged everywhere, from the Plaza San Martín in downtown Lima to the very public *micro*. The last time I saw her she had a scab across her forehead. She said she was in a *micro* sitting by the door when a man walked up the steps and snatched her prescription glasses right off her face, running away with them and leaving a long, thin scratch across her forehead.

This morning there was a report on the radio about a recent increase in taxicab assaults. Most commonly, the reporter said, the driver will force a detour and stop to pick up an accomplice waiting nearby ready to jump in. The Circuito de Playas, of course, is one of the favored detours, and there (the report said) rapes are not uncommon. I rarely ride taxis for this reason and have always felt safer in *colectivos* or *micros*, but the reporter said that even these are not assault-proof since the passengers that one normally takes to be good company could be robbers posing as such. And with the driver at the wheel and the three or four accomplices, once you're inside the vehicle . . .

Flavia came to visit this morning. Commenting on the morning report about taxi assaults, she said that her friend Mila, a petite and athletic ballet dancer who is used to getting around in taxis, has taught her how to jump out of a moving taxi in case it ever becomes necessary. Mila said that one should always sit in the backseat, very close to the door. To jump and not get hurt, she said, it is important to keep the arm on the side of the door bent and pressed tight against the upper body, and to land on it, rolling on the ground to reduce the impact. As Flavia spoke, she gestured with her body, pretending to follow Mila's instructions. We both laughed uncontrollably at the possibility of a situation so extreme that it was at once unnerving and utterly comical. Flavia said that Mila threatened to jump once when a cabdriver diverted from the main avenue near a descent into the Circuito de Playas. She grabbed the door handle and told the man she was ready to jump out if he didn't turn back. The guy got scared, begged her not to jump, and did as she said.

Today I put my camera in a backpack and went around the city taking shots of some of the places that figure in this diary; on my way back from downtown, I stopped by the house that my parents rented when I was a child after our little adobe-brick house on Avenida Pardo was declared inhabitable in the 1974 earthquake. This house is on a street that circles around a pre-Incan earth mound, a set of ruins untouched so far by development called Huaca Juliana. The house is right in front of the *huaca* ("sacred place" in Quechua), which, like most pre-Columbian *huacas* around the city, was virtually unexcavated when we lived in this house and seemed all but forsaken except for the occasional looting hole and the occasional boy riding his bike up and down the uneven terrain. A short distance from it is the Santillanas' old home, which back then also looked abandoned. With both parents dead, only Darío could be seen going in and out sometimes. We used to pass in front of it on our way to our neighborhood bodega, my brother Carlos and I, and pause to look at it, feeling mystified by the walled-in windows, the unlit rooms, the overgrown front garden, and frightened not because in it lived a madman, but because we knew he was our uncle. Neither Manolo nor Ricardo, both of whom left Lima long ago, want the house, but I believe it is accurate to say that they do not want anyone else to have it, either. So the house stands there, empty and falling apart. The house is the reason Manolo believes Uncle Antonio is being so awfully nice.

The house where we lived was a one-story, three-bedroom home with a red-brick front wall that gave onto the *huaca*. Next to it was a six-home apartment building and a large house with a front garden. Each morning my sister and I walked along the deserted *huaca* with Yolanda, our nanny, to the stop where we caught the bus to school. I have a fragmented but indelible memory associated with that bus stop: In it, my sister and I have just gotten off the bus and met Yoli, who every afternoon waited for us at the stop. We each grab one of Yoli's hands and start toward the house. She tells us that a surprise is awaiting us there, but she cannot tell us what. We walk in through the garage and, at that point, my sister and Yoli disappear from my memory. I am alone in the vestibule of the house, which is bathed in a dreary afternoon light, and I notice that my mother's purse and jacket are hanging from the rack. This meant that my mother was back from the hospital after one of her operations, much earlier than we expected. I drop my book bag and run, as fast as my feet would take me, to my mother's bedroom in the back of the house.

This morning Flavia said that the doctor is letting my mother remove the bandages permanently. She said "*la madre*," as we often like to refer to her, is doing well, still a bit disappointed, but well.

I could probably list in a single of these pages all the verbal exchanges I've ever had on this subject with anyone in my family, so few have there been since that terrible mistake took place. I was three years old, and I suppose that even a three-year-old knows when not to ask; without being told, she grows up knowing what never to ask. My mother was twenty-six and alone in the capital. She felt that most of the older adults around her had, in a way, turned their backs to her. Over and over she heard, "You'll be all right. It's God's test. Sh-sh-sh! Ya!" A young, handsome, promising doctor, the son of so-and-so, he mistook a breast HPV infection for something else and gave her a mastectomy. She heard, "God takes with one hand and gives with the other. Sh-sh-sh!" He extracted the mammary glands but didn't cut out the nipple, leaving a thick, vertical, purple scar on her flat chest. She heard, "God always has a plan. You don't know now but maybe later you will."

She never did. For years she would hide and cry. I only saw her twice, on the morning she cried because she felt that something was about to burst inside her bandages, and a few days ago when I told her that I am writing about it. I said, "It marked you; it marked us all." She said, "It did." It's still so raw and deep, the wound and the pain so fresh, so at the surface, "*a flor de piel*," she said with surprised, welled-up eyes, baffled by the fact that she hasn't gotten over it yet. She never understood how this could fit in anybody's plan. And she never forgave.

"So maybe this is it," she said. "What it'll take? Writing about it?"

"Just cry, Mother," I said.

"No," she said, fighting back the tears. The harm is done. "Maybe I won't ever, maybe it won't be me, nearing sixty, maybe I will never, but you will," she said, as she kept fighting back the tears.

She never forgot or forgave. When she felt the anger gnawing at her from inside, she hid and cried; she hid so as not to hear them say, "Sh-sh! Ya!" It has been a while now, although now and then, the anger gnaws at her again. Once, not long ago, she read in a local newspaper about a collective lawsuit filed against an American silicone breast-implant manufacturer. Her eyes flickered and widened, saying, "At last!" Saying, "I have to seize the chance!" She clipped the little square of newspaper with the news of the suit, at the bottom of which was the phone number to the Peruvian law firm that had joined the claim on behalf of women here. She had never had a problem with the implants; a little pain now and then, hardening spots over time, a small price to pay to never again have to use a prosthesis. As a matter of fact, she was thankful, imperfect as the implants were, especially back then, about thirty years ago, threatening of her health as they continued to be, the old implants she still had inside of her. She would agree to do it again and again, anytime in order to erase the horrifying image of her young, mutilated chest. But when she read about the suit, her eyes widened and she contemplated joining the claim, daydreamed about suing, too, like the other women, en masse with other women, fantasized about the idea of telling her story, of fighting, of raising hell, of unleashing all her stored-up anger and waging war for what was done to her.

She held on to the little square of paper for several months. It sat on top of other clippings and pending correspondence on her nightstand, with time turning sallow and brittle. But she never called. Three weeks ago she had surgery to remove the old implants and replace them with new ones.

———

Saturday, 11:00 a.m.: Last night, dinner at the lawyer's with Manolo.

To go from Miraflores to San Isidro, where the lawyer lives, the taxi driver took the most direct route, though not the fastest, and I was able to watch, love, and hate the new hustle and bustle of Friday nights in these two neighborhoods. Johnny, Manolo's friend, traveled in the front seat next to the driver and turned sideways to talk to us. All through Avenidas Pardo, Comandante Espinar, and Conquistadores, we spoke over screeching horns, which drivers here honk unthinkingly as if, together with pressing the gas and switching the gears, it were one of the fundamental components of driving. We remarked how congested the streets of Lima are nowadays. It seems that no one walks here anymore. With the unstoppable flow of vehicles into the country brought about by Fujimori's liberalization of imports early on in his government, I hear that there are thirty times more cars and buses in Lima, especially cheap secondhand vehicles from Japan, than there were ten years ago. Back in the late 1980s, one would see interminable lines of people waiting for a bus or a *micro* to go home in the *conos* on the outskirts of Lima, lines that circled around entire blocks and barely moved. Today, to the contrary, pedestrians are assaulted by empty taxicabs and half-filled *combis* and *micros,* which to remain in business have to engage in a constant, deathly competition for passengers for whom they will stop anywhere, any second, just with one slight wave of the hand.

Seeing them both in button-down shirts and jackets, I said mockingly, "So what's with the elegance?" Manolo frowned and said, "Do you know who Alfonso Forga is?" Until last night, I actually didn't. Manolo described his friend as a very successful lawyer, a big-game hunter, and probably one of the wealthiest men in Lima. "Old money," he said with a wink. I felt a tinge of intimidation. "He's married to Carmen Bryce—you know?—of the Bryce-Bryce," he said, meaning "the real thing." I suddenly feared I wasn't properly dressed—I had gotten back from spending the day at the city center with just enough time to dust off my boots and wash up from the day's grime when Johnny picked us up in the cab.

Manolo explained that many years ago, before he left Peru, he gave the lawyer private painting lessons; they had become good friends. Later, the lawyer financed some art projects and an art gallery that Manolo and a small group of artists, including Johnny, had run for a time. Last year, when the lawyer heard Manolo was back in town, he hosted a welcoming party for him. Manolo said that he couldn't wait for me to meet Edgardo, the lawyer's butler, a fascinating man who's been with the family for many years and who is like a character pulled out of a nineteenth-century *costumbrista* novel. Of all the luxuries and formalities one is met with at the lawyer's, it is Edgardo who makes the biggest impression on his guests. Manolo said he remembered watching him as he stood by the bar for hours on end preparing the most exquisite pisco sours, not in a blender but in a cocktail shaker, which he stirred without stopping until he broke into a sweat; and then serving the table with the precision of a master of some sacred ceremony, holding the heavy silver serving platter next to each guest with just one hand, never two, for as long as it was necessary, while the veins in his neck began to bulge and his arm vibrated in tension.

When we arrived at the lawyer's house, Manolo rang the bell and the maid let us in. "This way, señores," she said looking away and directing us to the vestibule where the lawyer, his wife, and a tail-wagging little dog greeted us politely. The lawyer was short and round and friendly, his wife tall and serious but gentle, and they both moved and talked and laughed with the self-assurance and control that I associate with the upper class. They took us to a small drawing room next to the vestibule, and the lawyer immediately offered each of us a drink, which he himself prepared. Manolo remarked the absence of Edgardo, and the lawyer said that he's on vacation, a well-deserved one. They miss him very much, the lawyer's wife said. "That's why Suzy, the maid of service, is very nervous," she said, "because for the first time she's on her own, and it'll be her, not Edgardo, serving us at the table."

Suzy brought in some hors d'oeuvres; she did look nervous. We sat down and small-talked for a while about the last corruption scandal, about an ambassador who has just arrived, about a bank that just went under. The doorbell rang again, and two more guests came in: a man in his fifties, who is a banker and, like the lawyer, a lover of the arts (he's the financier of the gallery where Manolo's show is taking place), and his much younger wife, also a Bryce, but according to Manolo from another branch, one that goes back to a man who was born illegitimately. As the lawyer's wife and the banker's wife said hello to each other, I think I felt some tension. The new guests joined us with a drink, and soon thereafter we were invited to pass to the dining room.

Suzy was donning her party uniform: a knee-length black camisole with white buttons and a white ruffled collar, and over it, a white apron tied with a bow around the waist and neck, the fringes of it also ruffled to match the collar. Just like Edgardo would have, although perhaps not as fastidiously, Suzy brought in the first course and went around the table, stopping to the right of each guest—first the women, then the men—and to the right of the hosts—first the wife, then the lawyer—holding before us the serving bowl and allowing us enough time to serve ourselves. It was cream of squash with homemade croutons. She held the heavy tray with both hands.

The conversation, meanwhile, flowed from one subject to another, from politics to history, from art to the Internet, from Peru to Europe. I noticed that no one touched their plate until the lawyer was done serving himself and Suzy had left the dining room. As we ate, the lawyer illustrated a point he was trying to make about communications technology today, the era of globalization, by recalling the day he and his wife flew from Moscow to Prague, arriving the day after the city had been seized by the Soviets. While today news would have traveled much faster, at the time it was not until they had entered the city and seen the Soviet tanks stationed everywhere that they realized something out of the ordinary was taking place. The lawyer's wife ate quietly, graciously, sporadically offering details that enriched her husband's story. As I listened to them speak, I noticed to myself how well traveled they are, and because of this, how cultured, how at ease and comfortable with themselves. In *L'Education sentimentale* Flaubert describes this attitude as a "confident simplicity," which is what set Mlle. Deslauriers's class apart from Frédéric's. It was indeed the unaffected quality of their deportment, consistently the same regardless of whether they were dealing with their guests or their servants, apparently free of the need to reaffirm their status, that made them utterly different from both the upwardly and the downwardly mobile middle classes to which I am used.

I was even quieter than the lawyer's wife. I know she wasn't, but somehow I felt that she was scrutinizing me. Then she stated across the table that she and my aunt Mari had gone to high school together, smiling and looking at me without blinking. I felt a bit uncomfortable, I'm not sure why—maybe my informal dress, my dusty shoes? While we ate, I was painfully aware of my table manners, painfully aware of theirs, and as much as I wanted it to stop, I couldn't control the flow of silent, self-conscious observations, the barrage of insecure thoughts that made me barely able to throw a phrase or two into the conversation before being sucked back into my own anxious thoughts.

Suzy came out again, now holding a plate of sliced roasted duck garnished with glazed baby carrots and turnips. As she went around the table, the lawyer refilled our wineglasses from his seat, which he kept doing all through dessert.

After dinner we went to the main living room for pousse-café. Manolo grabbed me by the arm and whispered, "This is what I want you to see." But before he was able to explain, I had already seen it, I was already caught in it: the gaze of thirty or forty animal-head trophies hanging from all four walls in the living room. Deer with horns that branched out like trees, gazelles and antelopes of all sizes, a lioness, a zebra, even a buffalo, all staring at us standing at the center of the room with their eyes as deep as water wells. The rest of the living room was black and white and wood, and besides a few other souvenirs from Africa were portraits of the lawyer on several African safaris, portraits of himself next to the carcass of these animals, rifle in hand. I could not help but feel that some of the animal heads had a human expression: The zebra, I swear, looked sad, the gazelle next to me was grinning, the buffalo up top looked at us with ears pricked and a slightly tilted head as if intrigued by something it was seeing. That is precisely the work of the taxidermist, the

123

lawyer said. The term *taxidermy* derives from the Greek: *taxi* meaning "movement" and *derma* meaning "skin," the true skill of the taxidermist resting on his ability to adjust the skin so that it appears lifelike. The best taxidermists, he said, are in Eastern Europe. I nodded, signaling comprehension, but thought, *And why the expressions? Happy, sad, curious?* Noticing my interest, he spoke with increasing excitement, his arms now flailing in the air to describe how he had come face-to-face with the lioness and shot it. The arms flailing in the air, and all I could think of was the tree-like horns, the pricked ears, the eyes like wells, looking, no, staring at us! I kept thinking, *Is it just me?* About thirty animal heads, all arranged on the walls by the lawyer's wife in such a way that their eyes looked down upon us. Thirty animal heads. Hegel says that increment in quantity, after a certain point, brings about qualitative transformations. I thought, *Why so many?* I thought, *Continuity*.

The Spanish philosopher José Ortega y Gasset says that hunting as a sport is an activity that, like bullfighting, humans have preserved through generations to be able to flee from civilization, to take, in his own words, "a vacation from humanity." He writes, "In all justice, the meaning of the sport of hunting is not to elevate the beast to the height of man, but something much more spiritual than that: a conscious and almost religious humiliation of man who leaves aside his prepotency in order to descend toward the animal. I have said 'religious,'" he goes on, "and I do not find the word excessive."[14]

Actually, neither do I.

What I understand from Ortega y Gasset's argument is that with the sport of hunting, humans attempt to re-create something of the numinous quality that the killing of any living being had to our ancestors. The true objective of hunting, Ortega y Gasset explains, what he calls hunting's in-itself (*"su mismidad"*), is not to kill or to kill in whatever manner or, even less, to kill in an efficient manner. If efficiency is desired, it is only the efficiency brought about by the hunter's skill and endurance, which ought to be displayed despite the atmosphere of risk and the fear and ambivalence the hunter feels before the animal he is about to kill. Efficiency is acceptable to the extent that it does not disturb the balance of power, the equilibrium of skill between hunter and prey that is required for the hunt to be perceived as fair game. That is why the sport of hunting has only slightly, and to a certain extent insignificantly, been affected by technical advances.

"A vacation from humanity." Bataille would have appreciated the phrase and would have emphasized the temporary and extraordinary qualities implied in the term "vacation." This is because, for Bataille, the longing that leads to the search for our lost intimacy with the animal world (in this case through hunting) does not entail the desire to return to animality by eliminating the limits that sustain the social world but rather the desire to cross those limits, which are there not so much to prevent their crossing as to charge it with the meaning of a sacred violation. This leads Bataille to reject the explanation of Neolithic cave paintings in Europe as magical devices to secure a good kill and to argue that we ought to see them instead as representations created *following* the kill, each of them the result of an act of atonement made imperative by the transgressive religious aura that surrounded the animal as it was done to death. Bataille writes, "The cave drawings must have been intended to depict that instant when the animal appeared, and killing, at once inevitable and reprehensible, laid bare life's mysterious ambiguity."[15] He thus suggests an interpretation of one of the Lascaux paintings found in what is known as "the shaft of the dead man," in which a dying bison faces from above the man, now apparently dead, who has probably wounded it, its head lowered and its eyes fixed on the man's vulnerable body. The theme of this representation, Bataille argues, must be murder and expiation, for the same feeling of awe concerning the death of a fellow man must have taken over the hunter as he killed his prey, since what hunters are really after is engaging animals that, at least for the moment that the hunting expedition lasts, he considers essentially the same as himself.

Is murder and expiation also the intention behind hanging hunting trophies such as these? And why so many?

"The lion," the lawyer said, "is one of the most respected animals you can hunt in Africa. Hunting a lion is dangerous; it is not like hunting a deer because a lion will hunt you as well." In Africa, it turns out, lions are among the most expensive animals a hunter can have in the scope, about $2,400 for each prey. This, on top of the cost of the safari itself, which begins roughly at $8,500 per person, plus $450 for a hunting permit, $300 for a firearms permit, $1,400 in conservation fees, plus the import duties for bringing into Africa one's own guns and ammunition, and at least another $1,000 for permits and fees if the hunter wants to bring this trophy home. Lions, "the most respected animal," apparently abound in Africa; they are not on the list of endangered species banned from hunting, in which the cheetah, giraffe, and rhino have been placed. Hunting in Africa, the lawyer assured me, is carried out under the strictest laws and regulations, which must be meticulously observed in the name of safety and conservation.

The lawyer said that it was he who spotted the lioness first. He and his guide were patiently observing it from their hideout, awaiting an opportunity to shoot. Then, all of a sudden, they lost sight of it and, alarmed, looked frantically around their hiding place only to realize some moments later that they were now being scoped by the animal. His arms flailing in the air, I believed him when he said that he was scared out of his wits. The guide had yelled, "Shoot now!" as the lioness sprinted and leapt toward him, and next thing, the animal lay on its side with a gunshot wound between its forelegs and surrounded by the hunters, who stood aghast looking at it in solemn silence. For a moment that might be worth calling religious, the killer was filled with ambivalence, with a sense of excitement and sorrow, conscious that he had committed an act that was both licit and illicit.

But isn't there countless evidence in modern society that the taboo on killing animals has disappeared in its entirety? Judging by the animal factories of today and the gruesome slaughter practices, couldn't we say that movements bent on raising ecological consciousness and enforcing animal rights are not so much expressions of the taboo or of its return but precisely a sign of its utter disappearance? Perhaps. Yet, it seems to me that the modern sport of hunting, with all its rules and formal limitations, allows for a taste of the original (for Bataille, non-Christian) character of social prohibitions, meant not to eliminate but to be completed by their deliberate violation. Such is the implication of Ortega y Gasset's essay. It is in the intensity of emotion, in the thrilling degradation afforded by the sport that, knowingly or unknowingly, big-game hunters seek to partake.

As we left the lawyer's house, I walked next to the lioness's-head trophy—its sharp fangs projecting out, its eyes deep and captivating—and thought of Lascaux. According to my calculations, that lioness alone must have cost the lawyer at least $17,000. Seventeen thousand dollars! I thought, *Money: today's form of expiation?*

———————

Later: This afternoon Vulture-man came to our door again. Three oddly short rings, and I knew it was him. I waited until Eulalia had opened the door and was talking to him to peer out the window. His wide eyes, greedy and disbelieving, were fixed on Eulalia as she tried to convince him that Manolo was not in.

"What about the señorita?" he said. "Is she in?"

By instinct, I stepped away from the window just as Vulture-man lifted his eyes to where he had seen me emerge the first time, even though Eulalia said that I wasn't in either.

He lingered in front of the house after Eulalia had closed the door. He walked impatiently back and forth in the space between the door and the clunky, ramshackle Dodge on the driveway, hands in pockets, occasionally directing a glance and a few words at the other man who stood still and quiet, his bony back to the car, the arms crossed in front, and facing the sea. Vulture-man seemed to me to be increasingly uneasy, turning his head left and right and back at the house, up to the window from where I was watching him behind the curtain. I had a feeling that he was determined to wait, however long necessary, for Manolo to arrive. Then he turned around on his feet to face the house again, looking up to the window and for a moment somewhere beyond the house with eyes that suddenly seemed anxious rather than greedy. His lips were pursed and his brow frowned; his short but portly demeanor looked beaten down, frail.

I thought, *Could it possibly be true?* Meaning, could it be true that Vulture-man is actually stuck with Paco's body, unable to cremate it without an autopsy clearance or to carry out an autopsy without Manolo's authorization? Or, what was in that puzzled, anxious look? I thought, *Could it be?* With distant eyes and absorbed in thought, it was as though he was weighing his options, thinking to himself, *Should I forge the authorization? Pay for an autopsy myself? Dispose of the body myself? Dump it? Bury it? Burn it myself?*

I finally decided to go down to talk to him. I walked down the stairs, unhurried, thinking what I would say. "I was napping upstairs," I would say. "Manolo leaves in two days," I would say. Or better, I would lie, "Manolo has already left." But I opened the door and they were gone. Vulture-man, the skinny guy, and the car—gone.

FIVE

Filth

Seen from the point of view of death, the product of the corpse is life.
—WALTER BENJAMIN, *THE ORIGIN OF GERMAN TRAGIC DRAMA*

From the threshold at the fourth door of Lima's Cementerio General, the first thing one sees is a marble sculpture of a Supine Christ. White and iridescent, Jesus' body lies limp over a sheet of undulating folds while his head is propped up on a pillow, showing forth his agonized grimace. The sculpture is at the crux of two straight, perpendicular avenues, which divide this early nineteenth-century necropolis into well-organized quarters, each with its marble mausoleums and tombstones, its oratories, and its L-shaped niche walls, where the corpses of the less well-to-do are neatly stacked up one above the other. Beyond two short palm trees one of those avenues shoots forth, flanked by several rows of individual tombs topped with amazingly beautiful marble sculptures: tiny neogothic steeples, obelisks, and catafalques; men's busts; mournful women in sensuous poses, draped in loose, lacy tunics; and myriad of angels, androgynous and sensuously positioned, too, some of them with their legs exposed and their long wings spread out, seemingly ready to take to the air. On the outer edges of this populous city of the dead, faintly visible through the haze, the low and barren hills of the westernmost Andes roll far and deep into the horizon, giving the cemetery an eerily bleak atmosphere and making the old and weathered white figurines look truly otherworldly.

Several meters down the same avenue, at another intersection from where more avenues shoot out in opposite directions, is the imposing, five-statue mausoleum of Marshall Ramón Castilla, one of Peru's nineteenth-century caudillo presidents. It was in front of the tomb of this legendary ruler that late one Sunday night in 1917 a visiting Swiss dancer, Norka Rouskaya, was made to perform a *danse macabre* before a group of entranced *Limeño* artists and intellectuals to the violin tune of Chopin's "Funeral March." The event, which was instigated by José Carlos Mariátegui, the future founder of Peru's Socialist Party, became one of the most notorious social and political scandals of the twentieth century, holding up important debates in Congress so that the meaning of the transgression could be hashed out by the lawmakers and throwing the entire city into a fit of "indignation coupled with vindictive hostility, anxiety, fear, and even shame," which lasted until after Mariátegui and his friends were thrown in jail.[1] In outrage, an editorial in the newspaper *La Unión* called it an act of degeneracy. It further stated: "A dancer performing on the tombs of our seniors, persuaded or contracted by a dozen amoral persons with meager intellect and low instincts! The fact is crude and shameful. Nobody would have suspected that *decent individuals* would shelter in their souls such mountains of garbage. . . . Even savages honor their dead and respect their graves. Only here it is reserved for us to be present at so large an infamy."[2] Rouskaya's performance may well have been the last expression of the long vanishing world of erotic-macabre phantasms that had pervaded the idea of death during the city's baroque period, before a shift took place at the end of the eighteenth century toward the sensual but less morbid and extravagant approach to death put forth by romanticism. Writing about Europeans' attitudes toward death, Philippe Ariès has characterized this shift as a sublimation of the baroque tendency to openly link the erotic with death. Others, such as John McManners, have described it as the rejection of baroque imagery depicting the inevitable horrors of death in favor of an individualistic and sentimental funeral aesthetic.[3] In the social and cultural life of colonial Lima, the construction and inauguration of the Cementerio General in 1808 had been the clearest manifestation of this ideological and cultural shift.

The Cementerio General, also called Cementerio Presbítero Maestro, was built over 150,000 square meters along a suburban road (today called Jirón Ancash) to the east of the city center, right where the Rímac River gives a sharp turn into the rising slopes of the Andes. Presbítero Matías Maestro was a Basque clergyman who settled in the colonies in the late 1700s, first in Mexico City and then, until his death, in Lima. Having had formal training in the arts, Maestro was put in charge of the renovation of the most important church altars in Lima after King Charles IV of the new Bourbon dynasty called for the eradication in Spain and in the colonies of all baroque forms of expression, which were now considered to be irrational, vulgar, and contrary to the rising modern and "enlightened" spirit. As a result of this measure, the main interior altar in Lima's Cathedral was torn down and replaced by one of neoclassical features, and its carved-wood baroque pulpit, endlessly praised for its beauty in the chronicles of the time, was substituted by one with round and fluted pilasters and adorned with bay-leaf garlands and other neoclassical motifs. Similarly, the main altar-*retablos* inside the churches of La Merced, San Francisco, San Agustín, and San Pedro were torn down by Maestro and replaced with neoclassical altar stands, while the church of Santo Domingo received the most dramatic makeover of all, both inside and out, as its baroque stone altar-façade was entirely rebuilt into a portico of clean, straight lines and smooth surfaces.[4]

Maestro was also made responsible for the design and construction of the city's first state-run burial ground, the Cementerio General, which radically reconfigured how the city would, from then on, relate to its dead. From the city's founding days until the turn of the nineteenth century, individuals had been buried in collective graves in churches and chapels in the middle of the city—under an altar or inside a nearby wall or in the atrium—from where their dry bones were eventually transferred to charnel houses and ossuaries to make room for new burials. But as in many European capitals, emerging scientific attitudes with regards to hygiene, sickness, and death prompted city officials to argue for the prohibition of church inhumations and order the transfer of all burial grounds, often only paces away from the main square, out to the periphery of the city. This idea was reinforced throughout Europe and in the colonies by an 1804 Napoleonic edict forbidding burials in urban grounds, which recapped several urgent calls to stop the interment of bodies inside the city of Paris after the collapsed walls of densely crowded churchyards had left thousands of human remains scattered about the city streets. With this edict came to an end what was really only a hiatus of a few centuries during which Europeans, driven by a newfound yearning during the early Middle Ages to be buried in close proximity to Christian saints and martyrs, had initiated a coexistence *in urbe*, that is, within the city, between the living and the dead, which had rarely, if ever, been seen before in the history of the West.[5]

In Lima, the opening of the Cementerio General, some distance beyond the Portal de Maravillas (one of the city wall's eight gateways), was met with a good deal of apprehension. The growing scarcity of burial space in and around Lima's churches had generated tension among the population and great competition for slots inside particular chapels or altars, or near particular saints or patrons. And this competition continued throughout the nineteenth century resulting in secret burials of individuals who had the means to influence church authorities and were willing to risk a state-imposed fine.[6] At the new Cementerio General, some of the old funeral customs persisted; for many years after its inauguration, save the space around the cemetery's central chapel, which was reserved for colonial authorities and the nobility, corpses were wrapped in a shroud (*mortaja*) and buried in collective graves, in no specific order. As it was also done in churches, their dry bones were later exhumed and placed in an ossuary. But as the last vestiges of the baroque concern with the drama of death dissipated, and as the idea of death as an individual, private affair took firmer hold, plots of land within the cemetery were sold for the construction of permanent personal tombs and family mausoleums. In the 1850s and '60s there was a veritable explosion of private funeral monuments at the Cementerio General with tombstones and marble statuary modeled after some of the best specimens at the Père Lachaise Cemetery in Paris and the Municipal Cemetery in Rome, whose purchase was made possible by the sudden prosperity brought about by the short-lived but powerful guano boom.[7]

For over 150 years, the Cementerio General was Lima's main official burial ground, until it, too, became saturated and closed down for new interments in 1965. (In 1999, the Beneficencia de Lima, a city government agency that runs Lima's public cemeteries, launched an "Adopt a Sculpture" campaign and, riding the wave of restorations and increased tourism in the city center under Andrade, turned the Cementerio General into a museum.) In 1959, another necropolis, the Cementerio El Ángel, was built across the street from the Cementerio General on the grounds of a former hacienda, stretching over 200,000 square meters. While it initially emulated the Cementerio General in its layout and iconography, it allocated significantly more space for affordable niche walls, a design also followed by the Cementerio Municipal de Surquillo, a working-class district that emerged in the late 1940s tucked between Miraflores and San Isidro. In the last thirty years, an array of modern and luxurious cemeteries have sprung on the edges of the expanding city in the form of tall, enclosed pavilions—such as the Cementerio La Planicie—or vast and artificially irrigated green lawns with room for mausoleums, individual tombs, and niche walls—such as the two Cementerios Jardines de la Paz, which resemble the one in La Planicie only in that they have a clean-cut, modern design and are almost completely devoid of statuary. Also in the last thirty years, numerous "clandestine" cemeteries have appeared on unoccupied swaths of desert, dotting and servicing the residents of the *barriada* settlements. A survey in the early 1990s accounted for at least thirty-one of these cemeteries, which José Tamayo describes as unruly and chaotic, characteristics that they supposedly share with the neighborhoods that surround them, from which, he says, they are often hardly distinguishable for lack of proper lines of demarcation. And like the *barriadas* once did, these "informal" graveyards, often signaled by scattered, thin, and windswept wooden crosses planted on the sand and nothing more, have a highly unclear relationship with the law and the city government: Their existence is not affirmed by them, but it is not denied either.[8]

———

The virtual lack of historiographic interest in Lima's changing relationship to its dead is striking in light of the central importance that burial grounds have had in the physical evolution and cultural life of the city.[9] Pointing to the critical role of the dead in the historical development of urbanism, Lewis Mumford begins his monumental *The City in History* by asserting that the only aspect in the early life of human beings that could have played a greater role than securing a regular supply of foodstuffs in their decision to establish permanent settlements was their "respect for the dead." "Soon after one picks up man's trail in the earliest campfire or chipped-stone tool," he writes, "one finds evidence of interests and anxieties that have no animal counterpart; in particular, a ceremonious concern for the dead, manifested in their deliberate burial—with growing evidences of pious apprehension and dread."[10] Mumford notes that in the unpredictable nomadic existence of Paleolithic man, the dead were the first to have claimed the privilege of a permanent dwelling, to which the living may have felt compelled to return regularly in order to commune with or placate the ancestral spirits. "In one sense," Mumford says, "the city of the dead is the forerunner ... of every living city. Urban life spans the historic space between the earliest burial ground for dawn man and the final cemetery, the Necropolis, in which one civilization after another has met its end."[11]

Georges Bataille was fascinated by the deliberateness of those early burials and, like Mumford, took them to be evidence of a budding interest and anxiety that he thought had "no animal counterpart." From the opening pages of *Erotism*, which hypothetically outline the emergence of the first taboos, we know that Bataille was most intrigued by the possible "meaning" of these early interments, which at the time he was writing, around 1960, was a source of contention (as it continues to be today) among archaeologists and anthropologists. Lacking any positive material evidence to confirm the presence of abstract thought, many of them do not dare to do more than suggest that the function of these burials was to prevent the corpse from being eaten by animals.[12] But, as Bataille compellingly asks, why would have these ancestors of ours cared at all about the fate of a dead human being if they didn't already find the idea of a gnawed-at decomposing corpse deeply disturbing? For Bataille, the presence of these burials, whose form is as simple as it is constant, can only signal human beings' incipient understanding of their own mortality. He writes, "For each man who regards it with awe, the corpse is the image of his own destiny. It bears witness to a violence, which destroys not one man alone but all men in the end." The ability to discern the transition from a human being's living state to the corpse and the tendency to view a rotting corpse as a tormenting and menacing object are, for Bataille, two of the most basic qualities that characterize human beings in contrast and in opposition to the animal.[13]

Bataille explains that the quality and intensity of the taboos that take hold of human beings in the presence of a corpse are a reflection of the distance they put between themselves and the violence that has taken possession of it, threatening the reality of their separate, self-possessed individualities as human beings. Against the emerging world of work and rationality, which in Bataille's Hegelian outlook is what gives birth to and what sustains the idea of the discontinuity of beings and objects, death means continuity of being. Death, he writes, "jerks us out of a tenacious obsession with the lastingness of our discontinuous being," bringing about the dissolution of the self and underscoring the futility of the separate individual.[14] Thus if death is dangerous, it is so only for those who are left behind, who dispose of the body ritually not so much to keep it safe as to keep themselves, those who have survived the dead person, safe from contagion. "The idea of contagion," Bataille states, "is connected with the body's decomposition where formidable aggressive forces are seen at work. The corpse will rot; this biological disorder, like the newly dead body a symbol of [our] destiny, is threatening in itself."[15]

The prohibitions surrounding the dead body—which is human and yet no longer properly human—have thus given way in all societies to a complex mass of beliefs, emotions, and behaviors, generally including a special language, a specific way of treating the corpse, and a need for what Robert Hertz refers to as "a correct burial."[16] Hertz's work on death pollution among the Dayak of Borneo is curiously ubiquitous in studies about death, in which the analytic power of Hertz's views about Dayak funeral rituals is evoked to shed light on practices and beliefs in places as far away and different from Borneo as China, Great Britain, France, and Bolivia.[17] This is perhaps because Hertz's descriptions of Dayak burials have the paradoxical effect of revealing as exotic even the seemingly obvious or necessary funeral practices in the West.

But more broadly and importantly than this, the value and relevance of Hertz's work lies in that he takes Durkheim's sociological theory to its limit to show that, beyond the brute reality of physical death, death is primarily a "social fact." As he put it in relation to the Dayak, when someone dies, it is as if the dead body, and by extension the whole of society, had suddenly become afflicted by a special infirmity, compelling those who are alive to regard the corpse, at one and the same time, as an object of solicitude and an object of fear. Hertz writes, "The deceased, both victim and prisoner of evil powers, . . . is violently ejected from the society, dragging his closest relatives with him."[18] For Hertz, this means primarily two things: On the one hand, death does not just end the bodily life of an individual. It also destroys the "social being" that was grafted upon that individual by society, putting to work "energies that are proportionate to the social status of the deceased [and] implying powers of the same order but of a negative nature."[19] On the other hand, not only do the relatives of the deceased and the entire community feel threatened by the presence of death's mysterious, antagonistic forces, but the process of destruction of the body by these forces is taken to reflect on the state of the survivors, in Hertz's own words, to "[express] concretely the state of bewilderment and anguish of the community." Among the Dayak, the rituals afforded by the disposal of the body and by the institution of mourning allow the survivors to deal with the danger and uncertainty of the situation. In the reduction of the corpse to bones the Dayak see the signal of the dead person's successful passage to the invisible society of the dead and an indication of their final deliverance.[20]

———

In the early colonial city of Lima, a similar correspondence was thought to exist between the status of an individual in life and in death. Except for the rare individual tombs of royal or church authorities, burials reflected the person's social standing in life and relationship to the church in the greater or lesser distance that was put between his or her body and the church's main atrium or altar. In Counterreformation doctrine, death was seen as the beginning of a chain of torturous events meant to purify the soul as it freed itself from the vile and sinful body.

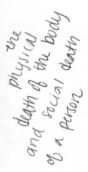

the physical death of the body and social death of a person

Interring bodies in churches was believed to ensure the process of pu-
rification since, as a thirteenth-century law by King Alfonso X stated,
"The devils will not be able to attach themselves to the bodies of the
dead . . . as they will to the ones that lay outside." Also according to this
law, the proximity and visibility of tombs and bones would ensure that
the relatives of the deceased, upon entering the church, would "remember to implore to God on their behalf."[21] In other words, nearness to
consecrated space or to the tombs of saints, like prayer and the church's
intercession, was believed to assuage the agonies of death and lessen the
time a soul spent suffering in purgatory.

In the Spanish baroque culture of the seventeenth and early eighteenth centuries, the theme of death and the physical corruption of the
body was a besieging concern exceeding the powerful attraction there
was toward these themes in the Middle Ages and succeeding in offering
an even more frightening version of it.[22] As the perfect counterpart to
baroque society's zeal for ostentation, voluptuousness, and laxity, great
satisfaction was derived from the contemplation of death's horrors, as is
attested by the vast repertory of macabre themes in Spanish and colonial
baroque art. Of these themes—many of which were shared with the rest
of Catholic Europe—perhaps the most recurrent one was the *memento
mori*. This was an array of iconographic motifs, meaning literally "Remember that thou shalt die," which depicted all sorts of scenes recalling
death by featuring an animated skeleton, some times winged, an arrange-
ment of human bones and skulls, or a single skull, next to or replacing
the head of a young woman, Vanitas, in an allegorical evocation of the
transience and irremediable decay of worldly things. As M. J. Mejías
Álvarez describes for Lima, the ephemeral catafalques built for various
royal obsequies during the baroque often had as the most prominent
motif a scythed, walking skeleton or a woman with a death's head.[23]

According to Elizabeth Musgrave, this morbid iconography, much
of which emerged in the Middle Ages, was keenly embraced by post-
Tridentine Catholic doctrine with a pedagogical or moralizing intention that emphasized personal mortality, judgment, and repentance.[24]
In Spain, for instance, the Jesuits recommended as a spiritual exercise
the contemplation of death through the gazing at a skull.[25] The *danse
macabre*, another kind of *memento mori* in which a skeleton (death) collects individuals from all sectors of society and dances them to the grave,
continued to be a popular motif during the baroque period, and the
churches' ossuaries continued not just to shelter but visually display dry
human remains in order to exhibit, as Musgrave puts it, the "wages of
sin."[26] The prominence of human bones and skulls in baroque funeral

art spoke less to the fate of those who had passed away (as would be later with the funeral representations of romanticism) than to the grim destiny of the survivors, of the still "living public that contemplated the funeral monument."[27]

With the first breezes of the Enlightenment arriving in Lima came a certain inhibition, what Ariès refers to as a sublimation, of the more gruesome, frightening, or repelling aspects of death. What's more, if during the baroque the role of the erudite intellectual—in Lima, characters like the scholar and dramatist Pedro Peralta y Barnuevo—was indispensable in helping the public depict and interpret hidden meanings in the signs of physical decay, by the end of the 1700s a similar role had been assumed by the scientist and the medical doctor. Based on Enlightenment scientific theories, the air infested with the odor given off by the corpses interred in or around the churches was increasingly seen as a source of pollution, infection, and epidemics. As it was conveyed by Diderot in his *Encyclopédie* as well as in the works of other European scientists who were often mentioned in Lima publications of the time, the health of individuals was believed to be directly associated with the purity of the air.[28] This idea was grounded on a "miasmatic" paradigm, according to which physical corruption and infection could make the air degenerate into highly poisonous, "sticky" miasmas that could kill a person through contact or inhalation.[29] In other words, a direct correlation was established between decay and its smells and the existence of infectious miasmas, a word whose etymology is the ancient Greek concept for stain or defilement.

In the late 1700s, the liberal, pro-Independence Sociedad de Amantes del País, through its printed organ the *Mercurio Peruano*, headed a feverish advocacy campaign, arguably the first one showcasing the notion of public hygiene, in favor of closing the city's churchyards; this was the beginning of the crusade that led eventually to the construction of the Cementerio General. The writings of a frequent and notorious contributor, who published under the nom de plume Hesperiophilo, make it clear that the public perception of the human corpse was shifting, assuming a new kind of corrupting and offensive character and making of it, in Hesperiophilo's words, "that which is most filthy about humanity."[30] In this, Hesperiophilo saw eye to eye with one of the Society's most prominent members, the scientist and doctor Hipólito Unanue, who also advocated the closing of churchyards, calling for the restitution of "decorum in our magnificent temples" and for the protection of "public health in the city" by no longer defiling the churches with human corpses, which he also called "the filthiest thing of the earth."[31]

On the one hand, Unanue thought that church burials were a sign of indignity and moral decay. He singles out as evidence of a debilitated rigor in the church's discipline the fact that what used to be a rare practice among early Christians, who restricted church burials to its martyrs (their bodies had "the smell of sanctity"), had in the last centuries become extended to "the lowest, most vulgar masses," who had saturated the soil with their dead bodies, violating the dignity of the consecrated space.[32] On the other hand, he believed that the presence of rotting corpses within the city was unhealthy since it turned the whole of it, for all practical reasons and purposes, into a "dirty cemetery," from where "pestilent vapors emanate, altering and corrupting the air that we breathe." If that would be true of any city with *in urbe* burial grounds, for Unanue, it was more so of Lima where vapors are corrupted by the warm and humid weather, both known to be chief agents in the decomposition of corpses and the reason why Lima's churches had become a "perennial source of contagion" that could lead only to debilitation, sickness, and death.[33]

In his writings, Unanue refers specifically to the Church of San Francisco, whose large number of devotees had made its churchyard, through the years, particularly dense. He noted that under the church's main altar, badly covered over, were close to four hundred corpses, "festering in the stench and the filth." The pavement of the atrium, including the presbytery, was crammed with crypts and sepulchers, which "no sooner had they been closed than they [were] open again to throw in the bodies of the recently dead on top of other bodies half-rotten." Unanue reports that, because of this, the temple itself had an unbearable stench and concludes that only the construction of a separate pantheon—located to the northeast of the city, opposite to the direction of the winds (*a sotavento*)—would free Lima of the churches' pestilent impurities that saturated the city air.[34]

It is important to remark that the problem wasn't so much that there was a sudden overabundance of bodies or that the conditions for their burial had unexpectedly worsened. It was rather that a drastic change in sensibilities was taking place. Prior to the debate about air and winds as potential corrupting agents, Jean-Pierre Clement points out, city dwellers seemed not to have perceived the putrid smell, not to have been conscious of it, or not to have minded it.[35] As Alain Corbin has observed about France—and this is also applicable to Lima—in the eighteenth century there was a "more refined alertness to smell" than before, a change that Corbin characterizes as a "far-reaching, anthropological transformation" in that it would take to new levels Western culture's rejection of olfaction as the sense most closely associated with savagery and animalistic behavior.[36] This "perceptual revolution," according to Corbin, was related to the growing scientific attention given to odors and to the theories that implicated them in the spread of disease and death, which, in turn, created new anxieties as well as "a whole array of taboos" on the uses of the olfactory organ and on smells arising from excretions of the body and material putrefaction. In other words, a "more refined alertness" to smells would lead to further repression of this sensory organ and to the modern notion that olfaction is a less important sense, compared to taste or sight.

From the mid-1700s on, as awareness grew among Lima residents about the odor of corpses, the concern also emerged, or deepened, about the smell of raw sewage and garbage, which were now viewed not just as spoiling the beauty of the city but also as threatening of public health. In the 1760s, the government of Viceroy Manuel Amat y Juniet announced a flurry of measures that sought to legislate street orderliness and hygiene, stating that "the cleanliness of the streets does not only lead to the adornment and beauty of this capital, but it is truly connected to the health of its inhabitants."[37] These measures included the 1769 *Reglamento de Policía* (still in the old sense of *policía*) and the 1785 *Nuevo Reglamento de Policía* (an addendum to the previous one), both of which made it mandatory for residents of the city to clean out the garbage from the section of the public sewage stream that ran in front of their houses and to take it to designated sites in the outskirts of the city. Likewise emphasizing the relation between street cleanliness and health, the *Nuevo Reglamento* instructed city authorities to cover the sewage stream with a metal mesh so that it would not clog with garbage. In the early 1790s, articles in the *Mercurio Peruano* that called attention to the smell of dead bodies often also referred to what one contributor to the paper described as "the stagnant water in some sections [of the city's sewage ditch], which in other sections overflows, and in all of them drags along domestic and natural filth [*inmundicias*], [that] cannot but add to the gaseous exhalations, which are noxious to the health of the residents" of this otherwise "beautiful Capital, worthy of a distinguished place next to the most opulent ones in Europe."[38]

The notions of hygiene and public health, and the stress put on both in the social policies of the Bourbon viceroys, were inextricable from the idea, dominant at the time, that the wealth of a nation depended on a numerous and healthy population, a notion that presupposed the social virtues of work, production, and economic progress. Clement notes that the drive in Spanish America to clean up the city streets extended to moral cleanliness, in relation to which idleness or lack of productivity, personified chiefly by vagrants and the poor, became not only reprehensible but also dangerous to city life. In his *Idea general del reino del Perú*, the report that Unanue wrote on behalf of Viceroy Francisco Gil de Taboada in 1796, he points to the insufficient growth of Lima's population as one of the main reasons for the "state of decadence" that afflicted the viceroyalty, which in turn had led many men and women to live dissolute or idle lives and turn to vice or thievery.[39] In the report, Unanue makes recommendations on ways that these most threatening and corrupting elements could be controlled and made useful to society (through work in factories and mines) and offers a list of city governing tribunals that should be charged with materializing these ideas. This list includes the new Corte de Policía, an institution that was created under the previous viceroy, Amat y Juniet, in 1786. This institution was presided by a lieutenant of policía who, aided by a foreman of architecture and four city mayors, was in charge of administering and keeping watch over the residents of the four quarters into which Lima had been divided, also by Viceroy Amat y Juniet, for a more efficient government of the city.

Under a section in the report subtitled "Policía," Unanue offers a detailed description of what Gil de Taboada had done to further enforce Amat y Juniet's *reglamentos*. From the information provided in this section, we learn that, in addition to the cleanliness and orderliness of city streets, the term *policía* now included the adequate supply and fair pricing of foodstuffs as well as the idea of public safety and security of property. Unanue says that, besides carrying out a census of city residents that included references to their class status and health state, Gil de Taboada had decreed important measures to prevent street delinquency and murder as well as to avert epidemic outbreaks and fires. On the issue of church graveyards, although he isn't explicit regarding the type of transgressions Gil de Taboada sought to impede, Unanue says that under this viceroy each of these burial grounds had been surrounded by a wall and gated so that they could be closed off at night to "the assaults of libertinage." The departing viceroy, says Unanue, had also fomented street lighting to prevent "nocturnal excesses."[40] But perhaps most important of all, Unanue goes over a long inventory of public works, with which the viceroy had contributed to the urban renewal efforts of the Bourbon viceroys before him, in particular Amat y Juniet, whose ultimate purpose was to control or redirect the flows of the ever-growing urban plebe, particularly around their leisure activities.[41]

To Amat y Juniet's works—which included the construction of the Plaza de Acho (the city's first and only bullfighting ring), the Coliseo de Gallos (a cock-fighting ring), the Paseo de Aguas and Alameda de Acho (public promenades), all of which were located in the periphery of the city, beyond the city wall—Gil de Taboada had added the Paseo Militar (a riverside promenade), repairs to the Cathedral Towers, to the tower of the Church of San Agustín, to the city's bridges and walkways, and, finally, to the city's open sewage stream, which prison inmates were made to clean on a daily basis. These works were intended to contribute, in Unanue's words, to the public's leisure and comfort and to a city center "free of the filthy and corrupted matter that used to offend our olfactory sense as much as harm our health."[42]

In Unanue's discourse, garbage and the plebe, the spread of material filth and of the masses' licentious behavior, had become two intimately linked subjects. Dirt and odors led to social disorganization and corruption. Based on the language of Unanue's report, one could say about 1700s Lima what Corbin says about the social implications of new perceptions of dirt and smells in 1700s France: "Abhorrence of smells produce[d] its own form of social power. Foul-smelling rubbish appear[ed] to threaten the social order, whereas the reassuring victory of the hygienic and the fragrant promise[d] to buttress its stability" and, we might add, its productivity.[43]

The earliest definitions of the concept of taboo by European scholars speak of it as a decree or ruling that physically separates ("marks off") a person or a thing from other persons and things, prohibiting contact between them. Being neither entirely religious nor civic, political nor moral, natural nor cultural, in these definitions taboo blurs the line between these pairs of concepts, partaking of the qualities of all these categories. Also from these definitions we learn that taboo implies the threat of physical contact, that in enforcing a separation between entities, taboo, in a sense, creates the danger of pollution and runaway contagion, where what is at stake is, to a greater or lesser extent, the very fabric of society. In Hertz's understanding of death as a "social fact" is contained, therefore, as in a nutshell, the Euro-American understanding of taboo as generative and potentially destructive of culture. Whether it is the evolutionism of Henry J. S. Maine or James Frazer, in which taboo figures as some sort of primitive system of law, the ancestor of modern jurisprudence, and the backbone of civilized morality; or the structural-functionalist paradigms of A. R. Radcliffe-Brown and Mary Douglas, in which taboo has a binding and a primordially ordering function in society; or the structuralism of

Claude Lévi-Strauss, where taboo appears as a catalyst of nature, bringing it to the exact point where it is able to transcend itself and become culture; in the history of anthropology, the widespread occurrence and observance of socially sanctioned interdictions has for a very long time been held to be at the root of human society, grounding and sustaining some of the oldest and most lasting social institutions.[44]

What intrigued Bataille about taboo is also the crux of theories of social origins, such as Lévi-Strauss's, and theories of social structuring, such as Douglas's: the negation of nature that taboo presupposes, what Bataille characterized as the denial and repudiation of "animal freedom." Taboo, for Lévi-Strauss, specifically the incest taboo, effects the transition from nature to culture, from the world of animals to the world of human society, by prompting social intercourse through the circulation of women and the ensuing set of positive rules and reciprocal obligations that this exchange makes possible, thus bringing about the "social state."[45] Focusing rather on ideas of filth, Douglas's stance is similar to Lévi-Strauss's in that she emphatically views the repression or elimination of filth as a positive effort by human beings to organize their surroundings. According to Douglas, this is not a movement generated by fear or anxiety, but a "creative movement" in which the world is made to conform to an idea of "social order."[46]

More than on the explicit prescriptions that taboos elicit or on the "social order" that they may generate, Bataille focuses on the observable *opposite world* to which the negation of nature through taboo gives form, that is, on the human world of prohibitions. "Humanity became possible," Bataille writes, "at the instant when, seized by an insurmountable dizziness, man tried to answer 'No.'"[47] The act of negation is so intrinsic to being human, he says, that in spite of the obscure complexities of the process of transformation from animal to human and of the remote date of the "event," nothing is better known to us than what distinguishes us from animals, nothing is so self-evident and so out of the question.[48] Yet, in contrast to Lévi-Strauss and Douglas, Bataille is interested less in the transformation by which human culture was achieved than in the "vicissitudes" of negation, the "constant movement of rejection" of nature, which has never totally been done away with and from which "[man] does not cease to have departed."[49]

One of the areas of culture where this "constant movement of rejection" is evident is in the education of children. "We take children out of the muck," says Bataille, "then we do our best to wipe out the traces of [our] origin."[50] He notes that infants tolerate odors and sights without spontaneously having a reaction. They may dislike certain foods and refuse them, "[but] we have to teach them by pantomime or failing that . . . curious aberration called disgust, powerful enough to make us feel faint . . . [and] passed down to us from the earliest men through countless generations of scolded children."[51]

The realm of disgust, Bataille argues, is solely the result of these teachings. It is impossible and in a way irrelevant to know whether the bad smell of excrement caused our disgust or whether excrement smells bad because of our disgust for it. We do know, however, that animals do not show any repugnance, and this makes shame and disgust chiefly human feelings. Adults have to work against the natural impulses of children, to "artificially deform them in our image" by instilling in them the horror of what is given in nature. Bataille writes, "We tear them away from nature by washing them, then by dressing them. But we will not rest until they share the impulse that made us clean them and clothe them, until they share our horror of the life of the flesh, of life naked, undisguised, a horror without which we would resemble animals."[52] If the filth were not constantly thrown out of the world around us, Bataille says, our entire social edifice would rot.

—————

In nineteenth-century Lima, the transition to a statistical treatment of death and the centralization of bodies of the dead in a single, state-managed institution were slow and erratic processes.

After the 1866 war with Spain, especially after the bloody Combat of Dos de Mayo, in which Spain tried to reassert its colonial authority over Peru, a series of epidemics of yellow fever and cholera coursed through Lima. Still dependent on church hospices and charities, the city was thrown into a serious medical and sanitary crisis that led to the construction of the first state-run hospital, the Hospital Dos de Mayo, in 1875. Built over the former rural estate of Cocharcas, on the fringes of the now wall-less city, the hospital housed Lima's cleanest and most advanced mortuary, which consisted of an open hall on the top floor of a frontal tower and a storage room below it, where the corpses were brought down by means of a pulley. But since dealing with corpses was considered to be a dirty and disreputable occupation, the mortuary operated with meager resources and second-grade, underpaid doctors. The building soon fell into disrepair, and the storage chamber got overfilled with corpses, to the point that the tower and the adjacent sections of the building were gradually engulfed in a cloud of unbearably pestilent stench.[53]

Later, in 1887, after a new sanitary crisis brought about by the occupation of the city by Chilean troops during the Pacific War (1879–83), an ad hoc Supreme Board of Public Health put into effect the first and much awaited *Reglamento General de Sanidad.*[54] This *Reglamento* reiterated the prohibition on burying the dead inside the city and ordered that the construction of cemeteries be carried out at least one thousand meters away from the last urban dwelling, in the outbound direction of the winds. Looking to strengthen the authority of the state (as opposed to the church) over the dead, the *Reglamento* ruled that cemeteries could be built with the permission of city authorities only after the issuance of a municipal license (art. 81). Likewise, it ordered that every death be verified and certified by a medical doctor and that cadavers be buried at the cemetery also only after issuance of a municipal license (arts. 85–86). Furthermore, it instructed that the recognition of bodies and the performance of autopsies take place in locales specially conditioned for these procedures either at the cemetery or at the new mortuaries and anatomical amphitheaters that had began to appear in city hospitals and the university (art. 84).

Besides this heightened anxiety about the fate of the dead, which was now clearly an affair of the state, the *Reglamento* exhibits a serious concern with borders and with the prevention of contamination and epidemics. It thus establishes a system to protect the city's seaboard by inspecting and labeling all docking ships according to their state ("clean," "dirty," or "suspicious") and by quarantining, expurgating, or disinfecting their contents before allowing them to come into the country (arts. 26–69). On dry land, another kind of purge was to be enforced, so that to the expulsion of burial grounds out to the periphery of the city was added that of hospitals for the treatment of infectious diseases (art. 72), of the city's slaughterhouses (art. 77), of all corrals for the rearing of hoofed animals (art. 95), of the burial of dead animals (arts. 93–94), and of all domestic garbage (art. 92), a rule that the city government was expected to enforce. According to the 1887 end-of-term report by the mayor of Lima, General César Canevaro, the entity that was then in charge of undertaking garbage collection worked under contract with the city and was known (as it is now) as *baja policía* (low or inferior police), a sign that the splitting of functions had begun for what would later become two separate state organs or services, one for sanitation and the other for crime prevention and law enforcement.[55]

The smell of decomposing corpses was the chief justification, although there were other emerging concerns as well, for the creation of the first city morgue in 1891 as an annex of the Anatomical Amphitheater of the Escuela de Medicina de San Fernando, on the premises of the city's Botanical Garden. At that point, the need for a centralized "house of the dead" was stressed by hygienists as much as by medical doctors, anatomists, and toxicologists, precursors in Lima of the budding science of forensic medicine, with its emphasis on the need to establish the cause of every death. This concern with the cause was not only a reflection of a fear of epidemics, now that there was a better understanding of the role of bacteria in the spread of disease, but also of growing scruples regarding murder, which until then would most often go undetected and unpunished. Just as important as these hygienic and ethical concerns, the creation of a morgue in Lima was also the result of a growing inclination to see death as a matter of secular (scientific) and of public policy interest and, therefore, as a chief responsibility of the state.

In 1903, a newly created Dirección de Salubridad Pública, operating under the authority of the city government, was put in charge of recording the occurrence and cause of every death, a task that, from then on, was out of the hands of the church.[56] In the new morgue, which was run by the Intendencia de Policía (itself an entity of the city government), would converge the bodies of individuals whose cause of death had not been determined by a physician, in order to be cleared before their burial at the Cementerio General. But with still insufficient resources, the morgue was also overrun, and the Escuela de Medicina soon reclaimed its amphitheater, whose original purpose had been a pedagogical one. From 1897 to 1915 neither the Escuela nor the city government was willing to assume full responsibility for the activities of the morgue and so it operated, with scanty personnel and equipment, from an improvised shack attached to the Botanical Garden's fence, on the side of the narrow Jirón Cangallo.

For all those years the morgue functioned without interruption. To combat the accumulating putrid smell, myriad solutions were employed: phenic acid, formaldehyde, quicklime, amyl alcohol. The stench, nevertheless, seeped out through the walls to swallow up the entire city block.[57] A 1916 article in El Comercio describes rotting corpses piled up in corners, gnawed away by rats, and guarded by a sinister man known as "Pajarito" ("Little Bird"), who walked around with blood-stained hands and a perennially lit cigarette, ostensibly to placate the smell. The article calls the morgue "una vergüenza para la higiene pública" ("a shame for public hygiene"),[58] revealing the extent to which the practical and medical concerns of prophylaxis were intertwined with moral anxieties and fears of transgression. Luis Jochamowitz puts it this way: "The pestilence, the stench that captured [the city's] collective sensibility . . . bestowed an almost tangible content to the urban notions of filth, sin, vice. At a moment of expansion of the city, the imaginary lines of corruption of the spirit and corruption of the flesh intersected over the Botanical Garden." Once a thriving sign of the impetus of the postwar reconstruction of the city, Jochamowitz concludes, "the house [of the dead] became another proof of exhaustion and barbarism."[59]

The first allocation of funds for a new morgue building was made in the annual budget of 1915, and by 1918 a house of neoclassical façade had been erected on the same spot where the shack had been. The house stood out, another *El Comercio* article noted, for "the immaculate whiteness of its walls and the purity of its lines." The building was provided with a refrigeration system, similar to the one that had been recently installed in the city meat market, which would use steel tubing to cool down the body storage room and the glassed-in "exhibition hall" for the recognition of corpses. The technological sophistication and aseptic, metallic finishings of the new building caused quite an impression among Lima's residents.[60] And from then on, the shameful corruption of the bodies of the dead would be one form of corruption that *Limeños* could cease to worry about.

Tracing the changes in mentality and their impact on Lima's ritual culture of death through the study of wills written between 1780 and 1990, Tamayo says that the most notable transformation in these texts is a marked process of "de-Christianization" of the discourse of death. He observes that, among *Limeños*, a pronounced "sense of the sacred" in relation to death and a fear of the afterlife devolved through time into a series of succinct, formulaic enunciations of faith and then disappeared almost in its entirety. The baroque obsession with religious mystery, with funerary rituals and ingratiation with the divine, which were still anxiously expressed in people's wills through the eighteenth century, gradually receded to give way to a more pragmatic, even indifferent attitude toward one's own passing. Direct references to the event of death and its transformations dwindled in favor of ones that merely reflected changes in the person's juridical status.[61]

Along with the simplification and secularization of wills, Tamayo argues that, through the nineteenth and twentieth centuries, funerary rituals and what he calls the "gestural culture" of death in Lima became trivialized, devoid of the slow cadence, the gravity and compunction, the majestic rigor and complexity that used to characterize rituals of death in previous centuries. Today, in the largely middle-class Cementerio El

Ángel, where more than fifty-five burials take place each day, Tamayo notes that ceremonies are extremely short and superficial.[62] And among the upper class, burials that once stood out for the pomposity and the open expression of grief, made more intense by the loud cries of hired women mourners (*lloronas*), the swiftness of the ceremonies is even more striking, as the family of the deceased is quickly transported in an automobile from the funerary house to the cemetery, where the body is buried with minimal protocol, often in utter silence (except for a brief prayer or recitation by a priest), and with scarcely any tears shed in public. Tamayo says that it is as though among the middle and upper classes there was a desire to accelerate the interment in order to readily free themselves of the dead person. Save in the cases of the most renowned political figures, he writes, "burials today lack the unction and expressions of pain that were so characteristic of Lima in days gone by. The ceremonies . . . are fast, speedy, as if the living wanted to get rid of the body of the deceased person in the quickest and least harmful or offensive way."[63]

Tamayo laments the lack of unction and formality of the burials of today, which he views as a cultural and moral impoverishment, a loss, a "veritable de-culturation." He attributes the inability or lack of interest of *Limeños* to replace their old funerary traditions with new, but equally rich ones, to the culture of irresponsibility, cynicism, and improvisation that, according to him, has come to replace the old "seigniorial" culture of Lima, loving of tradition, as well as to the intensification or dissemination of the "*cundería criolla*," a kind of practical, cynical, amoral outlook on life often attributed to *Limeños*, which for Tamayo smacks of the worst colonialist, self-subjected attitude.

Writing during the first years of the Fujimori regime, Tamayo says that the void left by the growing disinterest in death rituals and the afterlife has been filled by a compulsive attraction to the death of others, depicted in grim images in the media that no longer speak of our own death. He decries the violence and moral filth on which thrives what he calls "garbage TV," which he describes as a ceaseless stream of truculent images. The upper and middle classes mourn less and less and make the process of disposing of a relative's corpse ever more expeditious and abstract. Meanwhile, the masses reveal a disturbing appetite for morbid stories, the more gruesome and corrupt, the better, and are supposedly increasingly more attracted to but less caring about "the death of the other." If before, the intricateness of Lima's funeral culture was there to manage or contain the tangible and intangible effects of the rottenness of corpses and the contagious quality of death, today it is as if that very rottenness had impregnated all of culture, which for Tamayo is becoming ever more vulgar, dirty, and animal.[64]

Overtaken by the forces that it once sought to contain—material corruption, moral filth, general licentiousness, and lack of scruples— Tamayo argues that, at the beginning of a new millennium, the ritual culture of death in Lima is on the verge of disappearing.

SIX

Third Diary

Friday: This afternoon I went to Chorrillos to visit with Colonel Contreras and his wife, and on my way back to Miraflores, I was mugged! Walking on the *malecón*, I reached the small stretch of sidewalk that links the cliff with the Barranco Bridge, running along a slope of grass and bushes where garbage collects and where, on some nights, homeless men find shelter under pieces of cardboard. A young man with soiled jacket and messy hair was coming from the bridge, someone who people here would describe as having *pinta de malandro*, the look of a person inclined to do bad things. He walked very closely to the edge of the sidewalk, on the other side of which is the fenced back end of Barranco's municipal park. It was him and me walking alone on this isolated neck of road where only once in a while a car will speed by, coming off the bridge to cut through to the other end of the district. I moved to the edge of the sidewalk as well, but he moved even farther out, trapping me, as we came within reach of each other, between the bushy slope and him. He was looking at me straight in the eye and, with his right hand inside his jacket pocket, bulging with some object I could not see, he said forcefully:

"Give me your cell phone or I'll blow your head off!"

I said, "I don't have a cell phone," boldly stepping to the side and trying to walk around the man, somewhat taken aback by the reckless bout of self-confidence I felt knowing that I was telling him the truth. But he blocked me again.

"Give it to me, *carajo*!" he said.

"I told you I don't have a cell phone!" I said with what, to my growing surprise, seemed like a slight tone of irritation in my voice. "Do you want to take a look?" I said, opening the tote bag that hung from my shoulder and displaying for him a bundle of old newspapers clippings, a yellow notepad, and a dog-eared set of printout sheets with diary entries and other first dabbles at dissertation writing. I tried again to walk past him, now stating firmly that I swore I had nothing worth stealing and sounding convincing, apparently, because he let me go. I walked away and kept walking without turning, still amazed at my composure. But when I reached the bridge and got on it, the deafening roar of car engines racing down to the Circuito de Playas gradually receded and became nothing next to the *thump-thump*s of my heart, beginning to pound loudly in my chest and ears, crazy with fear.

I turned around to the man, who seemed to be leisurely walking away toward the boardwalk, and screamed:

"You're lucky I don't call the police!"—an idiotic and desperate statement that grew out of and carried all the sudden terror I had not been able to feel when I was face-to-face with him only a minute or two ago.

Hearing me, he turned around and stopped. I looked to see who was nearby, possibly hoping to find a policeman but seeing only two old gardeners working quietly on a sparse bed of flowers on the other side of the park. Sensibly, I turned away again, this time for good, and kept walking on the bridge, noticing that the heart thumping had extended out to my limbs and had now turned into full-body quivers.

I did not stop trembling until I reached my father's apartment building about half an hour later, where I was going to visit with him for a while and write some e-mails. I told him what had happened and, shaking his head in disbelief, he said that I had been lucky, insisting that it's simply dangerous for me to walk alone. I told him that I feel safe not carrying anything of value, but he reminded me that I could be robbed of my coat or shoes or be simply hit out of spite, as muggers are said to do with women when, precisely, they don't have anything of value on them.

My father lives in a building on Avenida Pardo in Miraflores, just three blocks down from El Haití. The building is where my family's first home used to be, a small, adobe-brick and *quincha* (a mix of mud and straw) house built in the 1920s when Miraflores was beginning to transform from a rural county into Lima's newest urban district. The earthquake of 1974 seriously damaged the structure and, soon thereafter, it was declared uninhabitable. In the early 1980s, my father sold the house to a construction company, which tore it down to build in its place a fifteen-story tower. As part of the payment for the lot, the company gave him an apartment in the new building, which is where he lives now on the twelfth floor.

After working for a while on his computer, my father and I sat in his living room. He brought up the news about Luis Castañeda Lossio, one of the recently nominated presidential candidates and, therefore, Fujimori's would-be contender, who is all over the newspapers today. Yesterday, the guy lost his cool trying to put an end to the relentless harassment he has experienced since he announced his candidacy a few weeks ago. The situation can only be described, at the risk of sounding trite, as Kafkaesque. The candidate and his wife had left their house in San Isidro yesterday when they noticed that, like the days before, they were being followed by an unmarked SUV and a pickup truck with smoked windows and a sign that said: "Placas en Trámite" ("Plates in Process"). A couple times, according to the candidate, the men inside the cars rolled down the windows and waved guns at them, menacingly. Then two men riding a motorcycle joined the other vehicles in following the candidate, performing scary maneuvers around Castañeda's car and also brandishing weapons. Performing scary maneuvers himself to dodge the guys in the motorcycle, Castañeda took a sharp turn onto a smaller street and stopped the car sideways, blocking traffic. He jumped out of the car with (what he said was) a toy gun and threatened the men in the motorcycle, who had stopped abruptly to avoid crashing into the candidate's car. One of the men got off the bike and ran away, but the candidate got a hold of the other one, whom he forced into his car at "gunpoint."

The candidate and his wife drove around the city for three hours, unable to decide what to do with the man, reluctant to go to the police since they suspected the man himself was a policeman. After consulting with his advisors by cell phone, the candidate decided to drive to the nearest newspaper, the San Isidro headquarters of the daily *Liberación*, where Castañeda called a press conference and, with the head-stooped man he had captured by his side, denounced the government's harassment tactics against all candidates of the opposition. (There have been many other complaints, especially by Andrade.) The man kept his head down and for the entire press conference refused to talk. The government responded immediately, confirming that he was in fact an officer of the PNP stationed at the SIN and filing a suit in the courts against Castañeda for "kidnapping" a member of the forces of order, a crime that could put him in jail for many years.

My father said he would have done the same, meaning not gone to the police but to the press, although, the political skeptic that he is, he believes that Castañeda and the other candidates are all awful people, thieves-in-the-making, and he could care less if Castañeda goes to jail for the rest of his life. I mentioned the rule of law but failed to convince him that you can't fight against a corrupt regime with its own corrupted tactics or achieve the rule of law through abusive, violent, or illegal means. In the present political context, however, I'm not sure I'm convinced of this myself.

My father and I sat by the window facing Pardo. The glass rattled every time a bus or a *micro* sped down the avenue below. Changing the subject, I noted the solid wall of apartment buildings across the street from his apartment and talked about one of the clearest memories I have of the time we lived on Pardo: the day I was roller-skating down the block, in what back then was a somewhat quiet and sparse boulevard, when the ground began to shake, first slightly, then violently. I pointed down to the spot in the street where, holding myself from a lamppost, I waited for the earthquake to stop and watched the only apartment building there was at that point across the street swinging wildly sideways.

On his side of Pardo, my father's living room window overlooks the roofs of two houses, the only ones now left on the avenue. The larger one is the residence where his mother grew up at a time when few families had left El Cercado to settle in Miraflores. Today, this mansion is the Lima headquarters of the far-right Opus Dei. The smaller one, now a commercial bank, was his parents' home, where my father himself grew up in the late 1930s and '40s. Much of the furniture and house ornaments in my father's apartment come from this house, the tall wooden chests and the large canvases, which in the low-ceilinged, boxy rooms of the apartment look gigantic, covering the walls from ceiling to floor and making the space look cluttered and dark.

My father said that as a young boy he used to climb over the creeper that covered the wall that separates both houses and wander around his grandparents' fruit garden and kitchen, where he hung out with Francisca, the cook, and with Dionisio, the family chauffeur. My father couldn't hide the nostalgia, the waves of excitement and sadness, that come and go when he shares his memories of the time when Miraflores was an enclave of tree-lined streets and suburban homes, many of which belonged to his grandfather, one of the earliest Miraflores pioneers. The grandfather was the son of a recent and poor immigrant from Spain who made a fortune from the highly profitable sale of a swath of land in the northern coast of Peru, which he transformed into a state-of-the-art hacienda. Having invested his entire inheritance in the bourgeoning real estate of Miraflores, the family fortune was lost when the value of property plummeted in the 1940s. In the 1950s, my father's parents, swept by the wave of socialist thinking, became disdainful of money; his father, José María, who was a lawyer, turned to attending indigent cases only, as the family went through whatever was left of his wife's inheritance. By the time my father was an adult, all that was left was his parents' house on a much-changed, busy, and commercial Avenida Pardo, which was sold in 1983 to a bank for a relatively small quantity (given the recession back then). Attempting to explain the family's financial downfall, my father remarked that his grandmother had a very strong personality, a stubborn and domineering streak in her character that had led her to press his grandfather to make unsound money decisions. Around 1921, something—my father doesn't know exactly what—pushed his grandfather to break with the governing (and at this point authoritarian) Civilista Party. To make a clean break, my father said, the family closed down the house in Miraflores and spent six years in Europe, in a sort of voluntary exile. He said, matter-of-factly, that the financial problems hadn't started until a year after they got back from Europe, when his aunt María Luisa left their home.

I was surprised to hear a new name thrown into what, within this side of my family, has been a told and retold story for many years.

I said, "Who's María Luisa?"

He said, "My aunt María Luisa," with the same understated tone. "The one who eloped with Jean-Pierre, the Jamaican."

Noticing my baffled look, he said, "I never told you?" And added, "Well, I learned the truth about it very late myself."

His last name was Dumont, Jean-Pierre Dumont, a young, tall, stunningly beautiful Jamaican man who worked as the family chauffer. With his finger my father went on pointing to the house below, to the garage where young and handsome Jean-Pierre used to park the car, a beautiful Marmon of four doors, to where he used to hang out and doze off during his breaks, before explaining that my grandmother Ema's sister, his aunt María Luisa, had lived in the house of her parents until she was in her late twenties. Smart but very shy and awkward around men, one day María Luisa disappeared, took off with Jean-Pierre. They soon got married and moved into the neighboring working-class district of Surquillo, where due to his generous donations in developable land, an avenue and the municipal cemetery bore the name of her own father, Octavio Corbacho.

I could not believe what I was hearing: a family secret so jealously kept for decades suddenly being disclosed, just like that.

It was a huge social scandal, my father said. María Luisa's father disowned her, and he and the entire family drastically changed their lifestyle, my father said, adopting new habits that made it seem like they were mourning a close relative. In a way, he said, María Luisa had died. Having until then been an important presence in Lima's society, the family stopped "entertaining" altogether, never again throwing a party or attending one. "The shame was so that they secluded themselves," my father said, "that they withdrew from society almost completely." And when his grandfather rode in the back seat of his Marmon, presumably with a new chauffeur, he did so with the side and back window screens lowered halfway, so as to further enforce the separation, extending his seclusion even to when he was out in the streets. My father's mother told him that once when she was still young, she was riding in the car with her parents, going to the city center to see a play in the theater, when by chance they drove by María Luisa standing on a corner poised to cross the street. Seeing them, María Luisa stood frozen, unsure of what to do, as the car went slowly by and my grandmother Ema burst into tears. Octavio Corbacho, my father said, died without ever seeing his daughter again, who from Surquillo later settled in La Victoria with Jean-Pierre and their three children. Every so often, María Luisa's youngest sister, Julia, a very pious woman who never married, would venture secretly into La Victoria to visit María Luisa and bring her money. But no one ever spoke openly of her again, my father said. The prohibition on her name was so extreme that, from then on, members of the family were forbidden to give their daughters the name María Luisa, which had been in the family for generations.

From the moment of María Luisa's escape, everything in the family appeared to go downhill. Marta, the oldest daughter, married a diplomat who was a homosexual; she then died of cancer, childless and in her thirties. Julia's longtime fiancé died in a car accident; after that, she became conservative and dogmatic, joining the Opus Dei and launching a war within the (largely liberal) family to donate her parents' home to the religious institution. Octavio Corbacho and his wife died long and painful deaths, as the money dwindled rapidly.

This part of the story I knew well. As my father finished retelling it, the sun was setting and the light in the living room dimming quickly, making the apartment look even smaller, boxier. My father and I fixed a light dinner for ourselves and later my sister joined us. She already knew the story of Aunt María Luisa and Jean-Pierre and was surprised to know that I had never heard it. She said that we should look them up, track them down, and meet them, our Dumont cousins.

———

Saturday, 9:00 p.m.: Had lunch with Manolo at El Suizo in La Herradura. He invited me out this morning, saying that he wanted to thank me for all my help. He leaves tomorrow morning.

La Herradura is the last beach in the Circuito de Playas, on the south end of the Costa Verde, a small inlet in the form of a horseshoe (*herradura*), right under the Morro Solar. In the late 1970s, that's where we would go for a swim on hot summer afternoons. My mother would leave work at lunchtime, swing by the house to pick us up as well as her lunch, and drive us there, where along with hundreds of other workers she would spend her lunch break dozing off in the heat or swaying back and forth in the surf before returning to work. Also shaped like a horseshoe and embedded in the rock at the foot of the cliff is a row of old, seedy night bars and restaurants. These are for the most part empty during the day, except for the Restaurant El Suizo, which stands out at the center of the horseshoe for its avocado-green walls. El Suizo is run-down like the rest, but there is almost always a small lunchtime bustle.

The last time I had lunch there a few years ago, I was waited on by the same old man who waited on us today. He approached our table in the terrace with slow, shuffling steps, bringing a damp, white rag to wipe our table and two menu sheets. He is almost entirely bald, except for a band of gray hair that connects one ear to the other through the nape of his neck, like Caesar's crown, and a long thin strand that he combs over the crest of his head. His tiny and squinty eyes looked somewhere in the direction of, but neither at Manolo nor me, as he mentally took note of our order of two beers and two *cebiches*. He nodded once and shuffled away, the wet rag hanging limp from his hand, and then came back with two starched cloth napkins and old, heavy silverware, which is what gives this place the "feel of yesterday" that makes it attractive to people, despite its atmosphere of decadence.

We were sitting about twenty meters from the shore. The sun bounced on the surface of the water in thousands of bright, wriggly speckles, like a shattered mirror, and a wet current of air blew steadily from the beach, making our tablecloth flap off the top of the table again and again. The waiter came back, slowly and painfully bent down to the floor, picked up two small round rocks from under the table, placed them over the tablecloth on either corner to keep it in place, and shuffled away again.

Manolo's *cebiche* included a side of *conchas negras*, a purple-black variety of seashell that, placed at the center of his plate, looked like a little heap of disgorged eyes. My order was a *tiradito*, which is a *cebiche* but with no raw onions. As Manolo poured the bottle of beer into his glass, he said, "Just when I was beginning to reconcile myself with this miserable city..." Forcing a smile, he lifted his glass to me, said "cheers," and took a sip. On the far right side of the beach was a lone bulldozer surrounded by mounds of rocks of the kind that have been beaching from the sea ever since the construction began, about four years ago, of an extension of the Costa Verde highway beyond the Morro Solar, for which the Morro was dynamited at the base. The shore of La Herradura is now muddy and rocky. Bathers don't come to swim here anymore because of that.

I said, "Will you come back, Manolo?"

He smiled again and shrugged.

I looked at the empty parking lot, at the bulldozer rusting away in the briny breeze, at the weary expression of a man who waited for clients inside his battered VW beetle taxicab parked in front of the restaurant, and at a young boy sitting alone, hunchbacked and spread-legged, on the short wall of the parking lot with half a cardboard box filled with candy and cigarettes hanging by a thin rope from his neck. All of a sudden, there was no difference, no way of telling what sets apart the face of this miserable city, as Manolo had called it, from the face of the men, women, and children who live in it.

"There's something about this place..." Manolo said, meaning La Herradura, meaning Lima, or the whole country, the people and the landscape, the indolence, the selfishness, the abuse and the pain that seems to have taken over every space at every moment. Again Manolo finished his thought in silence, shaking his head, unable or unwilling to say what he wanted to say. But I knew what that was, even if I couldn't say it either, even if I could only describe it too vaguely as a feeling of deep and irrepressible love for a place that you nevertheless know has wronged you in an irreparable way, an old and powerful affection that bitterly links you to it and that makes you want to escape and never come back, to exile yourself, but which only grows in strength and makes the link tighter the more you distance yourself from it.

"It makes it so hard to come back," Manolo said, as if he had heard my thoughts, shaking his head again, again expressing without words his frustration or disbelief. I wanted to ask him about Paco. Has he heard from Vulture-man? But never quite finding the right moment, never feeling like I had the heart, I asked him about his art, his life, his job in Paris as we finished our food and drank another beer. We then took the Volkswagen taxi stationed in the parking lot back to the house—the rattling machine hiccupped the entire way up the steep and curvy road and through the Chorrillos tunnel. When we were kids, my siblings and I believed that if you manage to hold your breath as you go through this tunnel and then ask for a wish, this wish will come true. Out of habit, I held my breath until the taxi rambled out the tunnel's other end.

———

Sunday noon: Manolo left this morning just like he arrived, in a yellow *Tico.*

I spent the rest of the morning trying to reach Mr. Gómez, on whom I had nearly given up since he had not returned any of my calls and seemed to be avoiding me. I finally got him on the phone. He said, "Oh, yes. I'll see the señora this coming Tuesday," appearing—despite all my messages—to have forgotten to let me know. We arranged to meet in front of the Church of San Francisco, across the street from the locale of SITRAMUN, at 3:30 on Tuesday afternoon. He asked me to wait for him and stated that I should not enter the union building. He'll be wearing a black leather jacket, he said, presumably so that I can single him out. I have no idea what to expect.

I just read in the paper that today is the last bullfight of the *Feria del Señor de los Milagros* (Fair of the Lord of the Miracles), Lima's bullfighting season which runs every year from early October to the last week in November. I'll call Héctor and see if I can talk him into going to the Plaza de Acho with me. If we go with some time to spare, we might find last-minute discount tickets.

———

Sunday night: Héctor was waiting for me in front of his building in Magdalena when I got there. We walked to Avenida Brasil, where we caught a cab. The driver, clearly a devotee of the Lord of the Miracles, had the characteristic purple insignia on the dashboard. He dropped us off a block away from the bullring since all the streets contiguous to it had been blocked off to traffic for the event.

In the 1980s, the *Feria*, like most other national pastimes, was seriously affected by the crisis, and for many years mediocre bullfighters fought mediocre bulls to an empty plaza. Briefly during the mid-1990s, the *Feria* experienced a revival, driven by the country's economic recovery and the heightened security in the city brought about by Andrade's recuperation campaign, which briefly reached the district of El Rímac. Some of that renewed enthusiasm about Acho lingers on.

The air on the right bank of the Rímac River, scarcely thirty minutes by car east of Miraflores, is crisper than on the coast, the sun brighter and warmer. Like most other *ruedos* (bullrings) in the world, Acho is split into two imaginary semicircles: *sol*, the eastern half, where one watches the entire *corrida* (set of fights) under the afternoon sun; and *sombra*, the western and more expensive half, which is always swathed in a breezy, bluish shadow. Héctor and I were willing to go to *sol*, mainly because of the cost, but since the *corrida* was less than an hour away, we were hoping to find a scalper ready to kill off his last unsold tickets to *sombra*. Sure enough, as soon as we arrived, a scalper rushed to us, offering two $60 tickets to *sombra* for $40 each. It was still too expensive. Something told me that we could bargain $40 *sombra* tickets down to $20 and get seats in the shade. So we looked around a little longer and, ten minutes before the *corrida* began, that's exactly what we got.

It was my first time at *toros*. But the fact that my father never brought me to see a bullfight when I was younger is an odd thing given that he is an aficionado (of sorts). As a young man, he attended *corridas* in Acho regularly, but when he became an adult he stopped going altogether, supposedly because the quality of the bulls had become so poor; they were coming from bad breeds, nothing like the enormous, ferocious *toros de lidia* (fighting bulls) that he saw when he was young. Once or twice, he also mentioned the prohibitive ticket prices and the stale and increasingly frivolous atmosphere of Acho, which he disliked. But if he never again saw a live *corrida*, throughout his entire adult life, as soon as October came along, my father would pull out a huge, dusty tome, some sort of encyclopedia of bullfighting, and leaf through its pages for the entire month, talking about bullfighting legends such as Joselito and Manolete and enacting for us each of their unique *suertes* (maneuvers). Perhaps because of their physical resemblance—the long face, the straight and pointy nose, the gaunt figure—he would do Manolete's *suertes* the best, standing with his feet closed together and fixed on the ground, his body straight like a pole, and turning slowly at the waist.

Our seats were close to the upper gallery, in the third to the last *tendido* (row), on the left end of the *sombra* section. There were several empty seats around us—surely the new recession—and most spectators were crowded in the lower *tendidos* at the center of *sol* and at the center of *sombra*, which was the most colorful, restless, and loud section. That is where socialites like to bunch together and where highbrow politicians like to make an occasional appearance to the cheers or the scoffing of the public, and where yesterday I saw none other than Alfonso Forga, the hunter and lawyer, Manolo's friend.

No sooner had I recognized Dr. Forga several rows down to the right of us than a band of the PNP, standing on a high *tendido* across the arena, began to play a tune, which got the first *cuadrilla* (a matador's team) of toreros busy behind the *barrera* (the wall that separates the arena from the first *tendido*). I said to Héctor, "I believe this is called a *'paso doble,'*" and the man sitting in front of us with his teenage son turned to confirm that it was indeed a *paso doble* and that it signaled the beginning of the *corrida*.

The portal to the *toril* (where the bulls are kept in complete darkness until the fight) suddenly opened onto the arena, and the first bull sprinted out to the light, stopping for a second and then starting again energetically and running around the ring in full gallops. I once read that, by law, the bulls that will take part in a *corrida* must never be exposed to any aspect of the bullfight before the afternoon in which they, for the first and last time, will confront a matador. The reason for this is that bulls seem to be able to learn the moves, even to become proficient at them. Bulls, like men, apparently learn. So as the first bull confidently surveyed the arena, I wondered to myself what kind of sense it was making of it all as its pupils adjusted to the light and the audience came gradually into focus, as its nostrils perceived the subtle scent of blood, that of thousands of its kind, and the excited roar of the public died out and yielded to silence.

Only when the bull's gallops had slowed down and stopped did the first *cuadrilla* enter the arena. The four toreros (none of which is yet the matador, the killer) scurried into the ring, swinging their capes to try to get the bull's attention, as the matador, still hidden behind the *barrera*, stood motionless, carefully analyzing the bull's ways. One of the old anecdotes my father used to tell is that, occasionally, during this moment of studious reflection, a matador nicknamed El Gallo would say that the bull had looked at him askance, believing perhaps that the examination was mutual. *"Me ha mira'o mal"* ("It's cast a bad look on me"), he would say and would simply refuse to fight that bull, letting the police take him away in handcuffs, without putting up the slightest battle, for breaching his contract with the sponsors of the event.

It was Emilio Muñoz fighting the first bull. He stepped onto the arena, and the other toreros hurried out. He was stunningly elegant in his skin-tight, deep blue-and-gold *traje de luces* (suit of lights). He walked toward the bull and positioned himself for the first *capeada* (move with the cape); absolute silence followed him to the center of the ring, where he began to swing his red cape in the direction of the bull, taunting it. The bull hesitated. But then, with a jerky start, it charged against the matador, lowering the horns as he approached the man and thrusting them against the fluttery red cloth instead. The use of the cape in this way is what, in the language of bullfighting, is called an *engaño* (deception).

The bullfighter's body was abnormally erect, to the point that his back was curving backwards as he taunted the bull again and a faint, breathy *Aha!* made it all the way up to our *tendido*. The bull threw himself toward the matador, burying its head into the cape once more. Then once more. And once more. I buried my face behind Héctor's shoulder, feeling too scared to look, but then I couldn't help it and had to look again. The bull's attacks were energetic but, to my very inexperienced eye, there seemed to be a tinge of hesitation in every move it made, as if another fight were being waged inside the animal, one between its instinct and its sense. My upper body and my legs felt stiff, and before I realized it, I had broken into a sweat.

Always ready to outsmart the animal, just at the moment when the bull could have been getting used to the *faena* (performance), just when it could have begun to intuit that it was being fooled, suddenly, without warning, the configuration of the fight changed. The *cuadrilla* stepped back into the ring as the matador turned his back to the bull, vainly and defiantly, to the enthusiastic applause of the public, to (shockingly) my own enthusiastic applause, and discreetly vanished behind the *barrera*. The four men taunted the bull all at the same time, and for an instant the bull seemed bewildered by this quadruple vision. After some unostentatious *suertes*, the men took turns with the *banderillas*, short metal spears capped with colorful ruffles. Sprinting toward the bull with two *banderillas* in hand, the men leapt over and away from the animal, in one single movement, thrusting the ruffled spikes into the back of the bull. Over, and away. Over, and away. Once six *banderillas* had been placed on its back, the men left the ring all at once. The bull, visibly in pain, stopped and looked around, appearing disconcerted, appearing to be contending with the echo of an impossible thought, *What is happening?*

I turned to Héctor, "What is happening?"

The bull stood still for a long moment, a thin, lusterless stream of blood pouring down the flanks of its body, its tongue sticking out stiff, thick and foamy drool dripping from its mouth to the ground. A few drops of cold sweat dripped, too, from my armpits down my sides inside my shirt. The animal was breathing heavily. Then the *toril* opened up again, and a man wearing a wide-brimmed straw hat came out mounted on a horse to join the *faena*, a sharp lance in hand. A pair of blinders limited the scope of the horse's vision, so as it circled the ring, it was unable to anticipate the bull's attack. The bull stood still while the horse was paraded alongside the *barrera*, its fury visibly mounting again. This time it wouldn't be the cape, it wouldn't be the *banderillas*, which now dangled on its back, but the horse against which it eventually had to charge. And eventually, it did. The picador forced the lance's sharp, stubby tip into the nape of the bull's neck, fiercely, right at the base of the skull, or wherever else he managed, stabbing him one, two, three, four times with short decisive *picadas* (thrusts) and then plunging it as deep as it would go, which wasn't too deep, and using the leverage afforded by the lance to push the bull away from the horse who, completely blind to the action, took tiny, bouncy sideways steps to keep its balance, as the bull, stubbornly not backing off, kept pushing the horns into the horse's body armature. The men in the *cuadrilla* intervened, luring the bull away from the horse with their capes. Once the bull had followed them, the horse left the arena and so did the matador and his *cuadrilla*.

Everything in my memory blurs after this point. What happened next is all mixed up in an indistinct sequence of risky but inelegant moves and painfully slow deaths, like the death of the fourth bull at the matador's third attempt, after the animal had wandered around the ring for endless minutes, looking delirious, with the sword halfway into the nape of its neck. It is all confused in senseless and disarrayed fragments, which I observed from time to time with one eye from behind Héctor's shoulder, while my body involuntarily tensed up, twitched, and relaxed in movements that partook of no clear rhythm or logic until the fifth bull made its appearance. Then, a certain rhythm and a logic began to emerge from the ring, and it became evident that my bodily reactions, my stiffened limbs, the sweat under my arms and on my palms, the tension in my face, both expectant and horrified, were following a pattern that was also that of the different phases of the *faena*, the different aspects or moments of what scholars of bullfighting like to refer to as "the ritual." The bull, the *banderilleros*, the horse, the picador, and the matador, never all at once in the bullring, entered it and left it, came together and came apart in a series of more or less well-timed configurations that varied in suspense and tragic character, building in intensity up to the moment of the kill. During the first four *corridas* my body had gotten rigid and relaxed, had stretched and twitched in perfect concordance with the internal rhythm of each phase.

The fifth bull, according to the program, was Landino, and it weighed 505 kilos. Heavily, proudly, its pitch-black hide glistening with silver streaks in the sun, the bull crossed the ring with earth-shaking gallops. The first few *suertes* were simply beautiful, as man and animal contorted in what seemed like perfectly choreographed moves. The man sitting in front of us turned to us and, clearly relieved, said that this one bull was "collaborating," which is how aficionados, somewhat perversely, refer to bulls who unwittingly make of the ritual that is leading to their own death a beautiful and moving one. Landino was indeed collaborating, forcing out again and again a frenzied *Olé!* from the public. It was Manuel Caballero, surnamed El Diestro de Albacete (The right-handed and/or skillful one from Albacete, a province in Spain), fighting the fifth. He was the only one wearing gold, gold and burgundy, while the bodies of the other four men in his *cuadrilla* were compressed into different tones and combinations of silver and blue. Once the *banderilleros* and the picador had left the ring, the bull wandered around for a few seconds, looking subdued, the six well-inserted *banderillas* dancing on its hump, its neck and head hanging lower because of the several *picadas*, and its tongue sticking out erect. When the matador came back into the ring, he positioned himself at the center with another cape, the *muleta*, and enticed the bull to charge again. The bull charged with his last reservoir of fury. It charged toward the man but impinged against the airy patch of red. The matador was getting dangerously close to the bull, but somehow he became more elusive the closer he was to the animal. *Olé! Olé!* The public was wildly excited. After a set of dangerous *suertes*, the matador's cape and *traje de luces* were stained with the bull's blood.

The matador then turned his back to the bull and stood still, with the animal no more than a meter or two behind him. In a gesture filled with dramatic effect, he turned his head slowly to the bull and looked at it beguilingly over his left shoulder. With the same control of movement, he turned his head 180 degrees in the opposite direction, holding the *muleta* and the cape in his right hand. In the gallery across from us, the band began a *paso doble*. With his back still to the bull, the matador watched it attentively from the corner of the eye. He stretched his right arm to the side, which was made longer by the sword still covered by the cape. He shook the cape a little, seeking to draw the bull's attention, and began rotating the cape forward and around, as the edges of it softly caressed the ground. The bull followed the cape with a bowed head, mesmerized by it, overpowered by it, as the man arched his torso gracefully over the bull. His legs, thin and long, were straight and fixed to the ground. The matador and the bull synchronically gyrated in the sun, and it suddenly struck me that, decked in his *traje de luces*, the matador was meant to resemble the animal: the stocky and firm body; the almost ridiculously thin and inflexible legs; the arms, also thin and inflexible, clinging from his sides like appendages and limited in their movement by the jacket's slender sleeves and stiff shoulder pads; the sparkles produced by the reflection of the sun; and then the hat, with its stubby mock horns and dangling tail in the back. The cape continued to brush the ground, and the bull followed it obediently around the body of the man. The two bodies lightly rubbed against each other until the animal had drawn a full circle in the arena and a loud *Olé!* had risen above the enraptured crowd. Our neighbor told us that this was *"un magnífico derechazo"* ("a magnificent right-hand move"), hence Caballero's nickname, El Diestro.

The matador then walked to the *barrera*, where he released the *muleta* from the cape and turned to face the bull. Sword in hand, he positioned himself in preparation for the kill. The band stopped the music and the crowd quieted down. He lifted the sword, placed the handle of it in front of his face at the level of the eyes, projecting the blade forward and parallel to the ground to provide him with a way of aiming, with an imaginary straight line between his eyes and the neck of the bull, in a studious gesture that aficionados call profiling. There was an eerie silence in the crowd. The matador was now the one to charge against the bull. Long sprints were followed by hastened little steps, a firm high leap in the air, and a smooth thrust of the sword into the bull's hump, right between the shoulder blades. The silence was broken by a single, fused sigh of relief. The bull took a few staggering steps and stopped before the *barrera* right in front of *sombra* but facing the center of the ring. The matador approached the bull with prudent but graceful steps, opening the cape and laying it down on the arena right under the bull's head. Always facing the bull, the man dragged the cape away slowly just as the animal's front legs faltered and caved in. The audience was in awe. Many sitting behind the *barrera* leaned forward, as if they were being pulled by a magnet toward the center of the ring. As the bull sustained this ultimate bow of submission, with its head on the ground and its hind legs and tail still standing, the matador walked up and stood right in front it, towering above it (the entire arena in absolute silence), not moving until the bull's hind legs finally yielded and the animal, now a carcass, was flat on the ground before him, bloody, inanimate, pathetic.

A group of seven young men in red and white uniforms, the colors of the Peruvian flag, ran out of the *toril* and tied the bull by the neck to a wheeled cart pulled by horses, dragging it out of the ring as the matador walked along the *barrera* with his arms lifted up displaying his trophies, the bull's two ears. He stopped at the center of *sombra* and tossed the ears up to the public. Carnations, leather wine-bladders, hats, even sweaters and purses flew down to the arena, which the matador picked up and, except for the flowers, politely tossed back to the audience.

After this fight, everyone watched the sixth and last one in a daze. Some in the audience got up and left halfway through. The rest of us, without booing or applauding much, got up from our seats as the dead

animal was being carried away. Héctor and I walked out in silence, overcome by what we had seen or maybe just exhausted. Down from our
tendido I saw the lawyer walking ahead of us. He was wearing a white
and blue pinstriped shirt and a lively kerchief tied around his neck. We
followed him and his friends, waiting for the crowd to thin out and
the chance to say hi. Nice cars and huge, slick SUVs were lined along
the streets' faded walls, two tires above the curb so as not to block the
narrow lanes completely. I was getting nearer the lawyer and was about
to call his name when he and his friends stopped in front of a tiny and
worn wooden door in the middle of the block and, crouching to go in,
disappeared inside, one by one. I have heard that during the *Feria del
Señor de los Milagros* neighbors around the Plaza de Acho open up their
homes for dinner of grilled meat (the bulls' meat?), allowing for a kind
of social mingling, a saturnalia that doesn't happen again during the
rest of the year and that some have described for celebrations that took
place during bullfighting season in colonial times.[1]

The lawyer did not see me. Héctor and I walked down to the closest intersection and stood on the street that turns into the Santa Rosa
Bridge to hail a cab. The traffic light on the corner turned to green and a
stream of ramshackle cars rushed by. One stopped for us, with the brakes
screeching painfully loud. "How much to Magdalena?" asked Héctor as
we hopped in.

―――――

Monday: Woke up to find out that Manuel Caballero, the fighter of
yesterday's fifth *corrida*, was named this season's best matador and given
the *Escapulario de Oro*, an award for which it is not enough to have fought
a bull many times one's size, or to have killed it, or even to have risked
death in the process. The "golden scapular" is given to the matador
who comes closest to bringing into the *faena* all the beauty and poetry,
the eroticism, agony, and violence that for Bataille made the Spanish
bullfight, in its blatant, sanctioned play of taboo and transgression, one
of his most beloved motifs.

Ortega y Gasset says that of all that goes on between the bull and the
bullfighter, it is the gore, the image of the bullfighter flying up into the
air and landing back on the arena with a punctured loin or abdomen,
that can be most easily understood by the public. A wounded matador is
just a man, his limp and bloody body the evidence of his mortality and
his inability to transcend it. The gore, what the public "most easily un-
derstands," is not what they are there to see, however, even if that's what

they secretly await and dread. What they are there to see and experience is the ceremony in which a human being takes on death in the form of an overpowering animal, confronts the threat of a pitiable destruction, and overcomes it through a ritual of killing, which is the person's objective to perform not as the bloody and gruesome gesture that it is but as an elegant, fearless ballet with death, which must be danced flirtatiously and appear effortless.

The symbolism of it is powerful, as is the depth of all the metaphorical meanings hidden in the surface of such an artifice, which is what students of the Spanish bullfight generally like to focus on. But this is not the aspect of bullfighting that fascinated Bataille, and it is not what he had in mind when he spoke of *tauromachie* as some sort of model for other forms of human behavior also based on sacrifice and loss, such as poetry, eroticism, and art, or what Michel Leiris evoked when, along the same lines as Bataille, he equaled *tauromachie* to the act of writing.[2]

In the bullfight, as a ritual of sacrifice and therefore of transgression, the matador (and by extension the public) faces real death without dying: He puts his life at stake and faces the anguish of dying but, through the animal, overcomes it, momentarily restoring in himself the non-alienated condition of beings who live "as if death were not." As he confronts what for anybody in the audience would be sure death with nothing so much for defense as a piece of cloth, the skillful bullfighter risks everything, undoes and escapes the limits of identity by seeking indistinctiveness with the animal, to whose fearless charges he must respond with more daring provocations and whose force he must outwit through skill. This is the objective of the bullfight. Short of this, it is the humiliation of being overtaken by fear, the shame of a nervous *suerte*, or the dishonor of a dubious kill.

————

Another piece of news is that yesterday morning a group of former ESMLL workers together with some members of SITRAMUN broke into the offices of SETAME (Metropolitan Taxi Service, run by the Municipalidad) where, in protest, they made *pintas* on the walls, destroyed furniture and computers, and then held battle against the municipal police. On the radio newscast they said that the workers had arrived at 11:30 in the morning, loaded in buses and pickup trucks. Armed with firebombs and metal bars, the protesters tore down doors and windows and rushed inside. Then they poured gasoline inside the building and were about to light it up with a match when the municipal police and the *serenos* showed up. The confrontation was violent, leaving about fifty people wounded, until a contingent of the PNP appeared and forced the workers out by throwing canisters of tear gas into the building. Most protesters ran away, somehow managing to light on fire a Serenazgo truck before fleeing the scene. A few wounded workers remained inside where they were beaten up by the police. At least one ESMLL worker, a woman, was stripped and left naked on the ground. This time, the worker was stripped naked by the police!

After a judge visited the SETAME offices to do a recognizance of the vandalized building, some of the workers of ESMLL came back and defiantly stood in front of it to demand reinstatement in their jobs. In response, the city's human resources administrator called for an exhaustive investigation into the actions of ESMLL and SITRAMUN. Later, the news report said, hundreds of current municipal workers took to the streets to also demand an investigation into the "pseudo-union" whose members, they said, are constantly attacking city workers (many of whom are currently working under conditions rejected by the union). The implication is, again, that this has been infiltrated by Montesinos's henchmen.

Tuesday: I was out the door at 12:30 this afternoon to make it to the library before it closes at 1:30 for lunch (you can stay inside, but you can't come in during lunchtime). A little after three o'clock, before my meeting with Mr. Gómez, I swung by El Cordano for a sandwich of *asado* and then walked on Jirón Ancash to San Francisco. Passing in front of an old mansion, I got a glimpse inside a squatted old solar. The two-story mud-brick building was in very bad shape; two buckling walls were propped up and barely held in place by wood beams fixed diagonally on the ground. There are thousands of houses like this in El Cercado, which could collapse at any moment, a situation that is made worse by the humid and drizzly atmosphere of Lima, which dampens the *quincha*.

The atrium and front plaza of the Church of San Francisco were filled with schoolchildren. Thin, shrill voices and frantic screams echoed down the narrow streets. In bright-blue uniform pants and skirts they ran in packs chasing away pigeons, hundreds of which have made a home in the crevices and folds of the church's baroque portal and bell towers. Because of this, the façade and the plaza are covered in bird droppings, and you can smell the birds' scent from down the block. In the sea of children there were several men, a few fathers with toddlers, tourists, peddlers of postcards and souvenirs, and men who seemed to be just passing the time, leaning against the gate or standing by the water fountain. I didn't quite remember Mr. Gómez's face. I'd seen him two weeks ago for about ten minutes, in the dark. And half the men in this city wear black leather jackets, I now realize. I asked a man standing near the entrance for the time; it was 3:25.

The asphalt on the last block of Jirón Lampa, where both San Francisco and SITRAMUN are, opposite to each other, was broken to pieces and piled in chunks on the side of several deep trenches where workers of SEDAPAL, the state's water and sewage company, were replacing the underground pipes. In front of the union, standing on a thin dirt pass, was a group of people, talking. Farthest away from the door and with her back to the church was a woman, short and round, completely dressed in black. Her hair, also black, was pinned up in a twirl. She stood with her arms behind her back, holding a plastic bag with both hands. From where I was, half a block away and across the broken-up street, I could see her long, aquiline nose, her protruding chin. From having seen, or rather studied, her pictures in the newspaper, I knew it was her, the street sweeper.

If it were not because Mr. Gómez had explicitly asked me to stay away from the union building, I would have walked up to her. It was past 3:30, perhaps 3:45, and I was beginning to fear Mr. Gómez would never show up. One of the men in the group turned to talk to the woman while the rest walked into the building. I looked at the guy intently, even though he was wearing tan pants and jacket, for the slight chance that he might be Mr. Gómez, but the man returned an empty glance. Then he also walked inside, and the woman stayed there alone, standing on the dirt pass, surrounded by the gaping ditches, her hands still behind her back and the plastic bag dangling. I just couldn't let this chance slip away. How many times had I looked at those pictures, wondered if she was real? I asked for the time again, 3:55, and waited a little longer, looking up and down the block for Mr. Gómez, when the woman began to walk on the dirt pass along one of the trenches and away from the union house toward Jirón Ancash, slowly and carefully looking where she stepped. It seemed like she was leaving. I rushed up the block and across the street and met her at the corner.

I stretched my hand out to greet her and asked her if she was there to meet Mr. Gómez. She held hers out to me and said yes, looking apprehensive, which is probably also the way I looked to her. I introduced myself as the student, the researcher Mr. Gómez had probably mentioned, and she asked if I would ask my questions right there and then, her look of unease becoming more like fear. I said that I didn't so much have questions as wanted to hear about her experience in the 1996 protests of ESMLL, whatever she could tell me. She said it had been "pure despair" what she did that day, flinching to emphasize the force of the feeling, the almost intolerable intensity of it. She had no teeth, so when she paused, her lips pursed and slipped into her mouth, her chin became longer, sharper. "They didn't tell us anything, señorita, nothing, just one day we didn't have a job," she said. She said, "I thought: 'And now, how am I going to feed my children? How?' It was pure despair, señorita." She brought one hand to her skirt and said she had wanted to take off all her clothes, suggesting that someone might have tried to stop her. She said, "I only took my top off." She said, "They threw tear gas at us, they hit us with their sticks, but nothing mattered to me. I wanted to kill myself, to die right there."

Her skin was fair and soft, peachy on her cheeks and forehead. I asked where she was from, and she said Apurímac, shifting her eyes and looking straight over my shoulder at Mr. Gómez, who was just arriving. Mr. Gómez suggested that we go sit somewhere, quickly putting himself in charge of the situation, perhaps a bit anxious to preserve his role of broker, while the woman took a step back and became quiet. I asked if they had time for tea or a cold drink and proposed Café Macchu Pichu across the street, catercornered from the church. We crossed the street in awkward silence, engulfed by the children's shrieks and laughs, and we went into the café through a pair of saloon-type doors, the woman lagging a step behind Mr. Gómez and me. They picked a table in the back, in the darkest corner, and we sat. On a shelf above us was a speaker with soft *criollo* radio music. After ordering our drinks, Mr. Gómez embarked on retelling the history of ESMLL's ongoing struggle, beginning in March 1996, when the workers had first heard rumors of the entering mayor's intentions and he, the mayor, had categorically denied them. I asked for permission to take my paper pad out and began to take notes, casting intermittent glances at the woman, who sat next to me, straight and perfectly still, her arms stretched out and her hands locked on top of the table.

Mr. Gómez said that, back then, of the 871 workers of ESMLL, 80 or 90 percent were women; of the 274 workers left now, it's over 90 percent, many of them single mothers, forty-three to sixty-five years of age, almost all of them street sweepers. He said that Andrade closed down the cleaning agency by appealing to Fujimori's privatization laws, even though the agency wasn't strictly a public enterprise. ESMLL was self-sustaining and managed its own earnings. He said that the new concessionary,

Relima, had committed to rehire 30 percent of ESMLL's personnel, but, in the end, it took in much fewer and only those in management positions. He said that those workers over forty and with a history of union activism were denied a job on the spot. The few street cleaners to whom they did offer a position had to take a huge pay cut, from 700 soles to 400 soles (a bit over $100), which is now the minimum wage.

Mr. Gómez knew the facts by heart, the numbers, the percentages, and listed them with the diction and firmness of a practiced activist expounding a cause. He said that ESMLL was created by congressional decree in 1982, along with other currently functioning municipal agencies, such as EMAPE (to manage the city's highway tolls), EMILIMA (the city's payrolls), and CERPAR (the city's parks). ESMLL's union was formed in 1983, and most of the 274 workers still in the struggle have been members of it since then. Mr. Gómez said that to privatize the service Andrade argued that ESMLL's workers were lazy and inefficient, but what he didn't mention was that back then the streets were packed with ambulant vendors, that, tried as they could, it was impossible to keep the streets clean.

I was straining to keep up with my notes when I heard the woman's voice, "1984." In twenty minutes she hadn't said a word. I turned to her. "The union, it was created in 1984," she said, correcting Mr. Gómez. She said, "With Señor 'Frejolito.'" That's how Alfonso Barrantes, the only left-wing mayor the city has ever had, was popularly known, as "the little bean," because of his short stature and dark skin. The woman had obviously been at ESMLL longer. "I worked there for fourteen years," she went on, "first sweeping the sidewalk of Avenida Abancay, from Congress to the river. Señorita, let me tell you, it wasn't the way it is now, all cement. Before it was pure dirt, pure garbage, dead dogs, dead cats, pure stink." She said that it was impossible to push the garbage cart in the dirt. Drawing a smile, she said, "It would always get stuck in the ground, so I'd strap it and carry it on my back to move it. It reminded me of being in the highlands."

She spoke eloquently. Through her thick Quechua accent streamed words and phrases with a sweet, subtle poetry that is difficult to preserve in English. "For a time I worked the dawning shift," she said, "down there in the Atocongo Bridge, until the night a car hit me as I swept the center island, under the bridge. A dog was crossing the road. I saw it coming toward me, and a second later I felt it hit me on the back, and then the car hit me, too, and I passed out. I broke my collarbone. This arm," she said rubbing her left arm, "doesn't work, just hurts since then. All the time either one or another señora was run over by a car."

While the woman spoke Mr. Gómez was quiet, sporadically looking away, over his shoulder, or down to the floor, perhaps distracted by a thought or feeling restless. He wore a pair of wire oval spectacles and, under the black leather jacket, a neat, gray mock-turtleneck shirt. His skin was olive and smooth, except for two prematurely deep furrows on either side of the mouth. His hair—long, black, and thick—was slickly combed to the back. He carried his briefcase, which he had placed on the empty chair next to him, and for the entire time we were at Macchu Pichu, he held a tiny cell phone tightly in his left hand. Mr. Gómez seemed young for a union leader, at one point he said he was actually the youngest one, and he clearly has not been a street cleaner himself.

They followed a certain protocol with each other, he as a union leader and she as a union worker, in which rigid structures of power pierced through the subtle intricacies of language and bodily expression. The woman is many years his senior, so he addressed her as "señora," but it was she who markedly showed deference toward him, allowing him to walk ahead, sit first, and speak first. This heightened, over and above their skin color, the contrast between her mountain, Quechua roots and his Spanish, urban ones, and broadened the gap this very contrast signifies in terms of social class, gender hierarchy, and education level.

From either side of this gap they offered vastly different perspectives. As he took sips from his glass of Coke, he never lost sight of the big picture, the goals of the union's negotiations, the points of pressure with the city government, and the labor laws that they sought to affect. As she sipped from her hot tea, it was obvious that her experience and memories of the same struggle were fused with the most concrete, the most base and irreducible of details, like the scent of dead dog, the pangs from a police stick, the tears of lachrymose gas.

She said that when the workers (*las trabajadoras*, or female workers) found out about ESMLL shutting down, they immediately took to the streets. In protest, they slept in makeshift huts on the damp ground in front of ESMLL's headquarters in the Via de Evitamiento, the city's highway belt, for seven straight months. She noted that this had been very bad for Francia, another longtime worker who had been there from the beginning and who had died a few months later of diabetes, for lack of money for the treatment. She said that on days of demonstration, they got up and marched down to the city center, gathering in front of the municipal building on the main plaza to protest. That's what they had done on the morning of the day she disrobed. "That day," she said, "the riot police were beating us, throwing tear-gas canisters at us, hitting us with their sticks on our backs and the sides of our legs." She said, "We were screaming, yelling, and rapidly I have reasoned to do that [strip]. I don't know what has coursed through me, like a—a desperation," she said, with a shudder. "'What are you doing?' Francia said to me. No one knew what I was going to do. I don't know in what moment, without compunction [*sin asco*], I took off my clothes."

Mr. Gómez and I listened without interrupting. An old Los Morunos bolero song, "Motivos," flowed softly from the speakers above. "I wasn't afraid," she said, shaking her head. "I was floating in the cold water they threw at me, swimming in it, as if it were nothing, moving through everything, the water, the sticks, the bombs [of tear gas], and I wasn't hurt. I was thinking 'Now what am I going to feed my children?' but then I didn't care about anything anymore. It was pure despair," she said again, as her face contorted in a pained grimace and she began to cry, sobbing over her words and making them unintelligible.

I looked at Mr. Gómez, who looked back at me, but he didn't seem as concerned as I was. Hesitating, I put my hand on her shoulder and thought I would just let her cry. After all, hadn't it been me who had made her break down? I mumbled something to her, I suppose trying to comfort her. I said I was sorry about her pain. I said I could tell it had all been very hard on her. But as I said these words, I hated myself a bit, hated my work, hated anthropology—meddlesome, voyeuristic anthropology. The tears kept sliding down her cheeks on either side of her toothless mouth, into which her lips had completely disappeared. I patted her softly on the shoulder, thinking to myself, *What the fuck are you doing, Daniella?*

Then, abruptly, she stopped crying, and wiping the tears off her face with her hand, she said, "Other señoras followed after me, but I think they kept their brassiere on." She said, "They [the police] were hitting us hard, and they have approached me and seen me like that, and they have retreated, they have restrained." I asked her why she thought they had reacted that way, and she replied, "Why, *pues!*" in a tone that suggested that the answer was obvious, at once unnecessary and impossible to put in words. She said she believes that she has a record at the police station of El Cercado. "My neighbor," she said, "he was a guard there and he has said to me, 'Señora Roberta, you have a *ficha* in the police station in the center. *Usted está fichada'* [meaning both 'You have a record' and 'They have their eyes on you']." I asked her if she was ever arrested and she said no, never. "They must have gotten my name from the Municipalidad," she said. "They also put my picture out on the papers. I felt so embarrassed! I sent my son out for bread that morning and the shopkeeper showed it to him, 'Your mother is crazy,' he said to him, and he came back home crying. A paper said that I am a Cicciolina," she said as her faced lightened up, "and now when I walk by the [police] station they say, 'There goes the Cicciolina.'"

At this point, she seemed excited, even cheerful. She smiled and, bursting into laughter, she recounted how, one day, a group of women workers who were taken to the Plaza de Armas in the back of a truck had gone by the Central Market to collect animal refuse to throw at the police, arriving in the plaza with buckets full of chicken blood, chicken feathers, and fish entrails. "It was pure waste, pure rot!" she said with a giggle. She then recalled how, from the back of the truck, the women had thrown the feathers and fish entrails and poured out the buckets of chicken blood over on the police below and, giggling again, she mimicked their astonished faces. Her words were now distorted by the gestures she made to describe how the refuse had fallen into the policemen's gaping mouths, gestures that were followed by an overpowering bout of laughter. She collected herself slowly, panting with the last chuckles, and said, "That day the police were the most violent."

In between songs the radio DJ said the time was 5:45. It would soon be two hours since I met Señora Roberta—only now I knew her name—at the corner. I said that I didn't want to abuse their generosity with their time, that I had only one more question, if they didn't mind. It was about the persistent rumors that the demonstrations of ESMLL have been infiltrated by thugs hired by the SIN to make things look bad and damage Andrade's public image. I hadn't finished my question yet and they were already shaking their heads vigorously, as if they had been waiting for it. They said that they have never seen anyone other than union workers at the protests. Mr. Gómez said that all sorts of things have been said about ESMLL, that Andrade has purposefully misinformed the press to confuse the public by saying that SITRAMUN has lent itself to the president's dirty games. Señora Roberta said that Andrade had gone even further than that, telling the press that the workers of ESMLL are actually terrorists of Sendero Luminoso. Andrade himself had said that! But they both reassured me that none of that was true.

I thanked them profusely, said that having met them and talked to them would help enormously with my work, and paid the check.

When we left Café Macchu Pichu the sun was out. The air was cool and crisp. We walked a block over to Jirón Azángaro, where we shook hands and parted ways. The last rays of sun shone over half of the street, warming up the sidewalk where I was walking south toward the Plaza San Martín. At the plaza there was a small CUT (Central Única de Trabajadores) protest; the workers had covered the base of the liberator's statue with a huge bright red banner. I grabbed a cab in front of the Sheraton Hotel. The taxi driver had the radio on, tuned to a show in which a psycho-analyst, Fernando Maestre, talks about psychological and sexual issues, answering calls from the public. Maestre was discussing the decline of sexual intercourse among married couples. Looking at me through the rearview mirror, the driver said, "One has to make time for everything, no, señorita?"

That was the last thing I wanted to talk about, sex and Maestre, whose conceited, sexist, and patronizing views I simply cannot stand. Turning up the volume, the guy asked me if I was married. I thought of Mila and scooted down toward the door. The sun fell warm on my shoulder through the side window. Exhausted, I threw my head back and closed my eyes, fighting not to doze off. Maestre's and the driver's words became like rumbling rocks in the bottom of the ocean.

———

Thursday morning: I just reread my notes about Tuesday afternoon, about my encounter with Señora Roberta, the meaning and intensity of which I will probably be teasing out for weeks to come. So, why do I feel a bit disheartened? She said it was just "despair." But, is that it? But, what was I expecting to hear from her?

The answer, if there is any, is probably not in the replies she offered, as directly as she could, to my unspoken but blatantly obvious question of why, of why she had done what she had done, but in the seemingly unimportant or irrelevant details of her story, like her son going out for bread the next morning and coming back crying or Francia dying of a treatable disease. In contrast to what I had presumed, even if unknow-ingly, that Señora Roberta would say, she expressed no sense of gain in her transgression, no awareness of the culture-shattering power of it, and no feeling of empowerment or sense of vindication from it.

The other day at the café, as she cried and laughed irrepressibly, as her sorrow folded indistinctly into delight, the object of both her tears and laughter dissipated into nothing, into nothing beyond the sobs and gasps of laughter that alone affirmed, in a way that words never could, her momentary but total escape from her subordinate reality. As I looked to her for precision about the meaning of her actions, for the reassurance of an articulated thought, my search for precision and meaning, I now realize, was part of her transgression's undoing, part of its slipping away.

The difference between my expectations of this meeting and what Señora Roberta offered is nothing else than the difference that for Bataille distinguishes the Hegelian putting at stake of one's life—which ultimately produces sense and knowledge, recognition and mastery, the recognition of mastery (as with the bullfighter?)—and his idea of sovereignty, an operation that, conversely, causes the dialectic underpinning transgression to dislocate, to lose its sense and its productivity. "Sovereign behavior," writes Bataille, "takes place only if the urgency for it appears: and if the operation does become urgent, it is no longer time to undertake efforts whose essence is to be subordinate to ends exterior to them, whose essence is not to be ends in themselves."[3]

The object I am after, therefore, does not exist, or if it does, its reality is of a kind that interrupts the flow of thought, that cannot be known beyond Señora Roberta's sobs and guffaws. Bataille likens our fits of laughter and tears to the rhythmed movements of poetry and music, which alone can recapture moments of rupture such as Señora Roberta's. If she was unable to objectify it and get to the bottom of her experience, to break it down into causes and effects, it was because that moment was a stepping outside of time and space, outside of the limits of discourse, resulting not in the neutralization of meaning but in its endless multiplication, in a kind of potlatch of signification that links the world of meaning to that of nonmeaning.[4] Conversely, my questions assumed causes and effects, anticipation and calculation in an action that anticipated nothing, that arrested thought and knowledge to proclaim only the "reign of the moment," which for Bataille is the heart of sovereign acts.

Bataille's understanding of sovereignty is not as "exception," as the prerogative of a single individual over a group of subjects, but as that of ordinary persons upholding a special value against the poverty of things and the poverty of life reduced to work and productivity. It is a quality that all human beings share and have only apparently lost, a fundamentally human value that a beggar has in common with a great nobleman and that is opposed to servility and subordination. "In order not to be subjugated, [sovereignty] *must* subordinate nothing. . . . [I]t must expend itself without reserve . . . [and] as the ultimate subversion of [Hegelian mastery], it must no longer seek to be recognized."[5] Thus human beings' "special value" manifests fully, sovereignly, only in the unpredictable, uncalculated brevity of a moment of pure loss. Like sacredness, this moment can never have the objectivity of things, and what is not a thing "is real but at the same time is not real, it is impossible and yet it is there."[6]

This sovereign moment Bataille describes as "the ocean into which the streams of labor disappear." In the plaza, before and around Señora Roberta, before and around her slackened strands of hair, her streaked and toothless grimace, her naked old body, was that ocean, and into it the world of toil and utility, of words and ideas, of servility and subjugation, of fear and death, of fear *of* death, simply vanished.

———

Later: My mother called this morning and asked if I'd like to have lunch with her today. She said she had something to tell me. She said, "I normally wouldn't tell you about this stuff because you think it's idiotic."

During lunch in her office she spoke about her last visit to *"la bruja"* (the witch), a new one, really good, recommended by so and so. I immediately recognized the pattern, in which even the "really good" fortune-tellers eventually fall in disfavor when on the second or third visit, as they begin to probe deeper, they inevitably get things wrong in their guesses and divinations and lose the client's trust, who moves on to another one in her infinite search for the real thing.

My mother said that *la bruja* knew right away that she had three children, knew right away that she's separated from my father but not divorced. She told her that we, her children, are doing well, but that of the three, I am doing best. She said that my brother has a bit of "a shadow" (*"está un poco sombreado"*), that my sister, too, has "a shadow." Then she said that, in fact, it seems like my mother has been touched by this shadow as well, that someone must have placed a curse on her (*"le ha hecho un trabajo"*). Taken aback, my mother said that it was impossible, that she does not know anyone who would do such a thing, who believes in such a thing.

The woman said, "Maybe a maid? A disaffected maid?"

My mother denied that categorically, just as she denied the woman's insinuations that possibly it was someone at her knitting shop, an envious or angry worker, or her estranged husband, with whom she still has unfinished business.

"Salvador? Impossible," my mother said, adding that the two of them actually get on well. Disappointed, my mother was about to thank the woman and walk out, when she asked her to wait, to hear her out because now she was sure that the source of the curse was actually her husband, but not him personally. The curse came from his family, the woman said.

She could now see clearly that a curse placed on them, the Gandolfos, had spilled over onto my mother and us from them. She said it was a massive job. My father and his entire family, she said, were completely "*sombreados.*"

As we ate our soup and talked, my mother said that this could explain the fate of that family, the paralysis they seemed to have suffered in the face of dire and mysterious misfortune.

"This is not from here," the woman had said. "This is not the kind of work we do here." The woman explained that the kind of curse that had been placed on that family was a much more powerful and deathly form of sorcery than anything ever practiced in Peru.

"It looks like from the Caribbean," she had said, "from Haiti or Jamaica."

My mother had stopped eating and was looking me in the eye when she said this last word. She repeated it, "Jamaica," pausing and giving me time to make the association myself between what the woman had said and Jean-Pierre, my great-aunt's husband. Flavia had told her that I had just heard the story, and she wanted to know what I thought about *la bruja's* spin on it.

I laughed and said that it all sounded like a soap opera, a really bad one. Never mind the racism!

My mother went back to eating and said that the woman herself had brought up my mother's "ongoing medical issues." Now completely mesmerized by her, my mother had told her the entire story of her breasts, the bizarre mistake the doctor had made that, like the debacle of the Gandolfos' fortune and home life, no one could ever explain adequately. In this light, all of it seemed to make more sense to her.

La bruja had said that, of her three children, I had almost escaped the curse. Not only was I the most different from my father, but I had also left the country, taken root elsewhere. My brother, Carlos, was definitely touched by it. "Does he have a hard time making decisions?" she had asked. But my sister, my little sister, the living image of my father, was completely taken ("*tomada*"), she had said.

Suddenly, it no longer seemed funny. It no longer seemed like a soap opera. But I am familiar with Mauss's work enough to know that the power of magic, its "facticity," is wholly dependent on its having a social reality, on its being collectively believed. So I was not about to affirm my mother's story by reacting with panic. I tried to stay relaxed, but feeling a bit nervous, a bit shaken inside, I said that under no circumstances she should tell this story to Flavia, appealing to the immense power of suggestion, to the idea that merely knowing that someone believes such horrifying things about her could actually have an impact on her, do harm to her, and, in a way, make the curse real.

My mother said that the woman had offered to take care of it. Initially my mother had accepted. But when she heard that the required ritual would involve going to her house and killing an animal, a chicken or a hen, my mother backed off. The idea of having to slash open a live animal right in the middle of her living room in order to do the *limpieza* seems to have scared my mother more than the curse itself.

———

Friday: At El Haití—the usual table in the back. Before me a cup of café con leche, a couple of feminist critiques of Lévi-Strauss, and a set of photocopies from African newspapers and journals.

I have noticed that, from early in the morning until about noon, there are only men at El Haití. Middle aged and older, they often come in alone with a newspaper folded under the arm; they take a seat, order coffee, browse the paper, and leave. Possibly retired or unemployed, they sometimes come to meet other men. In groups, they sit around a table, slouch on the chairs and smoke heavily, while they leaf through their newspapers and have loud conversations with each other or on their cell phones, as if they were alone in the café. At the only other occupied table in the mezzanine, there are five Chinese men. They got here a few minutes after I arrived. They're drinking coffee and smoking while they read Chinese newspapers and argue about something. The swelling cloud of smoke hanging above their heads slowly begins to engulf me.

For many years, before Sendero became active in the capital, El Haití was open around the clock. But as blackouts and car bombs increased in frequency, nighttime curfews were imposed, and El Haití, like most other businesses, began to close earlier and earlier. I remember I was here the drizzly, blacked-out August night I first left the country. That night the tables were lit with gas lamps and the ceiling-to-floor windows were crisscrossed with duct tape to keep the glass from shattering in the event of a bomb. My friend Aldo and I sat at a table, looking at each other in silence over the dim gaslight and two glasses of pisco sour, as my parents and my packed bags waited for me at home, ready to go to the airport.

"I think I'm fleeing from something," I remember whispering to Aldo. He nodded.

Of course I wasn't the only one; thousands of young people, of every region and class backgrounds, were leaving the country at the time, jumping ship. He didn't know it then, but Aldo himself would be packing up and leaving for Mexico City in a year's time. I was among the luckier ones, with a student fellowship awaiting me in the United States.

"But I don't know exactly from what," I whispered to him again, knowing that the reason wasn't as easily nameable as the violence that was ravaging the country, the mind-numbing inflation, the impunity with which those in power (Alan García and his cronies) had ransacked the country, the depressed labor market for those of us who were coming of age or graduating from college. It was something older, deeper, and more elusive, feeding an intense desire to begin again, to crawl out from underneath our colonial legacy of violence and injustice, out from under the weight of a society that slowly, tenaciously works the person since birth, works to break her so that she learns to abuse or to accept abuse, while almost everyone else just watches and condones it. I was scared shitless of Sendero, but somewhere, somehow, I think I understood the anger, pain, and frustration that fueled their bloody ideology that I, too, knew and bore, and that I was instead fleeing from—but from which, I soon would learn, there was no fleeing. Now that I'm back in Lima, I realize that truly returning is also impossible.

Going over this African material about the political use of nudity by women, a fact stands out: Time and again, the women are said to be "mothers" who stripped naked "before their sons" or "in front of their children," and it is clear that it is their status as mothers that gave their nakedness a special force and that made their actions abominable and shameful. The idea that the protesting women undressed before "their sons," while in most cases surely a metaphorical one, is upheld from Kenya to Cameroon to Peru, suggesting some powerful collective assumptions about motherhood, including that age can be a valid marker of motherhood as much as motherhood itself.

On this last point, Alexandra Tibbets, writing about the protests of the Kikuyu "mamas" in Nairobi, says that the act of *guturamira* (stripping) is an old form of resistance that is available "to older women only who are known or presumed to be mothers." She writes, "Curse by stripping is not a resource a young woman could employ even if she were a mother. Motherhood in this case is a resource when combined with the respect accorded to older women."[7] Similarly, writing about the Ondó of Nigeria, Elizabeth Eames says that women are believed to become more powerful with age, as their sexual energy and menstrual blood are thought to accumulate and turn into *àse*, a force that gives them the power to bring health, wealth, and fertility as well as ill fortune, barrenness, and drought. In the case of the stripping of the Ondó market women, Eames tells us that it was this motherly power, to give as well as to take life, that was put to work in order to curse the king.[8]

Questioned on the source of what I have here called the culture-shattering power of Señora Roberta's transgression and on the reason why the police reacted the way they did, Mr. Morales, the reporter at *La República*, offered an explanation that was concise and simple but, I think, profound: "Why?" he said matter-of-factly, "because a mother is a mother," as if it were not the answer but the question that was self-evident. And while I feel tempted to dismiss Mr. Morales's statement as redundant, I might as well pause and consider the kind of knowledge that is contained in that tautology—a mother is a mother—concentrated in it like high voltage in live wire and bearing such power when let loose. What sort of truth is implied in that seemingly absurd statement—a mother is a mother—that arguments that posit women's bodies as symbolic repositories of men's most primordial fears (such as psychoanalysis) do not so much clarify as take for granted?

What the African material and Mr. Morales's statement bring to the fore is a key anthropological problem, one that I am constantly contending with as I write and that can be summed up as the place of womanhood and motherhood in the structuring of culture as well as in its potential destructuring.

In this regard, Bataille did not so much differ with as stopped short of embracing the full implication of Lévi-Strauss's idea that taboo constitutes the social not just along the lines of the nature/culture divide but also along the lines of gender and sexuality. In *The Accursed Share*, Bataille reformulates Lévi-Strauss's thesis—that by means of taboo nature transcends itself to give way to culture—in terms of animality and humanity—where by means of taboo animality is repressed to give way to notions of proper human behavior that sustain, in turn, complex social divisions into classes and races. But Lévi-Strauss's point that humans' underrating and fear of nature, variously defined, and that the taboos that they place around it are the basis for the division of the sexes into genders and sexualities had to be taken up by feminist anthropologists in the 1970s, such as Sherry Ortner, who in a way completed Lévi-Strauss's argument, and Gayle Rubin, who blew this argument to pieces to reconstitute it in terms of a political economy of gender and sex.[9]

Ortner's thesis, which develops a critical but unstated aspect of Lévi-Strauss's argument in *The Elementary Structures of Kinship*, is that women everywhere are believed to be closer to nature, are seen as part of that "lower order of existence" that nature is in relation to culture. If, as Ortner

What are the taboos impressed upon us? And how do we trangress them?

THIRD DIARY

defines it, culture is the transcendence of natural givens through systems of meaningful forms, then women are "less transcendental" of nature than men. Women's assumed lower order of being is related to physiology, to the greater bodily involvement of women in the functions of reproduction. Drawing from Simone de Beauvoir's Hegelian critique of sexism in *The Second Sex*, Ortner argues that, because of this physiological reality, women's "animality is more manifest" as they are limited by their bodies "to mere reproduction." This is why reproduction and the life of the home, by extension closer to nature than the more public affairs of networks and alliances (viewed as "society" itself), enjoy less prestige than men's occupations, even though these often involve destruction (through hunting or warfare) rather than creation of life. Ortner explains that what gives these activities their value "is the[ir] transcendental (social, cultural) nature . . . as opposed to the naturalness of the process of birth. 'For it is not in giving life but in risking life,'" Ortner explains by quoting de Beauvoir, "'that man is raised above the animal.'"[10]

The structure of Ortner's (de Beauvoir's) point is that of Hegel's dialectic of the master and the slave, where it is the master who in the struggle for recognition risks his life by staring death in the face, and it is the slave through whom he achieves mastery. In fact, for de Beauvoir, the dialectic of the master and the slave is not just a helpful analogy: "Certain passages in the argument employed by Hegel in defining the relation of master to slave," she writes, "apply much better to the relation of man to woman." Much better? Whereas the captured slave, she argues, has also known the risk of life, "woman is basically an existent who gives Life and does not risk *her* life."[11] Ortner relies on de Beauvoir's assessment to argue that it is not so much that societies equate women to nature—even Lévi-Strauss knows that "in a man's world [a woman] is still a person," a full-fledged human being with a consciousness, who thinks and speaks. Rather, women are seen "merely" as being closer to nature, occupying an "intermediate" position between nature and culture and mediating men's and society's relationship with nature through their role in the socialization of children and as objects of exchange through which men build alliances and networks.

That women occupy a mediating position, in a dialectical sense, is also a central analytical point in what Rubin calls her Marxian analysis of sex/gender systems. But Rubin focuses on the possible political and economic implications of Lévi-Strauss's theory of exogamy and calls for a kind of theorization that examines the ways the "exchange of women" has not just brought forth "the social," in some abstract sense, but has enabled men to acquire power, prestige, and wealth, and even influenced larger-scale political processes, such as the maintenance of differential access to resources among groups, the consolidation of high-ranking persons into social strata, and even the development of early states.

Women's mediating role—that is, the role by which they "perform conversion functions" between nature and culture—would thus account both for their lower status and for the greater number and more limiting taboos placed on their bodies and social lives. Hegel's definition of the slave as the "other" consciousness, as the consciousness whose "reality is the animal type of life," applies especially well to women, says de Beauvoir. And "it is because humanity calls itself in question in the matter of living—that is to say, values the reasons for living above mere life—that, confronting woman, man assumes mastery . . . take[s] control of the instant and mold[s] the future."[12] It is precisely against this mastery that Bataille formulated his idea of sovereignty.

But something more than a mere replacement of "servile consciousnesses" seems to have take place in de Beauvoir's (and by extension Ortner's and Rubin's) treatment of the master/slave dialectic. From their texts it emerges transformed into a deeply gendered dialectic; it emerges dangerously close to Bataille's eroticism, signaling a place where we must read Bataille against Bataille.[13] What happens when the achievement of mastery is attempted through a servile (female) consciousness that, unlike the slave, will not fight to gain mastery herself, to take control of the instant and mold the future? Should we take this question even further and ask: Is "sovereign man" really a woman? An old woman? A mother?

———

Saturday morning: Woke up thinking about Vulture-man. He hasn't come by recently, and I wonder what he's up to. Today I will go by the morgue, see if I can straighten out Paco's story. Or did Manolo make arrangements with the guy before leaving Lima? I have called Don Julio, a taxi driver whom you can hire for an hourly fee. I got his number from Rosario, who hires him when she needs to travel with equipment for photo or film. In that situation, the car isn't so much what's needed as the deterring presence of a man. I'm going to the center with my camera, take all the shots I need today, and then stop by the morgue to see what I can find out.

———

Later: A little before eleven, Don Julio rang the bell. I found him dusting the side of his old white Toyota station wagon with a flannel cloth, which already looked sparkling clean to me. He's a lanky man; he has a gentle expression and droopy eyes. As we shook hands, the thought flit by, *He's the one to defend me in case of assault?* But as we drove around the city, stopping and taking pictures, I noticed that he is very confident at the wheel, that he knows every nook and cranny, every good route and helpful detour. What's more important, no one, not once, said a peep while I was with him.

It was about two o'clock when we pulled over in front of the morgue. A man was standing at the entrance of Vulture-man's funerary agency. I walked up to him and asked about Mr. Ventura's whereabouts, while Don Julio waited leaning against the car. The man said that Mr. Ventura doesn't come in on Saturdays. "He works by himself today," he explained, adding that he's probably at El Ángel and lifting his arm roughly in the direction of the cemetery. It took me a minute to realize that what this might have meant is that Mr. Ventura has a side business, as is fairly common here, probably an "informal" offshoot of his "formal" funerary agency job, selling gravestones, crosses, and flowers to those burying or visiting their dead.

Thinking I could save myself the trip up to El Ángel, I asked the man about Paco. I said that it's been a few weeks now since Mr. Ventura picked up the body from the morgue and that we have not seen the ashes yet. He looked up Paco's name in some kind of logbook. Nothing. "No, señorita," he said, "I really wouldn't know." He said I had to come back when Mr. Ventura was in, maybe on Monday morning, or on Tuesday, to be on the safe side, since he deals with this kind of matter "personally" (was this a euphemism for "under the table"?). I mentioned the contract Mr. Ventura and Manolo had signed. He said, "You mean a release form? Do you have it on you?" Of course I didn't.

I walked back to the car. Don Julio had pulled up the windshield wipers and was dusting the windshield with the flannel rag. I wondered out loud whether it made sense to go to El Ángel. Don Julio said that the cemetery was just a quick drive up Jirón Huánuco if I wanted to go. I wanted to go, and I did not want to go. I was at once eager to find out what has happened to Paco's body and terrified to know. Once I found out the truth, what would I do with it?

The main entrance to the Cementerio El Ángel circles around a small plaza, the Plazoleta del Ángel de la Resurrección, which on Saturdays and Sundays is full of vendors of flowers and all sorts of marble carved stones to place on niche openings. Don Julio parked across Jirón Ancash, on the side of the old Cementerio General, where there are also lines of wheeled carts filled with buckets of flowers. "Señor! Señorita! Flowers for your loved ones!" we heard from every angle. I crossed the avenue and walked around the vending stalls with very little hope (or perhaps determination) that I would find Vulture-man in the crowd. Thinking that it might be better to come back on Tuesday, when he's supposed to be at the funerary, I gave up.

Don Julio was standing at the door of the Cementerio General, looking in. Centered upon a small clearing, with a backdrop of smaller statues and old mausoleums, was a statue of Jesus lying on a shroud just down from the cross. "That's the Supine Christ," I said to Don Julio, pointing inside the cemetery walls. I somehow knew this statue. I remembered it, just like I remembered that my grandparents are buried in a mausoleum that is close to it although I could not say exactly where. I had not been to this cemetery since 1974, when both my *Limeño* grandparents died, within six months of each other. "Let's go in for a little while," I said to Don Julio. He locked up the car and followed me inside.

"I'm sure that's what this is: El Cristo Yacente," I said, taking a few steps back to take a shot of it with my camera. I went around it to get it from another angle, but as I was focusing the lens for my second shot I heard a coarse voice, yelling, "You can't do that, señorita!" An old, stubby man was running toward us, shouting that what we were doing was forbidden, that we needed an authorization. I asked for a reason since it is a public cemetery after all, and he said, rather tartly, that since the cemetery workers' strike, journalists have come and gone as they pleased, taking pictures of the most unkempt corners of the cemetery and writing scathing articles against the current administration. The man was wearing a button-down shirt that was worn thin on the back and chest. His sleeves were rolled up, as were his pants, which hung loosely from the waist, held by a thin belt. He wore old dressing shoes with no socks, and I noticed that his hands were dirty, that he had black dirt inside his nails, and that he was holding a shovel. If I hadn't known that there were no more burials at the cemetery, except at already-existing mausoleums, I would've sworn that he was a grave digger.

I told him that I was looking for my grandparents' mausoleum, the Corbacho Álvarez. "The Corbachos?" said the gardener with surprise, this time without a trace of bitterness in his voice. "Of course!" he said, pointing with the shovel and signaling us to follow him. We walked down a narrow path and into a labyrinth of mausoleums and niche walls, most dated in the late 1800s. We walked by the statue of a woman, whose head and shoulders were covered in a sheer Spanish shawl carved out of marble, which she clutched mournfully over her chest. We stopped before a square, flat-roofed mausoleum of gray marble that had the name of Tomás Corbacho Necochea in an arch of brass letters over the door. "The Corbachos," the man said, pointing with his shovel. "There was a burial here last month," he said. The brass letters and the brass door had been recently polished, and they stood out bright yellow in the grim atmosphere that surrounded them. I told the man that the name didn't ring a bell, that this was another Corbacho family, and looked around at the names of the mausoleums nearby.

Facing a wall of tiny niches for infant burials (called *parvularios*), there was one whose marble walls were so worn out that they had turned porous. The marble slabs on the roof were warped and chipped. The door to the underground crypt had been unhinged and reattached with pieces of jute cloth. The door handle was missing, and it was tied to the frame through the hole with another piece of jute. Some of the door's glass panels were missing and, covering the openings, was a sack of jute stretched over them. I walked to the front of the mausoleum, a bit perturbed by its patently violated state, and felt dismayed when I saw "Corbacho Álvarez" written across the front in dirty, brown brass letters. I turned to Don Julio, who was crossing himself, and then to the gardener, who said, "This is it, no?" as he looked around it, examining it up and down, rubbing the grainy surface of the walls and scratching it with his thumbnail. "No?"

I went up the steps to look through a peephole inside the main, aboveground chamber. Stacked one above the other, I saw the marble gravestones of my great-aunt, Ma. Luisa Murillo de Corbacho, and my great-uncle, Octavio Corbacho Álvarez (my grandmother's brother). That's all I could see from that angle. Don Julio shook his head in disapproval when I said that it looked dusty inside, appearing to feel uncomfortable for me, ashamed for me, as I bluntly put into words what by then was obvious to everyone, that the mausoleum has been broken into and that someone has been living or sleeping inside. He crossed himself again. "I think my grandparents' graves are down in the crypt," I said, bending down to see if I could catch a glimpse of the inside through the jute, then stepping down into the dark pit reluctantly, as if some nasty object might leap out.

The gardener kept surveying the mausoleum and scratching the walls. He said that since the 1993 strike of union workers at the Beneficencia de Lima, to protest the government's massive layoffs, the cemetery has been in frank decay. He said that during the days of the strike the cemetery was left unguarded and when the strike was called off the workers returned to find that the cemetery had been ransacked and that several statues were missing. He lifted his shovel to point to a round hole near the mausoleum's roof and said that the thieves, the desecrators, had also stolen numerous stained-glass windows. Those and the marble headstones are easy to resell in the black market, he said. But not the statues. For the most part, the statues were returned. He had heard that a rich man had bought a few of them in the Las Malvinas underground market, only to realize later that they had been stolen from the cemetery. He returned them instantly.

The gardener said that the marble in my grandparent's mausoleum was in very bad condition, that it clearly hadn't been given any maintenance for years. He said that, if I wanted, he could clean it up, treat and revamp the stone, even replace the stained-glass bull's-eye window. He said that, in total, it would cost around 3,000 soles.

"I need to call my father," I said to the men. "Is there a pay phone nearby?" I said, turning to the gardener. Don Julio unclipped his cell phone from his belt and handed it to me. I called my father at home, feeling certain that he would like to know what's going on. But as soon as I told him that I was at Presbítero Maestro, I realized that he already knew. "Oh god, it's falling apart, isn't it?" he said. He even knew that it would cost nearly $1,000 to fix it and seemed utterly mortified by the fact that he didn't have that kind of money now and wouldn't have it any time soon. I suggested that maybe we could get someone else to do it for less money and heard the gardener in the background saying, "How much are you willing to pay?" Eager to get off the phone, my father said that we could talk about it later.

It was soon going to be four o'clock. I told Don Julio that we would come back on Tuesday and that I wanted to go. The gardener didn't seem happy, but he walked us to the gate, perhaps to make sure that I didn't take any more photos.

When I got back to the house I had a message from Mr. Gómez. He had called early in the afternoon to say that he needed to talk to me urgently. I left a message on his cell phone, to call me back, and to do it soon because I'm leaving to go back to the United States in about a little over a week.

———

Monday, 6:30 p.m.: Manuela just got back from Ayacucho, where she's doing her dissertation fieldwork. We met today for lunch. I was about to leave the house when she called to let me know that on the front page of today's *Expreso* (a pro-Fujimori newspaper) there's a photo of a group of women protesting naked in the United States.

I left the house at about 12:30 and walked to the corner of Avenidas Larco and Benavides, where I bought a copy of *Expreso* and took a *micro* to Jesús María. On the front page, in fact, is a photo of the Seattle Lesbian Avengers, protesting at the WTO meeting in Seattle. They are all young and naked, except for their bottom underwear and an X of black tape covering over their nipples (to avoid being arrested for indecency; exposure of the areola or nipple is grounds for it). On their chest, back, and stomach, they had written "No BGH in the body," in reference to the bovine growth hormone injected into cows to increase their production of milk.

I got off the *micro* in front of the Ministerio de Trabajo (Labor Ministry) and was impressed, as if I had never seen it before, by the social-realist frontispiece on the main entrance of that building, built by General Manuel Odría's authoritarian regime in the early 1950s: larger-than-life, robust men and women of classic features, standing straight, disciplined, proud, and beautiful, holding huge hammers and sickles and looming over this otherwise chaotic entryway, which is traversed mostly by small, dark-skinned people whose labor rights have been tramped on since time immemorial and continue to be systematically tramped on by the present system and the present government.

I love the wide, quiet streets of Jesús María, with their modest, art deco houses and apartment buildings, their slightly neglected front gardens and parks, and the scrawny cats and dogs wandering around, lost or disowned, which give this beautiful district its air of forlornness. I met Manuela outside her office, and since we both felt like eating fish, we walked to the Jesús María market. Nibbling from a large dish of *cebiche* and another of *jalea*, Manuela and I caught up about our lives, talked about dissertation stuff, and eventually got on to the topic of the Seattle Lesbian Avengers and female nakedness in political contexts. In reference to the women of ESMLL, Manuela said that what they did was indeed unusual. After all, stripping is not an ordinary form of protest in Peru, where, she noted, it has been and is a more common practice to *undress someone else* as punishment or to denigrate the person. She said that, for instance, robbers and *abigeos* (robbers of livestock in the countryside) are often stripped naked by people in the community as a form of punishment through humiliation. She also said that in the context of the system of conscription for the construction of roads established by President Leguía in the 1920s, rural communities would ambush the soldiers who were coming to take their young men away, putting the women, presumably the most vulnerable members of the community, up front to throw stones at the soldiers, grab them, and then strip them naked. Finally, she said that in Ayacucho she has seen monuments to María Parado de Bellido, one of the few women officially recognized as a precursor of Peru's war of Independence, in which she appears fighting the royal army with her shirt torn open and her breasts exposed. Parado de Bellido was actually fusilladed by a royal squadron in 1822. Manuela said that someone at work has a *retablo ayacuchano* (a sculptural representation of folk or historical scenes in miniature) that features Parado de Bellido confronting the Spanish army in this manner. When we went back to her office, we walked up to her colleague's office and, sure enough, displayed on a shelf were two *retablos* depicting María Parado de Bellido leading a group of men with her arms stretched out and her shirt ripped open, confronting the bayonets and cannons of the royal army, very much like Delacroix's *Liberty Leading the People*.

Manuela and I had a cup of coffee before I left. Then I took a taxi back to the house because I wasn't feeling too well. I'm still not feeling too well.

Tuesday: Sick, sick, sick—bouts of diarrhea and, I suspect, dehydrated. Will go to the doctor for fear of cholera, though I suspect it isn't cholera. No vomit—yet.

Wednesday: In between long bathroom visits, I went yesterday to the emergency room of the hospital around the block. After running some tests, the doctor prescribed antibiotics. I decided to stay in bed today.

Friday: Fourth day in the course of antibiotics, I'm more than halfway through. Neither the discomfort and stomach pain nor the disgust at the idea that to get this bacteria I probably ingested something tainted with human feces compares with the mayhem that seems to have been unleashed inside me. With each dose, I can feel the antibiotic slowly dissolving and spreading throughout, seeping back into my mouth through my salivary glands and oozing out my pores. I can taste it, I can smell it, I can even hear it battling inside—a foreign body against another foreign body—both categorically Other, waging war, as it were, in pursuit of mastery. With each dose, I just lay still, imploring for either combatant to, once and for all, deliver the final blow.

After playing phone tag with Mr. Gómez, we finally talked this afternoon. He said he wanted to ask me, if I had it in my heart, to get medicines for Señora Roberta. He also wanted to know if I had any contacts in the press, who would, as a favor, cover ESMLL's story and its current predicament, for exposure. He said that since I study in the United States, I must know someone. I asked him what medicines, specifically, does Señora Roberta need, but he wasn't able to tell me. He said, "Anything would be good." *Anything?* We then agreed to meet at three this coming Tuesday, again in front of San Francisco.

I can't stop thinking about Mr. Gómez's request. What do I do about the meds? The sense of responsibility to do right by Señora Roberta only partially has to do with the fact that my burgeoning relationship with her is an important one to me and even more remotely with my altruistic desire to help. The sense of responsibility I feel has more to do with what I believe are the demands of reciprocity, of the circle of the gift, and with the (rarely acknowledged) fact that it is precisely the rules of gift exchange that govern our interactions during fieldwork. But is there a way to reciprocate the magnitude of the debt we incur? To address its complexity? I don't think so, just like I don't think there is a way to assuage the shame and guilt that will therefore become attached to this debt and that compel many of us anthropologists to avoid this topic altogether or to recast the relationships we develop while in the field as uncomplicated friendships.

For the rest of the day, I just lounged around and then, for the first time since I got sick, ventured out of the house. Walked to El Haití, managed to read a little.

Later: A composite from newspaper and journal articles collected over the years: Lima's 8+ million residents produce over 1.4 million cubic meters a day of sewage waters, of which 7.5 percent is treated while the rest is dumped into the river or the ocean. From 1861 to 1963, a network of ducts was built to collect the city's raw sewage and take it to the Rímac and Chillón rivers or to the ocean in front of El Callao, San Miguel, and Chorrillos. The outlet in Chorrillos is called Colector Surco, or La Chira, and is the city's largest and most modern. The collector is a pipeline of 1.8 meters of diameter that goes through the Morro Solar and opens onto the ocean on the other side of the beach of La Herradura, carrying the largest quantity of sewage water, 4.9 cubic meters per second, which is produced by nearly 3 million residents in the southern districts of Lima. When this collector was built in 1963, all of Lima had 2 million inhabitants.

The ocean's strong undercurrents are supposed to take this highly toxic waste offshore, but particles of solid matter often resurface and pollute the shoreline along the Circuito de Playas. Fishermen from the Muelle de Pescadores, a fishing dock in front of Chorrillos, refer to the La Chira outlet as the *boca del Diablo* (the devil's mouth) because of what comes out of it and the unbearable smell anywhere in its vicinity. One of the favorite spots for swimming along the coast of Lima is the beach of Agua Dulce, which means "sweet water," right in front of the fishing dock. On any given summer day, the clear, fine sand and tame waterfront of Agua Dulce are swarming with people gobbling down mouth-watering *cebiche* made with fish caught nearby and bought at one of the beach's many kiosks, while the vendor or a helping boy runs back and forth to the shore for water for the dishwashing bucket. These waters are a cauldron of bacteria and parasites that cause all sorts of eye, ear, and stomach infections. The cholera epidemic of 1991 ravaged these coastal districts.

———

Tuesday: It was a completely sterile morning. No, it was worse: I woke up in fairly good spirits and made a list of the things I have left to do before I go back to New York tomorrow. But no sooner had I finished writing everything down than I was prey to a terrible anxiety: Where do I begin? Have I done enough? I won't have enough time! So I spent the entire morning starting and stopping and starting again, moving manically from one unfinished item on my to-do list to the next, staring at it with overwhelmed eyes. A cat pursuing its own tail.

At noon I went for a run and, when I got back, took a long shower, which had the effect of an ablution. At about 1:30, I left the pension to go to the center, where I was meeting Mr. Gómez and Señora Roberta at 3:00. I had put some money in an envelope for Señora Roberta, not a huge sum but enough for a good supply of medicines, which here are not cheap by any standard. For Mr. Gómez, I had bought a book, a nice, illustrated history of the labor movement in Peru, in which I had written a thank-you note.

With the money securely tucked in my front pocket and the book in my bag, I set out to Avenida Larco to pick up the prints of the shots I took the other day with Don Julio. I walked past El Haití and around the Rotunda of Miraflores to Avenida Arequipa, where a *micro* abruptly stopped to pick me up. Screwed to a corner lamppost was a big sign that said, "This is NOT a bus stop." I jumped in.

I moved to the front and sat next to the conductor, sinking into the shallow pit of a vinyl-covered seat, whose springs had long ago collapsed. I flipped through my new pictures, as the *micro*, almost entirely empty, sped down the avenue. All traffic noise outside was stifled by the rattling sounds of the dented, rusted metal frame of the *micro* banging against a worn suspension. I could feel every tiny bump and hole on the asphalt, which made the bones in my body rattle, too, and my lower back hurt with the impact. We passed and were passed by other *micros*, some larger, some smaller, as they raced to pick up the scanty passengers that waited on sidewalk corners at this hour of the day. An old woman, hauling a large load bundled in a sack, got on. She climbed the steps one at a time, pulling the bundle into the bus with both hands, heaving. The driver hit the gas before she had taken a seat.

Looking out from the front of the *micro*, I had a view of the avenue like through a wide-angle lens. On either side of it stretched rows of old, run-down mansions and homes, many of them built in the 1920s and '30s, when Avenida Arequipa (then Avenida Leguía) was the first paved road outside the perimeter of the old fortress wall. Coursing through Miraflores, then San Isidro, then Lince and Santa Beatriz in a tall car like this, I could notice what is hardly visible from below. At a corner where the *micro* stopped at a red light, several worlds converged—that of a (possibly) college-educated, balding guy driving a taxi in his aged Toyota, of a street vendor sitting on a stool dozing off with a blanket on his legs, of a young and good-looking businessman in a suit singing to an English rock tune in his Peugeot, of a recent immigrant from the highlands walking in between the cars, going window to window, asking for money with an infant child wrapped in a *lliclla* on her back—the kid, who peeked out from over the woman's shoulder, had a glob of green, drying mucus stuck to her upper lip. I could see these and other very different and asymmetrical worlds coming together in that same spot but never touching, undoubtedly noticing but rarely acknowledging one another. Briefly, I had the thought, *How does it happen that someone stops caring?*

My mother once told me that many years ago she was driving in her car with her sister Ana and Ana's son, Frank, who were visiting in Lima from Arequipa, and they saw Darío, their cousin, as he was about to cross the street in front of them. Frank must have been six or seven. Hearing that this man was his mom's cousin, he watched Darío, tall and anonymous, walk across in front of the car, come and then go, and said, "But you'll do something, right, Mamá?" And as they drove away, Frank started to kick and scream in the back seat of the car, yelling at the top of his lungs, "You do something, Mamá! You do something!" crying and convulsing, as though it were not someone he didn't know but he himself who his mother had given up on, without stopping until they were back in the house.

At some point, one stops. At some point, someone else's distress no longer feels like one's own, someone else's predicaments leave us unmoved. Thus the world slowly begins to compartmentalize, split into unfamiliar, incomprehensible other worlds, which we can't touch or affect. And the love or the caring, the concern, the indignation, and the pain we once felt curdle into remorse and lassitude, and only sometimes they are violently stirred up again and they ache.

My meeting at the center didn't last very long. I got there early and waited sitting on the stairs of the atrium of San Francisco, talking to a shoe-shine boy who wanted by all means to shine my very haggard red boots with brown polish. He asked me where I was from (since only a tourist would walk around with shoes so tattered) and I said Miraflores, but I might as well have said France or China or Mars. I was telling the boy that it wasn't the right time or the right color to get a shine, when I saw Señora Roberta walking into the atrium, very punctual, right at three. I was happy to see her coming alone and gave her the envelope with the money right away. Her eyes sparkled when I handed it to her, and I truly hoped that she wouldn't be disappointed. We talked for about twenty minutes under the warm afternoon sun, surrounded by hundreds of wing-flapping pigeons—Señora Roberta, me, and the shoe-shine boy, who hung about and listened quietly to our conversation. She told me that the medicines she needed were for the youngest of her children who is fourteen and who seems to be a troubled and sickly kid. The worn, black plastic bag that she carried on the day we first met and that she had with her again was filled with candy and packs of cigarettes, which, she said, she tried to sell in the streets and buses that crossed the center to raise money for her son's medicines. She volunteered her neighbor's phone number and said that I should feel free to call her anytime.

When Mr. Gómez arrived and I gave him the book, I couldn't help but think that he felt let down. The three of us talked for several more minutes, chitchatted about this and that, about the perennial scarcity of jobs in Lima, about SEDAPAL's tendency to break open more streets and pipes than it will ever fix. Then Mr. Gómez said that they needed to go into the building for their meeting. As we shook hands, I told them that I'm leaving tomorrow night, but that I would stay in touch with them and keep up-to-date about ESMLL's struggle.

SEVEN

Nakedness

Contact can be established by means other than touching. One is in contact
with a thing simply by looking at it; the gaze is a means of establishing contact.
—ÉMILE DURKHEIM, *THE ELEMENTARY FORMS OF RELIGIOUS LIFE*

On the eastern end of the city center, fourteen square blocks
down the grid from the main plaza, is a cluster of lopsided
streets and *jirones*, the core of what used to be known as
the "Indian" pueblo of Santiago. One of Viceroy Francisco
de Toledo's first realized *reducciones*, the town had the function of gathering together, or "reducing," all "Indians" who
worked in Lima and who were scattered about the city, living in shabby temporary dwellings in the interstices of the
city grid. As it was provided by Toledo himself, the town
of Santiago was to house Lima's eight hundred or so indigenous people in *solares* distributed around the town's
distinctive rhomboid plaza, where they would live under
the "care" of a *corregidor* (royal administrator) and learn the
Christian doctrine under the tutelage of two Jesuit priests.
Striking an odd balance, as most of Toledo's measures managed to do, between his interest in the welfare of indigenous
people, his condescension toward them, and the colonial
government's need for their effective subjection, Santiago
was provided with an autonomous municipal hall, a sem-
inary for the sons of indigenous caciques (regional lords),
a jail for witches and idolaters, and a perimeter wall whose
two gates were locked at night so that neither "Spaniards
nor blacks, nor mestizos could disturb them [the Indians]."[1]

At the time Toledo dictated the provision for this *reducción* in March 1571, he was in the city of Cuzco, one of

the main stops in the long itinerary of his "general visit" through the viceroyalty's interior, which resulted in the vast and well-known body of ordinances that he issued while he was in power.[2] Intended to provide the disorganized colony with something like a structure, the ordinances contained instructions by region for the establishment of local governments and the regimentation of native life. These included, in addition to the resettlement of "Indians" in *reducciones*, the organization of work in the mines through re-creation of the pre-Hispanic *mita*—a state-mandated system of seasonal, reciprocal labor—as a forced labor scheme aimed at ensuring a year-round supply of workers. Also central to Toledo's massive legislative body were rules to enforce tribute among native peoples, to clarify the duties and curb the power bestowed by the Crown to Spanish and native authorities, and to protect the morality and sexual integrity of native populations, especially young women, by forbidding premarital sex, concubinage, incest, and drunkenness. The painstakingly detailed laws were also concerned with native people's physical appearance, and so sprinkled throughout the ordinances were statutes addressing their bodily hygiene and prohibiting the aesthetic deformation of heads, the painting of bodies or faces, and the use of certain elements in their dress. With this last group of measures Toledo introduced colonial legislation into the terrain of what, after Marcel Mauss, we call the "techniques of the body," setting off the long and complex process that, in the centuries that followed, would definitively transform native people's attire and physical comportment.[3]

The ordinances concerning the clothes of "Indians" came after the apprehension and execution of the last insurgent Inca of Vilcabamba, Túpac Amaru I, in 1572, when Toledo decided to set limits to the artful variety of tunics, hairdos, and headdresses that indigenous peoples of different ethnicities wore to affirm and distinguish themselves from one another.[4] In the Viceroyalty of Peru, Spanish conquistadors and missionaries were for the most part spared the trouble of having to convince native people to wear clothes since this was already a widespread custom—and for the Spaniards a commendable one—throughout the territory that had been previously under Inca rule.[5] Male Inca attire consisted of a sleeveless tunic, called *uncu*; a square cape tied over the left shoulder; a waistcloth, called *wara*; a headband or fillet, called *llauto*; and leather sandals, called *usutas*. The female Inca dress was made up of two mantles: the *anacu*, which women wrapped around their bodies and fastened with pins, and the *lliclla*, which they placed over their shoulders like a shawl. Female attire tended to be simple, lacking in the richness and sumptuousness of the male garb, which for men of certain status included large ear studs; nose ornaments of metal, bone, or wood; and colorful feathers. The Incas enforced this code of dress uniformly throughout the Tawantinsuyu (the four quarters of the Inca empire) while they let their subjects continue to wear hairdos and headdresses according to their group or province, a practice that they considered to be instrumental in the management of such vast territory.[6]

Stressing the cultural and economic importance that cloth and clothing had for the Incas, John V. Murra argues that textile production was considered just as important as agricultural production in enabling the complex system of reciprocity and redistribution that linked the sprawling Inca state with its subjects. Every year, Murra explains, every domestic unit was expected to contribute time and labor knitting for the state by means of a textile *mita*, which would result in the amassing of blankets, mantles, and articles of clothing in large state deposits scattered around the Tawantinsuyu. These garments were later distributed among the Inca army or—since textiles were second only to llamas as a favorite sacrificial offering—immolated to gods in the Inca pantheon.[7]

In Inca times, textiles were also a form of gift, key to renewing relationships of kinship during times of flux or social transformation (death of the Inca, initiation rites, and so on) when they were, in Murra's words, "lavishly consumed." The Incas would also use textiles to establish relationships of citizenship with newly conquered populations, who after being defeated would be presented with numerous gifts, chief among them textiles and clothing, a strategy that, Murra suggests, aimed to lock the new subjects into obligatory relations of reciprocity. On occasion, after a military victory, the Inca himself would appear before the conquered people donning the local costume as a mark of his new power and authority over them. Also referring to the power attributed to clothing, Murra explains that during the expansion of the Tawantinsuyu, Inca soldiers would strip prisoners and the dead of their clothes in order to make like-images of the enemy, which they would then strangle as a way to magically inflict harm on them. The custom of stripping naked those killed or wounded in battle, Murra notes, persisted against the Spanish army well into colonial times—a practice that Jan Szeminski has argued aimed at assigning the enemy, in this case the Spaniard, a nonhuman or an animal status.[8]

Given Andean people's widespread concern with cloth and clothing—Murra says it was almost an obsession—the Spaniards' main preoccupation in Peru, unlike many other European colonies, was not with covering native nakedness or getting native populations to conceal what chroniclers referred to as their "shamefulness" ("*sus vergüenzas*") or their "dishonest parts"—although native women were made to sew together the side openings of their *anacu* that left their thighs exposed.[9] Rather, what was at stake in this case were the social, political, moral, and economic benefits, as well as the dangers, of allowing indigenous people to adopt the Spanish costume. Turned chiefly into a question of social and economic policy, sixteenth- and seventeenth-century sartorial legislation in Peru was a confounding corpus of wavering and contradictory measures, in which statutes prohibiting the use of Spanish clothing by indigenous people coexisted with those encouraging it.[10] Toledo's ordinances, for instance, followed both a decision in the 1560s by Viceroy Count of Nieva to ban the use of Spanish garments by indigenous caciques and the nobility, and a nearly simultaneous but contrary recommendation by Juan de Matienzo, a Spanish judge whose chronicle *Gobierno del Perú* inspired many of Toledo's ordinances. Emphasizing the benefits of persuading indigenous people to adopt the Spanish attire, Matienzo stated that having "Indians dress with Spanish clothes is not only not bad, but very good for many reasons. The first, because they grow to love us and our dress; the second so that they begin to partake of the being of men [human beings], and this I say should be permitted to caciques and *principales* [indigenous nobility and the wealthier class]."[11]

The Spaniards' indecisive course of action in this matter was due, on the one hand, to competing interests that pinned the loss in the value of Spanish clothes items as markers of their status and authority against the likely economic gains in the local textile industry and the importation of fabrics, which were levied with high taxes.[12] On the other hand, the Spaniards' hesitancy on the subject of proper "Indian" attire also spoke to the social and political power that they themselves conferred to clothing as well as to their knowledge of the special value indigenous people assigned to textiles for social, political, and military maneuvering. In this sense, Spaniards understood that for indigenous people to don Spanish dress could be at once a sign of submission and an effrontery, an expression of obedience and a form of subversion, even a tactic by which the will and the might of the Spanish invaders could be garnered in their favor and deployed, through sympathetic means, against those very same men.[13]

For indigenous people, Spanish clothes were also the source of much ambivalence, the object of great desire as well as of repudiation. Many caciques and other Hispanicized individuals were quick to adopt garments like the Spanish pants and felt hat, which they favored over articles formerly imposed by the Incas, probably in the belief that those garments brought them socially closer to their new colonizer. Conversely, the plea to reject Spanish garments, oftentimes along with Spanish language, architecture, and food, was an important ingredient in resistance movements like the Taki Onqoy, the early colonial millenary movement of resistance to the invasion. A repudiation of Spanish clothing figured in the movement's cleansing rituals and in the speeches made by the movement's preachers following the episodes of entranced dance and possession that were the main feature of the movement. In those speeches, as sixteenth-century chronicler Cristóbal de Molina reports, preachers "threatened [the people] not to serve God, that it was not the time of God but of the *huacas* [native sacred powers], threatening the Indians if they did not fully reject Christianity, and scold[ing] the cacique or Indian, who wore a shirt or a hat, or *alpargatas* [Spanish-Arab sandals], or any other garment from Spain. . . ."[14]

The uncertainty that defined early Spanish clothing policy, however, came to an end after the rebellion of José Gabriel Condorcanqui, known as Túpac Amaru II, in 1781–82. Túpac Amaru II, a mestizo cacique and a merchant, was cognizant of the value of clothing in building credibility and networks of support in native towns and communities, and one of his first insurrectionary acts was to take over colonial textile production shops (*obrajes*) in Cuzco and to confiscate deposits of clothes, which he distributed widely to the people, emulating the "generosity" of the former Inca.[15] Some sources indicate that Túpac Amaru II appeared in public decked in the clothes of *corregidor* Arriaga, who he himself had executed in the plaza of Tungasuca (Cuzco) at the beginning of his rebellion. In resorting to this ancestral practice of donning the clothes of one's victim, Túpac Amaru II may have wished to summon in his favor the *corregidor*'s status and political clout and to flaunt his newly acquired authority not just before his indigenous supporters but also before other mestizos, creoles, and Spaniards.[16] Later, in visits throughout southern Peru, Túpac Amaru II was said to have worn an *uncu* as he sought to assert his affiliation with the Inca dynasty and his personal identification with Túpac Amaru I in order to secure support from indigenous peoples, on which depended the rebellion's chances of success.[17]

Túpac Amaru II was captured and executed by the general *visitador* (surveyor) José Antonio Areche in 1782. In the death sentence, which condemned the rebel to be present at the execution of his wife and two children, to have his tongue severed, and to be quartered by four horses in the main plaza of the city of Cuzco, Areche outlined the main offenses of the self-proclaimed Inca descendant. Notably among them was to have had his portrait made decked in an *uncu* and a *mascaipacha* (Inca royal headdress), motifs that, according to Areche, aroused great emotion among native peoples. Areche also used the occasion of Túpac Amaru II's sentence to decree mandatory changes in the behavior and customs of "Indians," which he believed had contributed to creating the conditions for such rebellion: From the moment of the reading of the sentence on, indigenous people would be forbidden to play the *pututo* and other native wind instruments, to stage plays dealing with pre-Hispanic themes, to build cannons or use gunpowder, and finally, but critically, to ever again wear native dresses, in particular those of the nobility, "which only serve to represent the ones worn by their old Incas, recalling memories that do nothing but bring about more and more hatred toward the dominant nation [the Spanish], in addition [to the fact] that their appearance is ridiculous and not in conformity with the purity of our religion, since in various parts [of their dress] they portray the sun, who is their main deity, [and] this resolution will extend to all the provinces of this South America, leaving those dresses completely extinguished."[18]

Areche's sentence is thus hailed as the turning point in the emergence in Peru of an indigenous "folk" or "traditional" dress. The Spanish costume was from then on mandated for all native peoples—but only that of the peasantry back in the Iberian Peninsula. This seems to have been the compromise that allowed the Spaniards and the growing *criollo* and mestizo classes to give commerce a boost and still preserve the social and political meanings denoted by some Spanish garments. In their new peasant dress, native groups were permitted to maintain regional differences in style and color, for which infinity of trimmings and accessories—embroidered ribbons, laces, fancy buttons, silk shawls, gauss kerchiefs, and velvet—were imported from Europe. Indigenous men gave up the *uncu* and the *wara* to replace them with pants and exchanged the *llauto* for the hat. Women stopped wearing *anacus* or adapted them to be worn under their new dress, which was modeled, with key local variations, after the Andalusian and Extremeño female peasant custom and consisted of a knee-high, multilayered skirt or *pollera* (sometimes ten or fifteen), an embroidered blouse, a small felt hat over a braided hairdo, a shawl, baggy underwear trousers, and heeled leather shoes.[19] From this point on, indigenous women's dresses would be more elaborate than the men's and would be made to carry, in the regional variations of hats, skirts, and shawls, a great deal of differentiated meanings proper to each town and ethnic group. The statement by anthropologist Marisol de la Cadena that women in the Andes are "more Indian" than their male counterparts derives in part from this role of carriers of ethnic identification and transmitters of tradition that, mainly through language and through dress, Andean women have been charged with.[20]

As in the rural areas, "folk" indigenous dress, particularly the female one, was also overtaxed with meaning, although of a whole different kind, when it was transported into the urban context by way of migration. In Lima, for instance, Deborah Poole remarks through her analysis of nineteenth-century representations of city women by European travelers that "Indian" women were thought of as fundamentally different from the other female "types" largely because of their dress. Poole shows that in representations of black or mulatto women and of *criollo Limeño* women (in the figure of the *tapada*, for example), the traits of their "typical" costume are secondary to the women's bodies and imputed sexuality. Oppositely, in the case of indigenous women, the artists' heightened interest in and minutely detailed depiction of their dress has "the effect of virtually eclipsing the existence of the body or woman inside the costume."[21] It was as if the dress masked their body and their sex; through their dress, indigenous women were fetishized, Poole writes, as "surface, as gloss"—or, one could say, as pure costume—and made visible only as the backdrop against which other, more "real" subjects were depicted.[22]

Through the nineteenth and early twentieth centuries, indigenous people's dress went on to experience further regional diversification and transformed to reflect mutations in the meaning of social categories, such as *indio*, mestizo, and *cholo*, brought about by increasingly more fluid transitions between the countryside and the city. A quick survey of the literature on migration and *mestizaje* in Peru reveals the weight that is now assigned to clothing—far and above phenotype and skin color—in effecting (or impeding) the emergence of new identities in the urban milieu. The style of the skirt or shirt, the type and quality of the fabric, its appearance and cleanliness, and the persistence of certain elements of indigenous "traditional" dress has produced what De la Cadena, writing about mid-twentieth-century *mestizaje* in the city of Cuzco, refers to as an "ethnic continuum." To illustrate the degree of self and social scrutiny that takes place regarding clothing, De la Cadena notes that Cuzqueño women "ranked" each other according to a scale that was largely based on women's attire and that went from indigenous or *mujercitas* (small women), to *mestizas simples* (simple *mestizas*), to *buenas mestizas* (good *mestizas*), to *casi damas* (almost ladies), to *damas* (ladies). The perception that mestizo women are different from indigenous women is thus not racial, De la Cadena asserts. "Rather, it approaches a conceptual understanding of ethnicity as cultural attributes that can be acquired and disacquired, and that distinguishes fluidly among individuals rather than rigidly among groups."[23] While the changing of clothes

does convey "de-Indianization," De la Cadena stresses that transformation through physical appearance should be interpreted less as a flat-out
rejection of indigenous ways than as a sign of changes in the person's
social and economic power.[24]

In Lima, as in most other urban centers, features of indigenous dress
are generally met with ridicule and rejected by individuals of all social
standings. For this reason, immigrant men, upon arriving in the city, often give up the hat and the poncho, and women shed their shawls and
polleras in favor of a skirt with less or no flare, a simpler blouse, no hat,
and a plain, cropped hairstyle.[25] With this change, migrants also seek to
shed the "Indian" identity—the ethnic affiliation that was imposed on
them with the Spanish conquest and that positioned them in the last
echelon of colonial and postcolonial society—for membership in the
broader, more amorphous, and ever elusive category of mestizo.

———

In one of the better known anthropological works dealing specifically
with the subject of dress, Terence S. Turner refers to clothing—to the
forms in which individuals of all societies cover or decorate their bodies
according to notions of everyday propriety—as "the social skin."[26] In
this text, Turner argues that the surface of the skin functions as the
frontier of the individual, both of the biological and psychological self
as well as of the social self. As such, the skin is where the "drama of
socialization" takes place through the cultural medium of dress, which
according to Turner is the medium "most specialized in the shaping and
communication of personal and social identity."[27]

Zeroing in on the code of dress of the Kayapo people of the southern
edges of the Amazon forest, Turner argues that even apparently naked
bodies, such as those of the Kayapo, are covered in a fabric of cultural
meanings that convey social status, beliefs, desires, and ideals. He explains that Kayapo propriety in bodily appearance is anchored in ideas
of cleanliness, particularly in relation to bodily hair and substances such
as food and blood, which are thought to bring illness when left un-
washed. While the Kayapo idea of health is a state of full and proper
integration into the social world, Turner explains that illness is "conceived in terms of the encroachment of natural, and particularly animal
forces upon the domain of social relations."[28] Thus cleanliness, tidiness,
and proper adornment according to gender and life stage are key expressions of a person's healthy level of sociality—with the Kayapo distinctive
hairstyle of a forehead shaved upwards to a point at the crown of the

head representing the highest level of social integration that can possibly be attained by a human being.

What can be gathered from Turner's observations is that, for the Kayapo, it is mainly their dress and their adornments that effect the transformation from the primal, animal world into the human world by imposing the boundaries and the discontinuities of social form on an indistinct, unsocialized, and continuous reality. From Turner's article it is possible to infer that a Kayapo concept for nakedness would imply the unshaping of the social world, its reintegration to the realm of unsocialized nature, and its dissolution into animality, a state associated with children and with those in mourning and to which the Kayapo periodically seek to return ritually not by revealing body parts but by further adorning themselves and "animalizing" their human dress with painted animal designs, feathers, and blood, and by enacting dances and songs believed to have originated among wild animals and birds.[29]

Today, in the Quechua-speaking communities of the southern highlands of Peru, dress has a similar ability to shape and unshape the social world, a function that is made manifest in the multiple meanings of the Quechua word *qala*. *Qala* translates literally as "naked" or "peeled," and is used to refer to individuals viewed as outsiders, in contrast to *runa*, a self-descriptive term that means "person" or "people." The different uses of the word *qala* have carried over into the Spanish *calato* to mean not just naked or bare (as in *pata cala*, "bare feet," or *poto calato*, "bare butt") but also, metaphorically, to refer to a dispossessed person or to a young child. In communities like the Ayacuchan village of Chuschi studied by Billie Jean Isbell in the 1960s and '70s, the term *qala* was also used to refer derogatorily to residents of the village who spoke Spanish and wore Western dress, as opposed to *comunero* (commoner peasant).[30] Isbell says that she was once told that *qala* used to refer to villagers who had left to the city and come back wearing shoes instead of sandals; when the group of wealthier, mestizo residents in the village grew in size, the term *qala* and *qalakuna* ("peeled" or "naked" people) was extended to them to convey their non-*runa* status and the fact that they were prone to identifying themselves first as Peruvian nationals rather than *Chuschinos*.[31] Today, the term *qala* is still used as an insult in towns of the region to refer to migrants who return from a stint in the city dressed in mestizo clothes.[32] This is more markedly so with young women returnees, whom the village's older señoras greet with sneers and comments such as "Poor thing, she must no longer have enough to even buy a *pollera*."[33] *Comuneros* believe that the clothes acquired in the city are not only more revealing of the body but, first and foremost, made of a thinner, lighter, and therefore

cheaper material than the heavily woven woolen fabric and the embroidered cotton cloth employed in the making of local dresses. The implication is that with the shedding of *comunero* clothes there is an impoverishment of the person, a thinning or peeling off of the sheath that transforms
a being, a nonperson, into a human and cultural being. "One might say,"
writes Isbell to explain the *comunero* perspective on this issue of dress, "that
the *qalakuna* have peeled off their indigenous identity."[34] But this statement is only partially accurate, for the *qalakuna* have also peeled off their
personhood, some fundamental aspect of their condition as humans.

Isbell remarks that in Chuschi the opposition between *qalas* and *runas*
resembles that between rival ethnicities in the sense that the two groups
do not intermarry and do not belong to the same circles of exchange.
In fact, in the eyes of *comuneros*, *qalas* are "foreigners" who are not tied
to the community by the same bonds of reciprocity and ritual responsibility that *runas* are. *Qalas*, without exception, live on or near the town
plaza (in many cases the core of an old *reducción*) where all things foreign
are located, including the municipal and district offices, the schools, the
church, and the stores. *Qalas* are thus residents in the same village; however, in their rituals, *comuneros* represent them as embodying a negative,
outsider power against which the community must defend itself. In the
personification of a priest, of soldiers, or of schoolteachers, they appear
in ritual dramas next to other outsiders of dubious or suspect humanity,
such as the indigenous people of the lowland tropical forest known to
the villagers as *chunchus*, who according to the villagers also go about
"naked" and who are believed to epitomize antisocial behavior.[35] Along
with the *chunchus*, *qalas* are ritually classified together with the dreaded
naqaq, the supernatural being who is said to go around stealing body
fat, eating babies, and castrating men. Isbell argues that these representations of *qalas*, *chunchus*, and *naqaq* as foreign entities, threatening of
the community, express and reinforce the closed, corporate quality of
Chuschino society, which is also continually reaffirmed by the *comuneros'* endogamous marriage patterns as opposed to the *qalas'* exogamic
preferences, which lead them to establish links with nonvillagers or seek
alliances with persons from the district capital. *Runas*, by contrast, favor
marriage contracts within the community between members of different *ayllus* (bilateral kindred) and *kuyaqs* (exchange circles). Unions with
outsiders are viewed as perilous to the integrity of the community and
are avoided, just as are the unions between members of the same *ayllu*
or *kuyaq*, which are tabooed and considered incestuous.

It is in the context of Isbell's treatment of the incest taboo among
Chuschinos that one gains insight into the place of nakedness in the

enforcement of social rules and in the punishment of the transgression of these rules. According to Isbell, villagers believe that individuals who engage in incestuous relations are condemned to wander at night in the bodily form of a domestic animal, a dog, a pig, or a donkey, wearing human clothes or a bell around their necks; if touched, the condemned ones transform back to human shape and reveal their identities. Isbell relates the story of a man and his adolescent daughter who were caught by the village *varayoq* (mayor) seducing each other and playfully pulling off each other's clothes while up in the *sallqa* (the highest regions of the Andes, which *Chuschinos* consider to be savage). The man and the young woman, the story goes, were apprehended by the *varayoq* and taken down to the village plaza, where for two days they were publicly displayed naked and barefoot for all the villagers to see and revile. Isbell says that, as the *varayoq* whipped the couple, the crowd pelted them with vegetables and garbage.[36]

In a study of consuetudinary law in peasant communities of the Andes, Hans-Jürgen Brandt mentions forced nakedness as a common form of punishment—he calls it a "penalty of honor"—which he lists among other types of retribution, such as beatings, ostracism, and death, used by communities to sanction transgressions of the law.[37] Brandt tells of the case of three men in a peasant community in Ancash (north of Lima) who were caught as they were about to steal cattle from a herder. According to Brandt, the men were locked away in the town's jail, tried later in a public assembly, and sentenced to walk naked three times around the town's plaza in front of all the *comuneros*, before being expulsed and banned from ever returning to the community. Brandt states that the purpose of this punitive action was to intimidate the men, to ridicule them so that they wouldn't dare to come back, and remarks that this form of public scorn is nowadays rarely applied, particularly since the heavily regulated *rondas campesinas* (armed peasant policing rounds) have been officially put in place, oftentimes not just for policing but also for the administration of justice. The *rondas'* regulations, Brandt states to back his point, forbid the use of insults and the humiliation of detainees.[38]

The forced stripping of clothes as a form of punishment might indeed be applied today only in rare cases. However, in the drawings accompanying the early seventeenth-century narrative by mestizo chronicler Felipe Guamán Poma de Ayala, the nakedness of bodies stands out in the context of his description of common forms of punishment of "Indians," used both in pre-Hispanic as well as postconquest times. Judging from the images and from Guamán Poma's text (even though textual

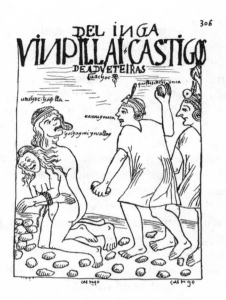

"Of the Inca. Punishment for (female) Adulterers."

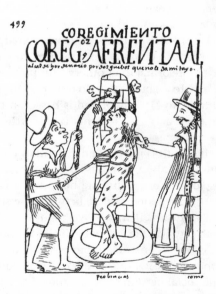

"*Corregidor* [Spanish justice administrator] confronts the mayor for two eggs that he did not receive from *mitayo* [taxpayer]."

references to the use of forced nudity are few and very general), it seems that the forced stripping of clothes often complemented punishment by whipping, stoning, and ostracism, for offenses as varied as adultery, lust, stealing, drunkenness, murder, perjury, and laziness. One of the images shows two individuals during Inca times as they are stoned to death for adultery and another one a man as he is lashed by order of the *corregidor* for defaulting in a payment of two eggs. It seems telling of the "meaning" of nakedness that the only other context in Guamán Poma's chronicle where naked bodies are also prominent is in his depictions of *chunchus* from the eastern *suyu* of the Inca empire, who appear in the drawings wearing waistcloths and displaying bare torsos and breasts next to wild, jungle animals or entirely covered in feathers like birds. These images stand in stark contrast to the representations of individuals from the other three *suyus* who appear heavily decked in *uncus* and *llicllas*.[39]

Benjamin Orlove, in his study of ritual battles between communities of the southern highlands of Peru, says that the stripping of clothes is an integral aspect of the violent treatment directed at "prisoners" taken by either of the rival communities during these confrontations.[40] Orlove's main focus is the different kinds of violence used in *Ch'iaraje*, one of the most common forms of periodic, ritual fighting, where the taking and killing of prisoners, as he explains, is governed by the same logic of reciprocity that regulates communal labor and the sponsorship of feasts. From local accounts of these battles, Orlove infers that there is, for both *comuneros* and mestizos, a gradation of violence, in which certain acts are perceived to be more brutal than others. This progresses in ascending order from (1) insults, to (2) blows that do not break the skin, to (3) blows that make blood flow, to (4) killing, and is based on the perceived degree of harm that these acts inflict (rather than on the intention or the weapons used).

Orlove states that both *comuneros* and mestizos consider the forced stripping of clothes and the public display of the naked body to be a violent act, whose degree of cruelty and harm lies somewhere between the third and fourth categories, that is, between the shedding of blood and the infliction of death. If in the West emphasis is placed on the skin as the natural, physical boundary of the body and the person, and the stripping of clothes is construed more as an act of humiliation than of violence, in the Andes, Orlove remarks, "cloth and clothing [are] constitutive of the social person, so that removal of a person's clothing resembles wounding a person's body." The perceived injury, he notes, is extended further to the loss of the clothing itself; whereas in the

West the feeling of exposure and vulnerability ends once the person's body is again covered or decently dressed, in the Andes this is only the case when the clothes that were stripped off are returned to the injured person.[41]

More recently, during the war between Sendero and the Peruvian army (1980–c. 1993), which started in Ayacucho and ravaged this region of the country, forced strippings were part of the punishment inflicted to alleged *soplones* (whistle-blowers) or *chismosos* (gossipmongers), as is illustrated by a painted *tabla* of Sarhua, where a woman, entirely naked, has been left for display in the plaza and a man with bare torso is being whipped on the back by an authority. The caption to the painting reads:

A difficult moment arrived one couldn't speak circulate rumors gossip about occurrences—plans mistakes of the "*onqoy*" [sickness] terrorists was completely forbidden when they found out they punished cruelly in the public plaza forcing at gun point in the presence of the community they gave 25 to 50 strokes with the whip—cut hair and ear of the men according to possible fault cut braided hair and stripped naked the women amid tears terror relatives had to withstand horrendous punishment—never occurred in history—that destroy the good customs of the community generating unpardonable hatred and chaos.[42]

Lastly, in the context of the city, especially Lima, the forced stripping of clothes is known to be a component of acts of lynching, with which residents of the relatively new, outer districts of Lima have come to sporadically settle robberies, sexual offenses (especially if it involves minors), and other crimes. This modality of punishment by lynching begins with the apprehension of the suspect by a crowd of *vecinos* (local residents), who most often strip off the offender's clothes, shave his head, and either (try to) bury him alive, burn him alive, or tie him to a pole where he is beaten or stoned to death. In an article dealing with the subject in *Caretas*, all the men depicted in pictures while in the process of being lynched have had their clothes totally or partially removed.[43] Hernando de Soto, in his book on Peru's burgeoning "culture of informality," and A. T. Revilla and J. Price, the authors of a text dealing specifically with the issue of "informal justice," list public nakedness, along with the shaving of heads and banishment from the district, among the forms of punishment often inflicted by urban lynch mobs against common delinquents and sexual offenders, even when these acts do not lead to the person's death.[44] For these authors "popular execution" and other kinds of communal punishment are the obvious

"Punishment for the *soplones* [informers]."

result of notorious shortcomings in the country's formal legal system, although none of them explain why they take the form that they do.

In the illustrations accompanying a contemporary "chronicle" modeled after Guamán Poma's early colonial account, Eduardo Vidal has represented this kind of urban lynching in the image titled "Linchamiento / Justicia por propia mano." The legend next to the image reads in part: "When a robber is found 'in fraganti' [red-handed] on a street block, people quickly arrive. They surround him, kick him, beat him, and drag him to a place where he is buried alive. The police, who couldn't cover that area of the city, alerted by phone, arrive and save the 'victim.' Sometimes they do not arrive, and no one ever learns [what happened]."[45]

As stated earlier, Guamán Poma openly depicts the chastising nakedness of "Indians" but speaks little about it; Brandt affirms that forced and public nakedness as a penalty is applied only rarely today in communities

"Lynching."

of the Andes; and the caption from Sarhua's painted *tabla* asserts that the punishment inflicted on the woman by terrorists had "never occurred in history." It should not be surprising, then, that the authors of this contemporary chronicle, when speaking about the new modality of urban lynching, leave out from the text one of the most striking aspects in Vidal's image: that the man in the process of being lynched is completely naked.

———

If, as all these sources suggest, clothing helps turn individuals into social beings and the act of unclothing them strips them of their personhood, under what circumstances does public nudity, used in Peru as a socially sanctioned punitive measure against offenders, become an act of aggression against society? Or, more pointedly, how does the bearing of one's body in public, which is most often degrading of the person who disrobes, become instead degrading of others?

This last question drove much of Shirley Ardener's work in the 1970s, which she developed in the context of a still active protest culture in England and the United States. Ardener was intrigued by certain dissent strategies used at that time, whose political persuasiveness seemed to depend on their ability to "invert normal codes of conduct" in those societies.[46] In particular, Ardener was concerned with acts of nudity and vulgarity, such as "bra burning" or "mooning," that were deployed against entities of power perceived to be offensive or oppressive. She turned for explanations to ethnographic descriptions of what are said to be customary techniques of dissent involving nudity among women in Cameroon and Kenya, which they employ to confront male relatives and state authorities in retaliation for actions and policies thought to be aggressive or unfavorable to women.

In the first article that she published on the subject, Ardener lays out the crux of her argument: If in every society there is a zone of social interaction that prescribes polite and deferential behavior, she says, there is always also an "underside" of that zone, whose exposure constitutes what we call "vulgarity" and "obscenity." Most frequently, the exposure of this underside brings shame and humiliation onto the person who is effecting the exposure. But on occasion, as indicated by the African ethnographic material she reviews, acts of lewdness perpetrated by women and directed toward men can produce a transformation, whereby, as she puts it, female shame is replaced by honor, and male honor is replaced by shame.[47] In those African settings, when one or more women expressed their anger or discontent by stripping naked or by displaying and directing their vagina, buttocks, or breasts toward the offender, the gesture conveyed disrespect and denial of dominance and placed a curse or carried a death wish toward the man or men to which it was directed. These acts, which Ardener describes as "militant techniques," often took place alongside the chanting of obscene songs and gesticulations that, like their naked body parts, women directed toward the men, causing them to turn away, avert their eyes, or flee.

Patricia Chuchryk, Temma Kaplan, and Jennifer Schirmer refer to the same kind of transformation—from female shame to honor and from male honor to shame—in their work on women's political cultures in the context of the violent military dictatorships in Latin America in the 1970s and '80s. They all focus on the fact that the effectiveness of women's actions against these regimes seemed to stem from their decision to mobilize not just as women but, more importantly, as "mothers."[48] As with the well-known case of the Madres de la Plaza de Mayo in Argentina, who protested the disappearance of their sons and daughters in the hands of the state, women across the region have used their bodies and resorted to activities traditionally associated with motherhood and domesticity, typically absent or undervalued in the public sphere, to precisely have a stronger impact in it. The political force of the mother, according to Kaplan, resides in her ability to make a "spectacle" of herself with the intention of "embarrassing those who have placed them in their current predicament."[49]

In relation to what Schirmer refers to as the "protectiveness of motherhood," Kaplan makes the important observation that rank-and-file soldiers and policemen generally share women's perceptions of themselves in their role of mothers and thus do not welcome occasions when they have to confront them around what they claim are survival issues. The reluctance to attack women who are pursuing their families' survival interests, Kaplan argues, gives women a leverage that men of their same class and race could never have. This leverage is attained, as Chuchryk explains also for the case of Chile, through the inversion of women's and especially mothers' traditional public invisibility by appearing in the political scene and drawing attention to their troubles through unconventional methods of protest. These may include dancing, going on hunger strikes, or chaining themselves to the gates of government buildings. They also may include dressing up, for example, as "upper-class" women to demonstrate in the streets, or wearing distinctive articles, such as the familiar white head scarves of the Madres de la Plaza de Mayo, who turned a symbol of women's modesty into a sign of subversion. By manipulating conventional meanings of sex, gender, and class, Chuchryk argues, the women deployed an aspect of women's identities that is normally excluded from the political arena, such as motherhood is, precisely in order to justify their presence in it and to make their demands legitimate just "because they *were* wives and mothers."[50]

Writing about women's use of obscenity in political contexts, Ardener argues that the very existence of terms of propriety and of signs for demonstrating respect and submission through particular forms of address, speech, and behavior allows for the generation of contrary expressions, marked with the opposite value, and for antithetic behavior rooted in the symbolic force of obscenity and the inherent power of vulgarity.[51] The consistency and effectiveness of actions involving female nudity, particularly that of women who are or are perceived as mothers, would derive from the potent symbolic value that societies place on certain parts of the body—of what Ardener calls the "symbolic sexual body"—like the vagina and in some instances the breasts, which are required by society's terms of propriety to be hidden.[52] When offended or unfairly treated, instead of conforming to the terms of propriety, women deliberately draw attention to their otherwise concealed bodies, shaming the offender by resorting to the same logic of propriety to transform the symbol's meaning from a negative to a positive one, making of the women's "hidden secrets a dominant and public emblem."[53]

The capacity to switch the meaning of an action or an object from a negative to a positive one is crucial to Ardener's interpretation of women's use of obscenity in political settings. Much of her attention is on the potentially libratory or empowering outcomes of these "militant techniques." She refers, for instance, to a 1955 case of *Anlu* brought about by Kom women in Cameroon against a government measure that would force women to adapt their traditional farming techniques to include practices that were more sustainable but also significantly more arduous. After the great upheaval produced by *Anlu*, Ardener notes that "eventually... things settled down, although to a new order," as the police, who were enforcing the new measure, decided to take no further action and the *Anlu* leader was invited to be a part of the local council.[54]

Like Ardener, others have emphasized the positive results obtained by female participation in community or national politics through analogous forms of behavior.[55] Most recently, Turner and Brownhill write about the benefits brought about by the 2003 takeover of several petroleum plants in the Niger Delta by peasant women whose major threat to company and government officials was that they would shed their clothes and expose their naked bodies to the men so as to inflict upon them "social death." According to the article detailing the events, with their "curse of nakedness" the women had implicitly stated that they would "get their demands met or die in the process of trying" and had in fact managed to have many of their claims addressed, such as more schools, more jobs, and more participation in decision making.[56]

Conversely, other literature about women's political cultures in Africa and Latin America paint a more complex picture. For instance, in an article dealing with *Anlu* among the Kom, Audrey Wipper reviews other works on women's use of nakedness in Africa and concludes that, at best, the results of the women's political actions have been mixed and often difficult to ascertain.[57] Having to resort to extra-legal channels to voice their grievances, she says, their ventures into the political arena generally come at great cost to them in time and effort. Already overburdened with demands as wives and mothers, farmers and traders, for African women to engage in a riot is "a drain on their already taxed resources," a reality that makes their participation over an extended period of time impossible for most women. Wipper also notes that in forms of female militancy like *Anlu*, the leaders most often remain anonymous and go unrewarded, unlike men at the forefront of grassroots political struggles, who are often acknowledged and later co-opted into formal or public positions. She concludes that

although these sanctioning devices [use of nudity, for instance] worked well when applied to individuals, they were not so effective when used against the colonial regime. A basic weakness of female militancy is that when the explosive aspect is over, there tends to be a return to the status quo or a slightly altered status quo. Women tend to rely on the grand gesture, ad hoc ventures into the political arena that require verve and audacity, are dramatic and heroic, and may temporarily immobilize the system but which lack the sustained effort needed to bring about deep rooted structural change.[58]

Schirmer arrives at similar conclusions about women's mobilizations as mothers in Latin America. Writing about the Grupo de Apoyo Mutuo in Guatemala (GAM) and the Agrupación de Familiares de Detenidos-Desaparecidos in Chile (AFDD), both groups formed by women in the context of brutal state repression, Schirmer remarks that, having achieved "coherence and continuity," these movements grew to represent a temporary suspension of all institutional control by symbolically embodying the rule of law in lieu of the government, which came to represent the institutionalization of death. On the other hand, she notes that after having claimed important political space, these groups tended to be "eclipsed by the dominant political forces." Once processes of re-democratization were under way, many of these groups, Schirmer explains, have been charged with interfering with the democratic process and have not been granted institutional hearing. "In the act of re-democratization," she writes, "these women [were] once again marginalized politically, and the traditional gender roles which had been transformed by the immediacy of repression [fell] back into place."[59] Diana Taylor, for her part, sees similar results in the activism of the Madres in Argentina. While they challenged traditional maternal roles by becoming visible outside the confines of the home, physically and politically, and while they succeeded in calling attention to the social (not just the biological) construction of motherhood, the Madres "have not altered the politics of the home, for example, the gendered division of labor; after coming home from their demonstrations most of them still cooked and did housework... even in those cases in which the husbands were at home full time."[60]

What these more sober conclusions underscore is the eminently transgressive nature of the women's presence in the political arena in the various contexts discussed and the fact that this transgressive element is at once the reason their participation and methods of action were effective and the reason they ultimately failed in effecting lasting change. For, as Wipper suggests, the women's actions did not so much bring them into the political fold as temporarily broke through the logic of reasoning that excluded them from it. With their actions it was as if the "mediators" of de Beauvoir's critique (and of Ortner's and Rubin's arguments) had stepped out of this role and dislocated the dialectic that positions them as intermediaries between nature and culture, as mere catalysts of the political sphere. What the cases of political activism reviewed here suggest is that rather than effecting an inversion of social meaning, as Ardener would have it, rather than turning a negative into a positive, the women's transgressions were acts of self-extrication from the realm of meaning, a thrusting forth of what de Beauvoir calls women's "more manifest animality" and a risking of life that opened up a space where all meanings are possible and therefore none are.

When Wipper says that the "explosive aspect" of women's militancy and their reliance on dramatic gestures "may temporarily immobilize the system" but fail as a long-term strategy, she is referring, even if unwittingly, to the problematic relation between transgression and politics, the issue of the advantages and limitations of using transgression as a means to political ends, and the challenge of articulating transgressive acts within the discriminating and calculating consciousness required by political action. In other words, Wipper's concluding remarks set forth for our consideration the political utility of transgression with its dependence on a delicate balance between unexpectedness and expectedness, between its condition of unreasoned impulse and its reliance on the existence of firm rules. The violation of a taboo is shocking (that is, effective) insofar as it is an extraordinary breach of an ordinary rule, insofar as it is an unpredictable contravention of a predictable custom loaded with long-standing personal, cultural, and historical significance—such as are the rules, ideas, and customs regarding motherhood. In this shaky balance, transgression depends on that unexpected element to produce "a breakdown—an interruption—of the rules [in which] the regular course of things ceases [and] what originally had the meaning of limit has that of shattering limits."[61]

As the shattering of limits, transgression undoes Ardener's distinction between positive and negative. It undoes the distinction between power and powerlessness and brings forth a sovereign moment that abolishes the anticipation of political strategy.[62]

EIGHT

Last Entry

Thursday: Last night my father's car broke down. At the last minute, I had to get myself to the airport in a cab. As I was running late, I asked the driver to take the Costa Verde freeway and thus cut through the impossible rush hour traffic between Miraflores and Maranga.

Down below, night was quickly falling on the water. Surfers in their wet suits walked near the road looking like dark, long-winged birds ran ashore after a day's stint in the sea. Some loaded their boards up on their cars while others got ready to climb the cliff by foot. The headlights coming from behind the curves threw light intermittently on the crashing waves, which were fluorescent white against the darkening void. Leaving Miraflores and San Isidro behind, at the end of a steep, downward slope we were greeted by a weather-beaten billboard that said, "Playa Contaminada" (Contaminated Beach). There, the dirt and debris go right to the edge of the water, which is a flat, murky brown. Bright plastic bags and old tires top the mounds of garbage and slip into the water when the tide is high, floating on the surface until some obstinate limp wave spits them out again. The entire way I rode with the window rolled down, wistfully taking mouthfuls of the ocean's slightly fishy smell.

Once back up, we drove down Avenida La Marina through a stretch that has exploded into a vast compound of department stores, fast food restaurants, slot machine houses, casinos, Turkish baths, and night clubs of tawdry façades and Anglicized names, which give tangible form to what the United States looks like in people's fantasies. They read (in English): "New York Casino," "Crazy Sandwich,"

"Full Body Spa," in countless dusty neon tubes protruding from the front of each business. In this section of the city, which is said to be the commercial artery with highest sales in all of Peru, prosperity has a sordid, decadent face as the sudden bonanza of a few years ago has crossed the line into excess and turned areas of the city like this one into hubs of modernity's favorite vices.

Despite a bottleneck of cars where Avenidas Faucett and Colonial intersect, the taxi driver got me to the airport with enough time to check in and buy a couple bottles of pisco for gifts before going to the gate. I traveled with José María Arguedas's last novel, *El zorro de arriba y el zorro de abajo*, which was published posthumously and in which (drafts of) chapters are flanked by diary entries he wrote as he struggled to sort out the threads of the novel's plot and as he, carefully and self-consciously, also plotted his suicide. The setting of the story is not the sunny, rural landscapes of the Andes, as is the case with most of his other novels, but the grim and fetid industrial atmosphere of the fishing port of Chimbote, some two hundred miles north of Lima. The narrative, set in the 1960s, centers on life in one of the *barriadas* surrounding the port and on a group of uprooted highland migrants, who make a living as fishermen, fishmeal factory laborers, and prostitutes, as they find themselves in the grip of contradictory and alienating forces regarding power and corruption, forestalling the urban *anomie* that many believe has been the hallmark of Lima from the 1980s on.

Waiting for the plane to take off the ground, I browsed through the novel once again, noticing how the lives of its characters surge in intensity at the same pace as Arguedas's own life sinks into hopelessness, a process that unravels in the diaries along with his solidifying desire to die and his emboldening tone of raw candor, honesty, and surrender, which he adopts, ironically, as he confessedly is "unable to stop thinking that [the diaries] will once be read."[1] Digging himself deeper into this contradiction, he later writes,

I think I am speaking with "audacity" only because of my utterly sick soul, and not because I believe that these pages will be published only after I have hung myself or blown off the top of my skull with a bullet. . . . It may also be that I get cured here, in Santiago [de Chile] . . . and if I do get cured and some friend I respect says that the publication of these pages would be useful, I would publish them. Because if I don't write and publish, I shoot myself.[2]

This book by Arguedas draws much of its strength and beauty from this paradox, from the mix of self-consciousness and honesty that is a kind of aporetic element in diary writing. This element was at the center of the debate among Anglo-American anthropologists after the publishing event of the most infamous diary in the discipline, Malinowski's *A Diary in the Strict Sense of the Term*. Of course, when he says that his is a diary "in the strict sense of the term," he's referring to the frankness and presumed lack of intention with which he writes about experiences that, in the context of doing fieldwork, many of us endure and go on to suppress in our ethnographies, the personal minutiae of tensions and distractions we confront when away "in the field" and the compulsive worries and habits with which we seek to ease them—which, in the case of Malinowski, involved drugs, unrelenting depression, unrelenting insecurity, and unrelenting dislike for the people among whom he worked. But, I don't think it was these alone that put Malinowski's reputation on the line and that rocked the foundations of an entire discipline. These diaries had the effect they had only in light of the other texts he published after that trip, particularly *Argonauts of the Western Pacific*, which some of us anthropologists love to juxtapose with the diaries to see how they alter the picture Malinowski had rendered of Trobriand life, of the all-important *kula*, of the *kula*'s legacy for the study of the gift. As I write this, however, I am inclined to turn this question around and suggest that what diaries like Malinowski's and Arguedas's bring into relief is the extent to which, no matter how excruciatingly intimate or how close to death, writing is itself a kind of *kula*, is itself like the gift, being fueled as much by selfishness as selflessness, an expression of total generosity and disinterest, yet always in expectation of a return.

After a long wait on the runway, in what seemed like the middle of nowhere, the plane finally took off. As it climbed higher, the lights on the ground gradually became smaller and sparser, shining dimly in random clusters, like stars in an inverted sky. Shaking, the plane pierced through the thick bed of clouds that hangs above Lima and wisps of white mist hurried past my window. I thought of the whiteness of Melville's whale, of his description of the city as "ruins forever new." I thought of Señora Roberta and of Andrade's intention to wed, in a single, redemptive stroke, the apparently irreconcilable notions of tradition and modernity with the idea that modernity will be achieved only by reclaiming tradition, and in the process reconfigure the convulsive history of the city into a version of the past that is bleached out of all racial and sexual violence and class conflict.

As for Señora Roberta, her transgression, if nothing else, is a blotch of ink in this bleached-out picture of Lima's past. Unlike the Nigerian mothers, who are said to have used the threat of nakedness effectively against the transnational oil industry, stating that "they would get their demands or die in the process of trying," Señora Roberta, by contrast, achieved neither. None of her demands were met, and she met no death. Before and after her stripping, there seems to have been only pain and anguish—"pure despair" she called it—the terrifying depths of an abyss into which, as far as she could tell, she had jumped, like one of those desperate Chinese women often described in the Western press as seeking escape from their dire conditions by jumping into the village's water well, drowning, and polluting the water supply. But Señora Roberta did not die; she jumped only to find herself in a continuation of the same despairing reality, back in the downward path that is leading her to what, without a secure job, with a chronically sick son and an aching and rapidly aging body, promises to be more pain and more despair. With her transgression, law and its infringement crossed paths and totally exchanged their beings in the person of her bursting forth "like a flash of lightning in the night which . . . loses itself in this space it marks with its sovereignty and becomes silent now that it has given a name to obscurity."[3]

This realization goes right to the heart of the inclination that, as an anthropologist, I initially had to interpret the street sweepers' transgression not as an act of abasement, of utter and unreserved self-degradation, but as an act of resistance and vindication; it goes to the heart of my desire to construe it not as the already lost search for life and justice through self-annihilation, through the denunciation of all human worth, but as a redeeming pursuit that, with or without Señora Roberta's knowledge, elevated her over and above the mundane quality of her suffering. More than about her, the idea of resistance strikes me now as part of our very own reservoir of hope from where we, as anthropologists, somewhat desperate ourselves, draw amply to address our own sense of helplessness about a people for whom we grow to feel genuine concern, whom one way or another we grow to love, but for whom we feel we cannot do anything. For Señora Roberta there is really no redemption, just as there is no redemption for this lost city. She polluted an already-tainted well.

"Lima, the way it once was." So what about the longing for a city that has truly never existed beyond the urban panegyrics of the seventeenth century? Salazar Bondy, through his notion of "Colonial Arcadia," says that the idea of an idyllic period in Lima's past is indeed a historical mirage but suggests that its perdurable force stems from the fact that such wealth, abundance, and ostentation were once true for a very small colonial elite, a reality that blinds us to the harsher one of a colonized people divided along caste lines. Alejandra Osorio, for her part, argues that Lima's idyllic image was deliberately created back in the city's early baroque period through the writings of self-flattering paeans and through their public enactment in city streets as a tactic vital to the city's fight for power and dominion in a fragile hierarchy of strategically positioned urban centers in America. Osorio believes that *Limeños'* concern with creating and projecting this image during the city's early days—affirming and holding in magical balance its propensity toward order and excess, religiosity and mischief—was part of the eminently modern process of identity making, which, as Osorio argues, was (and is) a process hugely dependent on simulacra, on the public performance of power and beauty as a way of making them real.

Mirage or simulacra, this constructed image of Lima's past is now intertwined in the history of the city. It might well be a fallacy, but it is as integral to the city as are its oldest or most admired buildings and plazas, as much a landmark of its identity as are its river and surrounding dry hills. And it seems to be integral not just to the history of the city but to the personal histories of many of its residents in that, as with Mayor Andrade, it has somehow become a part of the Lima of our childhood and of the childhood of every passing generation, whose memories inevitably draw from the picture of Lima as "it once was." Lima's idyllic self-image behaves like a floating signifier, moving from century to century and surviving the realities of stench and chaos described by Durán Montero and Unanue for the seventeenth and eighteenth centuries, the realities of war devastation and sanitary crises of the nineteenth, and the realities of "people overflow," poverty, and decay portrayed by Matos Mar and Salazar Bondy in the twentieth, mutating its meaning and shifting in its intentionality but apparently getting further cemented in our imaginary the more critical or ravaging the crisis is.

This is the story I have wanted to tell in this book—the story that sparked out of the clashing discrepancies between the city's representation of itself and its reality, and that I could have never conveyed better than Señora Roberta herself in that momentous crossing of limits. It is also the story that was sparked out of my conflicted return home and of my decision to write about it at a time when, with the war between Sendero and the military over and the dismal crisis of the 1980s temporarily overcome, some of the city's deepest social and racial tensions had bubbled up to the surface. Nothing had prepared me for how difficult this task would be as much as my readings of Arguedas, who, being both a writer of fiction and a trained anthropologist, spent his life looking for the terms with which to write about "home," that place that occasionally he refers to in his writings as *querencia*—a word that, meaning both "love" and "desire," designates the place where we know we belong, but from where we know we have to leave, and where, as if by instinct, we feel compelled to return.

As the child of white parents who, after being orphaned by his mother, was raised in an isolated hacienda of the Andes by Quechua-speaking servants, Arguedas grew up straddling largely antagonistic worlds: those of the highlands and the coast, of *runa* and *criollo* life, producing in him a ripping sense of dislocation that would also mark his relationship to both literature and social science. In his debates with the media-savvy, cosmopolitan writers of the so-called Latin American boom, who promoted experiments with form, Arguedas would stress the importance of *arraigo*, of maintaining an intense, physical rootedness in one's world (like he said he was rooted in "the very *oqllo* [breast, chest, heart] of the Indians" who brought him up), for it is this rootedness that, according to Arguedas, allows us "to transmit into words the matter of things." Conversely, in his polemics with social scientists, who were still under the spell of structuralism and on a quest for a method that would capture reality objectively, Arguedas would insist on the importance of artifice in the creation of realist effects, an ability for which he drew on indigenous forms of storytelling and song making that produce narratives that are, as he put it, "absolutely true and absolutely imagined."[4]

As both a novelist and an ethnographer, throughout his life Arguedas held on to the belief that the writer's lived experiences function as some sort of conductor through which a substratum of reality can be transferred into language to be communicated, in all its concreteness, by virtue of the infinite malleability of words and textual form. Perhaps nowhere did he better put this idea to work than in *El zorro de arriba*, whose writing he handled with the thoroughness of an ethnographer and the inventiveness of a novelist. More than in his other works, which were celebrated everywhere for their "realism," in *El zorro de arriba*, Arguedas draws attention to the process and conditions of its creation as a text as well as to the made-up, "artificial" character of his style by inserting throughout the novel intimate diary entries written on recommendation of a doctor for their potential therapeutic effects. The end result—and best "effect"—is that from the triangulation of stories told through the alternation of genres emerges a reality that is neither entirely fictitious and external nor entirely individual and private, but one in which fantasy and certainty, memory and fact, feeling and idea, condition one another to create a world that is inextricable from the strange and wonderfully unique position of an ethnographer/novelist writing about his own home.

Tightly strapped into my seat, I looked out the plane's window again. The wing cut sharply through the air, zoomed through it as if weightless thousands of meters above the ground, challenging gravity on every fraction of a second and every fraction of an inch of what would be a seven-hour, six-thousand-mile trajectory. Below there were no more stars, just a pitch-black emptiness. I was left with just my thoughts and with a growing intuition that the diary form would be the best means to attempt to perform the social and deeply personal dimensions of the "drama" that Bataille talked about in reference to our daily, repetitive efforts to draw and redraw the boundaries that make up our social worlds and that, occasionally and momentously, offer us a glimpse of what's beyond them. This would require dwelling in the breaking down of thought that such a glimpse produces, in the startling impact of its chance occurrence, and in the upsetting fact of irresolution, all of which a diary might lend itself to seizing through words in a way that is, of course, "absolutely true and absolutely imagined."

Notes

1. See *La República*, "Madres obreras protestan desnudas" and "Protesta a lo Cicciolina." (All quotations from texts in Spanish are my translation unless otherwise indicated.)
2. The term *criollo*, as I use it in this book, refers to individuals generally native to Lima who claim Spanish ancestry (and therefore some degree of "whiteness") and at the same time deep cultural roots or a strong sense of belonging in the city. For a more comprehensive explanation of the term *criollo*, see chapter 1, note 3.
3. "Informal" markets and "informal" transportation refer, respectively, to sites of commerce and forms of transportation in which transactions take place and/or services are rendered outside of state regulation. For a more comprehensive explanation of the term "informality," see chapter 1, note 8.
4. Bataille, *Erotism*, 38.
5. Congresswoman María Jesús Espinoza declared, "They [the women or the mothers] cannot be left out in the streets from one day to another. We need to find a solution to this grave problem. We cannot continue to see these mothers reclaiming their rights, many of them stripping naked in the middle of the street, in a depressing scene." See *La República*, "Piden que Congreso se pronuncie."
6. Arguedas, "Novel and Literary Expression," xvi–xvii (as translated by Horning except for the last phrase, "la posibilidad, la necesidad de un absoluto acto de creación," which she renders as "the possibility of, the necessity for a more absolute act of creation").
7. Bataille, *Erotism*, 63.

8.   Bataille, "Psychological Structure of Fascism," 143.
9.   Geertz, "Thick Description," 15.

CHAPTER ONE

1.   Günther and Lohmann, *Lima*; Pulgar Vidal, *Geografía del Perú*. The ring of the Peña Horadada broke off some years ago due to erosion.
2.   Günther and Lohmann, *Lima*, 219.
3.   In Peru, as elsewhere in Latin America, *criollo* originally referred to the off-spring of Spaniards as well as of Africans born on the American continent and to the new cultural traits and behaviors associated with these populations (see Arrom, "Criollo"). Starting in the early nineteenth century, however, with the emergence of nationalistic sentiments throughout the continent, the term acquired narrower, more local meanings. In Peru it described cultural creations (with respect to food, music, dance, humor, etc.) and tastes that were considered to be "truly Peruvian" or, more specifically, "truly *Limeño.*" In this regard, Simmons states, "Lima has been traditionally considered, by both its inhabitants and those of the provinces, as the source and pulse of *criollismo*" (Simmons, "Criollo Outlook," 110). Today, the term *criollo* is to a great extent associated culturally and ethnically with the ur-ban, fair-skinned and mestizo middle classes of Lima; in certain contexts it can be said to more emphatically mean not-Indian or not-indigenous. Even though, as is the case with most ethnic and class markers, the term *criollo* cannot be unequivocally defined, it is in reference to the fair-skinned and mestizo middle classes of Lima that I use it in this book.
4.   Instituto Nacional de Estadística e Informática, Censos Nacionales 1940, 1961, 1972, 1993; Zolezzi Chocano, "El Centro de Lima," 201.
5.   Matos Mar, *Desborde popular*.
6.   Günther and Lohmann, *Lima*, 15.
7.   Driant, *Las barriadas de Lima*, 66–67.
8.   "Informal" businesses exist de facto, are not registered with the city or state, do not pay taxes, and most often do not abide by labor laws. The term "in-formality" was first disseminated in English-speaking academic circles by Keith Hart (1973) through his work on Ghana's informal economy and later popularized in Peru by Hernando de Soto et al. (1986). Far from being a tech-nical or academic term, "informality" in Lima is now a colloquial term with which people of all social backgrounds refer to business transactions oc-curring in the conditions described above. Throughout this book I place "informality" in quotes to draw attention to the false assumptions that the term, as it is often used in opposition to and exclusivity of a "formal" econ-omy, might lead to. Wherever "informality" is common practice, as it is in Lima, there tends to be a great deal of fluidity between it and the economy's so-called formal sector: First, individuals hold occupations and rely on strate-

gies that are alternately "formal" and "informal" depending on need and efficacy; second, the "formal" and "informal" sectors of the economy tend to rely on one another in day-to-day operations; and third, some sectors of the economy are entirely dependent on "informal" business, to the extent that "informality," and not "formality," could be said to be the norm.

9. Matos Mar, *Barriadas de Lima, 1957.*
10. Ibid., 17–18.
11. Riofrío, "Barriada y ciudad," 211.
12. Portocarrero, "Fantasmas de la clase media." Portocarrero's study is based on a survey of students at Lima's top-tiered universities: Universidad del Pacífico, Universidad de Lima, and Universidad Católica. The survey directly addresses the possibility of an invasion of Lima (from the highlands). It is also based on a separate survey of thirteen-year-olds at a private school in Lima. In this survey, students are asked to narrate a recent dream, which Portocarrero analyzes.
13. González Cueva, "Ciudades paralelas: imaginarios urbanos en Lima." This thesis was published as "Ciudades paralelas: una investigación sobre el imaginario urbano."
14. González Cueva, "Ciudades paralelas: una investigación," 11.
15. Frazer, "Taboo."
16. Smith, *Religion of the Semites*; Durkheim, *Elementary Forms of Religious Life.*
17. Frazer, "Taboo," 18–19.
18. Durkheim, *Elementary Forms of Religious Life*, 35.
19. Ibid., 306 and n. 7.
20. Ibid., 36, 312–13.
21. Ibid., 16.
22. Freud, *Totem and Taboo.*
23. Elias, *Civilizing Process.*
24. Lévi-Strauss, *Elementary Structures of Kinship.*
25. Douglas, *Purity and Danger.* See also Douglas, "Pollution."
26. Bataille, "Attraction and Repulsion II," 118.
27. Ibid., 121.
28. Ibid., 114.
29. See Michelson, "Heterology and Critique."
30. Bataille, "Notion of Expenditure," 125.
31. Bataille, *Accursed Share*, 3:339.
32. Ibid., 3:67–68.
33. Ibid., 3:333.
34. Ibid., 3:57.
35. Bataille, "Notion of Expenditure," 125. See also "Psychological Structure of Fascism"; "Counterattack: Call to Action," "The Threat of War," and "Toward Real Revolution"—all three in Bataille, *Writings on Laughter;* and all the manifestos on the College of Sociology and on the practice of "sacred sociology" in Hollier, *College of Sociology.*

36. For more about the military during the 1990s, see Rospigliosi, *Montesinos y las fuerzas armadas.*
37. Ibid., 41–42.
38. This was the outcome of the election's second round. Fujimori ran against Peruvian novelist Mario Vargas Llosa. The late 1980s were years of national economic and political turmoil: In July 1990, the month Fujimori was sworn in as president, the rate of inflation surpassed 7,600 percent, and the number of unemployed or underemployed workers rose to 70 percent. Additionally, in 1990 the Shining Path's urban and rural terror attacks peaked in number (*Caretas*, "La ruta del terror"). There was a generalized sense among politicians and intellectuals that Peru, as a nation-state, was on the verge of collapsing. See Degregori, *Década de la antipolítica*; and Grompone, "Vertiginosa irrupción de Fujimori."
39. Grompone, "Vertiginosa irrupción de Fujimori," 191.
40. Ibid., 191–92. This argument is based on the idea that, in a country with weak financial, political, and civil society institutions, "informality" is for millions of impoverished immigrants in the city a resourceful alternative to full, integrated modern citizenship. See also Villarán, "El fenómeno Fujimori."
41. Quoted in Oliart, " 'The Man Peru Needed?' " 417.
42. Rospigliosi, "Un Presidente Combi."
43. The year of 1996 was the apogee of Fujimori's regime and the beginning of its collapse. On the one hand, the budget for social programs had grown 65 percent to 3.3 billion in 1995 (*Caretas*, "Por qué ganó"), but on the other, the GNP had slowed down from 12 percent in 1994 to a mere 2 percent at the end of 1996. The 1995 electoral extravaganza of public works, carried out with revenues from the privatization of state enterprises, had by 1996 turned into total fiscal and political debauchery. Rumors were spread that pieces of luggage packed with dollar bills were being handed to ministers and other favored authorities around the country to finance popular programs and projects. There were also rumors that Fujimori liked to travel, even abroad on official business, carrying huge bags of dollar bills with which he paid all his expenses, including his hotel bill, often running in the thousands, to the dismay of more than one hotel clerk. (For the regime's handling of privatization and other revenues, see Coordinadora Nacional de Derechos Humanos, "Dossier Fujimori.")

    In August 1996, it emerged that Montesinos had bought off several public officials and personalities, and in September, shortly after Fujimori's puppet Congress decreed the "Law of Authentic Interpretation" to allow him to run for president for a third consecutive time, thugs hired by the SIN attacked three judges who opposed the law and bombed the facilities of the outspoken Red Global TV.
44. See also Degregori, *Década de la antipolítica*. Here I am indebted to Jeffrey Mehlman's Bataillean reading of *The Eighteenth Brumaire*. Mehlman, *Revolution and Repetition.*

CHAPTER TWO

1. Melville, *Moby Dick*, 180–88.
2. The idea of recruiting the services of the Bratton Group LLC, William Bratton's security consulting firm, was under consideration by the Andrade administration since 1998. Bratton finally visited Lima for a week at the end of May 2002 and issued a plan of action for the city of Lima. The recommendations included creating a system analogous to New York City's COMPSTAT (described above), which maps the occurrence of crimes by district in order to identify patterns and anticipate trends. See the Bratton Group LLC, "Plan de acción para la Ciudad de Lima." Bratton and Rudy Giuliani have lent their policing consulting services to several Latin American municipal governments, including those of cities in Venezuela, Brazil, Chile, and Honduras.
3. Caillois, "Festival," 302.
4. Portocarrero, "Ajuste de cuentas," 14.
5. See Marisol de la Cadena's study of the politics of race and culture in twentieth-century Cuzco for an in-depth examination of the notion of decency as a marker of "whiteness" through deflection of attention to skin color and appeal to class distinction and education level. De la Cadena, *Indigenous Mestizos*.
6. Ibid., 14–15.
7. *La República*, "Madres obreras protestan desnudas" and "Protesta a lo Cicciolina."
8. Bataille, *Accursed Share*, vol. 2.
9. *Caretas*, "No da más Lima." It is worth noting that throughout the 1990s, *Caretas* was markedly supportive of Andrade and his urban renewal plan.
10. *Caretas*, "Limpias intenciones."
11. Municipalidad Metropolitana de Lima, "Lima . . . ensueño."
12. A series of measures hostile to provincial municipal authorities was epitomized in the 1993 Law Decree No. 776, enacted during the government of Mayor Ricardo Belmont (1990–95), Andrade's predecessor. Decree No. 776, introduced as a "decentralizing" measure by Fujimori, redesigned the transference of funds to municipalities to favor districts over provinces. For a detailed analysis of Fujimori's efforts to break the spine of regional and provincial governments, see Tanaka, "Dinámica de los actores regionales."
13. *La República*, "Ex-dirigentes politizados rompen el diálogo"; *Expreso*, "¡Andrade mentiroso cumple con la ley!"; *El Comercio*, "Contra agresiones del SITRAMUN."
14. Bataille, *Erotism*, 18.
15. Bataille, *Erotism*, 17–18.
16. Bataille, *Accursed Share*, 2:149–53.
17. Tibbets, "Mamas Fighting for Freedom," 34.

18. This and previous quotes from *Daily Nation*, "Mothers Vow to Continue Strike" (my emphasis).
19. This and previous quote from *Daily Nation*, "MYWO Criticises Women Strippers" (my emphasis).
20. Eames, "Ìjà Obìrin Ondó."
21. Ardener, "Sexual Insult and Female Militancy." See also Ritzenthaler, "Anlu" and Wipper, "Riot and Rebellion."
22. See Chuchryk, "Subversive Mothers"; Howe, "The Madres de la Plaza de Mayo"; Kaplan, "Community and Resistance"; Kaplan et al., "Women and the Politics of Spectacle"; Schirmer, "Seeking of Truth" and "'Those Who Die for Life'"; Stephen, *Women and Social Movements*; and Taylor, *Disappearing Acts*.
23. Schirmer, "'Those Who Die For Life'"; Howe, "Las Madres de la Plaza de Mayo."
24. Schirmer, "'Those Who Die for Life,'" 27.
25. Schirmer, "Seeking of Truth," 33–34.
26. Radcliffe, "People Have to Rise Up," 207.
27. Ibid.
28. A small portion of the elevated train has recently been equipped and put in operation.
29. Andrade's urban renewal campaign, however, built on a corpus of legislation passed during Ricardo Belmont's double stint as mayor of Lima (1990–95). In it, Belmont for the first time made reference to a "historic center" that corresponded to the sections of El Cercado with large concentrations of colonial and early republican buildings and plazas that his own administration zoned as the area for intervention. Belmont already referred to this intervention initiative as the "recuperation" of Lima's historic center. See Ronda, "Estrategias de legitimaciones."

CHAPTER THREE

1. Also see the description of the Church of San Agustín in Pacheco Vélez, *Memoria y utopía*.
2. Wolfflin, *Renaissance and Baroque*, 30, 58.
3. Andrade, "Prólogo," 11–12.
4. *Diario Oficial El Peruano*, "Plan Maestro Centro de Lima."
5. Following historians and theorists of the Spanish and Latin American baroque, I treat this period as an early modern period, which followed the initial wave of European expansion, conquest, and migration that set off what we know today as globalism. In Spanish America, this period was characterized by the slow development of markets out of the mercantilist phase, the growth of bureaucracy, and urbanization, antecedents of the political, economic, and technological modernity advanced by the Enlightenment and the Industrial Revolution. See Maravall, *Culture of the Baroque*; Rama, *The Lettered City*.

6. Picón Salas, *Cultural History*, 100.
7. Ibid., 99. See also Benjamin, *Origin of German Tragic Drama*, 55.
8. Maravall, *Culture of the Baroque*, 102.
9. Ibid., 243–45.
10. As quoted in Rincón, "El universo neobarroco," 365–66.
11. Ordinance 138, quoted in Fraser, *Architecture of Conquest*, 49–50.
12. Osorio, "Inventing Lima," 29–34. This view of the Spanish colonial city, in particular Lima, as a "stage" is well developed and substantiated throughout Osorio's excellent dissertation.
13. Ibid., 1–26.
14. Ibid.; see also Acosta de Arias Schreiber, *Fiestas coloniales urbanas*; Mejías Álvarez, "Muerte regia en cuatro ciudades."
15. Beverly, "Dos caras del barroco," 19.
16. Osorio, "Inventing Lima," 42; see also Wuffarden, "La ciudad y sus emblemas"; Bonet Correa, "La fiesta barroca."
17. In her study of the Libros de Cabildo de Lima, the colonial city government records, Durán Montero shows that the idea of a city wall was discussed many times since the foundation of the city and the need of it was justified either as protection against pirate incursions or as defense against an Indian invasion. Every time, it was rejected as superfluous. However, a wall was finally built between 1684 and 1687. Durán Montero remarks that this wall might have worked as a deterrent for an Indian invasion but was useless against pirate incursions. She also notes that the wall inexplicably cut through the neighborhood of Santiago; she speculates that this may have had to do with the fact that the builders prioritized the shape of the wall for aesthetic reasons (rather than maximized its defensive potential) in order to bring Lima's profile closer to Seville's. Durán Montero, *Lima en el siglo XVII*, 85–90.
18. This image served in turn as inspiration for one of the better known panegyrics of Lima, the 1688 *La estrella de Lima convertida en Sol sobre sus tres coronas* (The star of Lima turned into a sun over its three crowns) by Francisco Echave y Assú, providing an account of the feasts in celebration of the beatification of one of Lima's saints, Toribio de Mogrovejo. Wuffarden, "La ciudad y sus emblemas," 68–71.
19. Pacheco Velez, "Esplendor barroco, larga decadencia," 154.
20. Echeverría, *La modernidad*, 41–42.
21. Picón Salas concurs: "In spite of two centuries of enlightenment thought and modern criticism, we Spanish Americans have never managed to escape altogether from the Baroque labyrinth. It still heavily influences our esthetic sensibility and the many complex aspects of our collective psychology." Picón Salas, *Cultural History*, 87. See also Carpentier, *Razón de ser*; Rama, *The Lettered City*.
22. Echeverría, *La modernidad*, 35–57.
23. Osorio, "Inventing Lima," 6.

24. Kagan, "Piety and Polity," 26–28.
25. Ibid., 27.
26. This refers to a use of the term in the work of Bernardo de Sahagún, as quoted by Lechner, "El concepto de 'policía,'" 402.
27. The concepts of "culture" and "civilization" do not appear in Spanish writings until the eighteenth and nineteenth centuries, respectively. See Lechner, "El concepto de 'policía,'" 397.
28. See Kagan, "Piety and Polity."
29. This refers to the instructions issued in 1516 by the Spanish Crown to the Hieronymite missionaries. Fraser, *Architecture of Conquest*, 42.
30. Although these meanings of *policía* lasted through the nineteenth century, the use of the term as enforcement of social order and the law appeared as early as 1590 when Phillip II, in an effort to rid Madrid of criminals and vagabonds, established a "Junta de Policía." Kagan, "Piety and Polity," 209 n. 41. A 1611 dictionary by Sebastián de Covarrubias already suggests this relationship between city life, courtliness, and enforcement: "Policía: A civic and courtly [or polite] term. Police council, that which governs the small things of the city and its adornment and cleanliness. It is a Greek term 'politeia,' *res publica*. Polity, the urban, the polite." Cited in Lechner, "El concepto de 'policía,'" 398.
31. Cobo, *Historia del Nuevo Mundo*, 52. Also quoted in Fraser, *Architecture of Conquest*, 21.
32. Burke, *A Philosophical Enquiry*, 105.
33. Ibid., 39.
34. Ibid., 53.
35. Phillips, introduction to *A Philosophical Enquiry* by Burke, xv.
36. Ibid., xxiii.
37. Bataille, *Erotism*, 144. See also Bataille, *Theory of Religion*.
38. Bataille, *Erotism*, 143.
39. Ibid., 143.
40. Bataille, *Accursed Share* 2:149.
41. United Nations, "The Habitat Agenda."
42. Andrade, "Prólogo," 11–12.
43. Povinelli, "Radical Worlds."
44. Ibid., 327.
45. Beverly, "Dos caras del Barroco," 24.
46. Velarde, "El neo-barroco en Lima."
47. Ibid.
48. Picón Salas, *Cultural History*, 89–90.
49. As quoted in Pacheco Vélez, *Memoria y utopia*, 253.
50. Pacheco Vélez, "Esplendor barroco," 159–61.
51. Lohmann Villena, *El Conde de Lemos*, 95–100. See also Basadre, *Conde de Lemos y su tiempo*.

52. Glave, "El virreinato Peruano." See also Lohmann Villena, "La memorable crisis monetaria"; and Andrien, *Crisis and Decline*. Andrien attributes the crisis in the viceroyalty of Peru to a financial and political decline in Spain, the diminishing productivity of the mines, the recession in the Atlantic trade, the diversification of the colonial economy, the corruption among colonial functionaries, and the catastrophic consequences of the 1687 earthquake.

53. Durán Montero, *Lima en el siglo XVII*, 79–85.

54. Durán Montero, "Lima en 1613."

55. Cobo, "Historia de la fundación de Lima," 306.

56. Moreyra y Paz Soldán and Céspedes del Castillo, *Colección de cartas de virreyes*, 18; and prologue by Céspedes del Castillo, xvi.

57. Salazar Bondy, *Lima la horrible*, 12–13.

CHAPTER FOUR

1. Hertz, *Death and the Right Hand*, 50–51.

2. Bataille, *Theory of Religion*.

3. *Caretas*, "Prensa y monitoreo."

4. Ibid.

5. See Protzel, "El paradigma del príncipe."

6. Evans-Pritchard, "Collective Expressions of Obscenity."

7. The expansion of the Internet during the 1990s rekindled old debates about this issue. In 1996 the U.S. Congress passed the Communications Decency Act. Among its critics, a close second to the concern that the CDA would threaten the freedom of speech was the concern that its vagueness and am-biguity made it inapplicable. Modern obscenity definitions in the United States stem from the 1973 U.S. Supreme Court decision in *Miller v. California*, which set forth a multipart test for determining whether an act or a work of art is obscene: (1) It must depict or describe sexual conduct in a patently offensive way; (2) the average person, applying contemporary community standards, must find that the act or work, taken as a whole, appeals to the prurient interest; (3) the act or work, taken as a whole, must lack serious liter-ary, artistic, political, or scientific value. The result is that obscenity is a crime that cannot be defined in advance and whose actuality is wholly dependent on a jury's decision.

   In Peru, the legislation language is even vaguer and, being a code-based legal system, there is no such court decision to serve as precedent.

8. Bataille, *Accursed Share* 3:53 (my emphasis).

9. González Cueva, "Ciudades paralelas: imaginarios urbanos."

10. Mehlman, *Revolution and Repetition*.

11. Both "The Notion of Expenditure" and "The Psychological Structure of Fas-cism" were published in *La Critique sociale*, numbers 7 and 10 respectively.

These essays, according to Denis Hollier, reflected a "conscious shift" in Bataille's writings toward political themes linked to "the failure of *Documents*" and to changes brought about by economic hardship and the upsurge of fascist forces in Europe. Hollier, *Against Architecture*, 125.

12. Bataille, "Notion of Expenditure," 125–26.
13. Matos Mar, *Desborde popular*, 104.
14. Ortega y Gasset, *La caza, los toros, y el toreo*, 77–78.
15. Bataille, *Erotism*, 74.

CHAPTER FIVE

1. Stein, *Dance in the Cemetery*, 123.
2. Ibid., 86, quoted from *La Unión*, November 6, 1917.
3. Ariès, *Western Attitudes toward Death*, 58; and McManners, *Death and the Enlightenment*, 445. See also Howard, *Architecture and the After-Life*.
4. In these churches, for the most part, only the baroque side altars were left intact, and in La Merced, San Francisco, and San Agustín, also the front façades.
5. Ariès calls this coexistence of the living and the dead inside the city "a new and surprising phenomenon." He tells us that the practice was unknown in pagan antiquity and even in early Christianity. The ancients feared being too close to the dead and, although they honored their sepulchers and kept these nearby, they made sure they were separate from their cities. In Rome, human burials inside the city were forbidden by law, and thus cemeteries were located along suburban roads. Ariès traces the European custom of burying the dead in and around churches in the historic heart of cities back to the fifth century when a desire took hold of Christians to be buried in close proximity to the tombs of Christian martyrs and saints (who were traditionally inhumed in churches). In medieval speech the word *church* thus came to include the entire space around the church building, including the "chimiter" or cemetery. Ariès notes that this custom became alien again to Christians in the late eighteenth century. Ibid., 14–18.
6. Tamayo Herrera, *La muerte en Lima*, 47; and Casalino Sen, "Higiene pública y piedad ilustrada," 338.
7. Tamayo Herrera, *La muerte en Lima*.
8. These cemeteries have been shut down many times by municipal authorities, but they have invariably, if always clandestinely, been put back into operation. Tamayo refers to the status of these informal cemeteries as "semi-official." Ibid., 60–64.
9. Besides primary sources, including journal and newspaper articles that argued in favor of the expulsion of Lima's burial grounds to the periphery around the turn of the nineteenth century and of the creation of a city morgue at the turn of the twentieth, I have just found the following essays dealing with death in Lima (only the first one, Tamayo's, refers to

attitudes toward death and the dead in contemporary times): Barriga Calle, "Experiencia de la muerte en Lima"; Casalino Sen, "Higiene pública y piedad ilustrada"; Jochamowitz, "La morgue"; Tamayo Herrera, *La muerte en Lima*; Zapata, "Historia de la muerte en el Perú." There is much overlap of information and perspectives in these articles.

10. Mumford, *The City in History*, 6.
11. Ibid., 7.
12. On the other side of the spectrum were those who affirmed that intentional burials are the marker of early humans' symbolic (that is, ritual) capacity, which of course doesn't explain why the ritual takes the form it takes, like that of depositing the corpse underground. For a great summary of past and current dominant interpretations of these early burials, see Riel-Salvatore and Clark, "Grave Markers."
13. Bataille, *Erotism*, 44.
14. Ibid., 16.
15. Ibid., 46.
16. Hertz, *Death and the Right Hand*, 27.
17. To name a few. See, for instance, the articles in Jupp and Howarth (eds.), *Changing Face of Death*; see also Bradbury, *Representations of Death*.
18. Hertz, *Death and the Right Hand*, 78.
19. Ibid., 77.
20. Ibid., 83.
21. Quoted in Barrós Arana, "El entierro de los muertos," 228.
22. Maravall, *Culture of the Baroque*, 164.
23. Mejías Álvarez, "Muerte regia en cuatro ciudades." Tamayo describes a print found in a Lima archive called "A picture from hell," which depicts Vanitas with a beautiful human head and a skeleton for a body, as she writes in a book a verse about burning in hell forever. Tamayo says that images like this one were commonly found in the oratories of colonial eighteenth- and nineteenth-century mansions. Tamayo Herrera, *La muerte en Lima*, 78–79.
24. McManners refers to it as "the baroque pedagogy of death." McManners, *Death and the Enlightenment*, 445. The excellent historical essay by Elizabeth Musgrave focuses on the *memento mori* in Brittany. Musgrave, "Memento Mori."
25. Hall, *Dictionary of Subjects and Symbols*, 284, 291; Roberts (ed.), *Encyclopedia of Comparative Iconography*, 223–24.
26. Musgrave, "Memento Mori," 67–69.
27. Maravall, *Culture of the Baroque*, 165. See also Mejías Álvarez, "Muerte regia en cuatro ciudades."
28. Clement, in his study about the emergence of the notion of hygiene in Latin America, says that the work of Antoine L. Lavoisier and Joseph Priestly, the discoverers of oxygen, was well known among doctors and scientists in Peru and Latin America. Clement, "Nacimiento de la higiene urbana," 80.

29. Ibid., 79–82. See also Cipolla, *Miasmas and Disease*, 4.

30. Hesperiophilo, *Mercurio Peruano*, February 13, 1791.

31. Unanue, "Discurso sobre el panteón," 48.

32. Ibid., 44.

33. Ibid., 50–51.

34. Ibid., 46.

35. Clement, "Nacimiento de la higiene urbana," 86.

36. Corbin, *The Foul and the Fragrant*, 4–8.

37. Quoted by Clement from Amat's *Auto de Buen Gobierno*. Clement, "Nacimiento de la higiene urbana," 84. Also see Ramón, "Urbe y orden," 295. These measures were part of the effort undertaken by the new Bourbon King Charles III to restructure the cities of Spanish America. Ramón writes: "In the sphere of urban life, the Bourbon viceroys fomented a drastic alteration in the official use of the city. Eager to modify the colonial administration system . . . they utilized each urban center as a key element in this effort. On the one hand, they promoted the creation of new cities, with the objective of re-conquering territories that were only nominally within the Hispanic jurisdiction. On the other, they decisively exerted their influence in the existing ones with the objective of transforming them into centers for the irradiation of the [new] colonial message."

38. *Mercurio Peruano*, February 17, 1791.

39. Unanue, "Idea general del reino del Perú," 71–72.

40. Ibid., 76–77.

41. Ramón describes the Bourbon administration's urban policies in the city as aimed at "recuperating" Lima, which was thought to be in frank decadence since the fragmentation of Spain's possessions in America and its deposition as colonial "head city." Ramón, "Urbe y orden," 308.

42. Unanue, "Idea general del reino del Perú," 78.

43. Corbin, *The Foul and the Fragrant*, 5

44. I am here referring to the following texts: Douglas, *Purity and Danger*; Frazer, "Taboo"; Lévi-Strauss, *Elementary Structures of Kinship*; Maine, *Ancient Law*; and Radcliffe-Brown, *Structure and Function in Primitive Society*.

45. Lévi-Strauss, *Elementary Structures of Kinship*, 8–11, 490.

46. Douglas, *Purity and Danger*, 2–6.

47. Bataille, *Erotism*, 62.

48. Bataille, *Accursed Share*, 2:52–53.

49. Ibid., 2:62.

50. Ibid., 2:63.

51. Bataille, *Erotism*, 58.

52. Bataille, *Accursed Share*, 2:63.

53. Jochamowitz, "La morgue."

54. Lavorería (ed.), *Prontuario*, "Reglamento General de Sanidad, 1887."

55. General Canevaro (Alcalde de Lima), *Memoria del Honorable Consejo Provincial de Lima*, 44.

56. Lavorería (ed.), *Prontuario*, "Estadística demográfica, 1915."
57. Jochamowitz, "La morgue," 438.
58. *El Comercio*, "La pretendida Morgue de Lima," quoted in Jochamowitz, ibid., 439.
59. Jochamowitz, "La morgue," 439.
60. Ibid., 441.
61. Tamayo Herrera, *La muerte en Lima*, 15–20.
62. Ibid., 69–70.
63. Ibid., 73.
64. Ibid., 92–99.

CHAPTER SIX

1. Iwasaki, "Toros y sociedad en Lima colonial."
2. Leiris, *Literatura como tauromaquia*.
3. As quoted in Derrida, "From Restricted to General Economy," 269.
4. Ibid., 274–75.
5. Ibid., 265.
6. Bataille, *Accursed Share*, 3:206.
7. Tibbets, "Mamas Fighting for Freedom," 37.
8. Eames, *Ìjà Obìrin*, 70–76.
9. Ortner, "Is Female to Male"; and Rubin, "Traffic in Women."
10. Ortner, "Is Female to Male," 74.
11. de Beauvoir, *Second Sex*, 64.
12. Ibid., 64–65.
13. Derrida, "From Restricted to General Economy," 275. See Guerlac, " 'Recognition' by a Woman!" for a well-developed argument that Bataille's notion of sovereignty in *Erotism* remains close to Hegel's mastery.

CHAPTER SEVEN

1. Cobo, *Fundación de Lima*, 126; Günther and Lohmann, *Lima*, 122. For an overview and assessment of the impact of Toledo's policies, see Hemming, *Conquest of the Incas*.
2. Toledo, *Disposiciones gubernativas*.
3. Ibid.; see, for instance, "Instrucción de los jueces naturales," 1:465, and "Instrucción y ordenanzas de los corregidores de naturales," 2:414–20. Mauss, "Techniques of the Body."
4. Castañeda León, *Vestido tradicional del Perú*, 63; Patiño, *Vestidos, adornos y vida social*, 4:23.
5. According to Lynn A. Meisch and Ann P. Rowe, in the area of what today is Ecuador, some degree of nudity appears to have been common before the Inca conquest, some fifty years prior to the Spanish invasion. Based on pre-Inca clay figurines, they say that men probably wore loincloths and women

simply wrapped skirts, and that both complemented these garments with body decorations in the form of painting, jewelry, and headdresses. The authors write: "Inca dress was influential in highland Ecuador, since if the Incas did not consider newly conquered peoples sufficiently clothed, as apparently was the case in the northern highlands of Ecuador, they ordered people to wear something similar to Inca dress." Rowe (ed.), *Costume and Identity*, 44.

6. Castañeda León, *Vestido tradicional del Perú*, 24–37.
7. Murra, "La función del tejido," 145–70.
8. Szeminski, "Why Kill the Spaniard?"
9. Castañeda León, *Vestido tradicional del Perú*, 36.
10. Patiño, *Vestidos, adornos, y vida social*, 4:173.
11. Matienzo, *Gobierno del Perú*, 69–70.
12. Patiño, *Vestidos, adornos, y vida social*, 4:173.
13. Patiño refers to a successful siege of the newly founded Spanish city of Santiago (de Chile) by the warrior Araucano Indians who, wishing to bring upon themselves some of the power of the conquerors, dressed in Spanish garments before attacking the city and killing Pedro de Valdivia, its founder and governor. Ibid., 4:172. A similar ritual use of the colonizer's clothes has been described for other colonial contexts. See, for example, Comaroff, "Empire's Old Clothes," 406–7.
14. As quoted by Cavero, *Los dioses vencidos*, 66.
15. These deposits were now run by *corregidores* (royal administrators). The *corregidores*, via a system of debt-bondage called *repartimientos*, would force-sell textiles and clothing by credit to people who had to accept them and later pay for them in kind, money, or labor. For Túpac Amaru II's actions against the *corregidores* and the *repartimientos*, see O'Phelan, *La gran rebelión en los Andes*.
16. Ibid., 158–59.
17. Ibid., 158–60.
18. Durand Florez, "Sentencia expedida por el visitador general Areche," 268–77.
19. Castañeda León, *Vestido tradicional del Perú*, 63ff; Canavesi de Sahonero, *Traje de la chola paceña*, 25; Otero, *Vida social en el coloniaje*, 131ff.
20. De la Cadena, "Women Are More Indian."
21. Poole, *Vision, Race, and Modernity*, 99.
22. Ibid.
23. De la Cadena, *Indigenous Mestizos*, 222–23.
24. Ibid., 230.
25. To my knowledge, no one has written in detail about this transformation of dress among migrants in Lima. However, the fact that immigrants in the capital adopt new attire as well as new tastes in food and music is mentioned invariably in studies about migration. In what is perhaps the most detailed account of the experience of city-ward migration, *Conquistadores de un nuevo*

mundo, the authors say: "In fact, in their advance toward Lima . . . the Andean population sacrifice language and dress, the two exterior signs by which they are more easily recognizable [as individuals from the highlands] and, moreover, despised, since discrimination is more cultural than strictly racial." The authors quote one of their interviewees, Andrés, as stating: "I think that (for their insults) they base themselves wrongly on the dress. For example, there is a girl here, nice, but provincial; she arrived with her *ponchito* and they called her *serrana*. . . . I think that they mocked her because of her dress. . . . Well, my dad, my mom, they dressed with that kind of dress. That is why they bothered them. So that many times when they didn't dress like that, they could say I am *Limeño*." Degregori et al., *Conquistadores de un nuevo mundo*, 164.

26. Turner, "The Social Skin."
27. Ibid., 114.
28. Ibid., 116.
29. Turner states that, for Kayapo men, having a penis erection in public or exposing the *glans penis* from under the penis sheath is as embarrassing as it would be for Westerners to walk naked through their town or workplace.
30. Isbell, *To Defend Ourselves*.
31. Ibid., 70–71.
32. Personal communication with Olga González, who in 1996 lived and worked in the highland community of Sarhua in Ayacucho.
33. Ibid., from an interview with "Carmelita" in González's fieldnotes. Carmelita, a migrant returnee in Sarhua, speaks of the pressure she felt to change back to her *pollera* when she first arrived back in the village and states that, were it not for the insults and the gossip, she would more comfortably wear pants and sneakers. She told González to notice how in the month of August migrants who return for the village's annual rituals will dress back "like we do in Sarhua."
34. Isbell, *To Defend Ourselves*, 71.
35. Ibid., 218. González says that, in Sarhua, lowland *chunchus* are ritually represented by *comunero* children with a naked torso, wearing raffia skirts and feather headdresses. Personal communication.
36. Isbell, *To Defend Ourselves*, 135–36.
37. Brandt, *Justicia popular*.
38. The *rondas campesinas*, which have existed in the rural Andes to protect private and communal property since before the Agrarian Reform of the 1970s, were endorsed and enlisted by the state in the 1980s for the fight against Sendero Luminoso. Ibid., 152.
39. Guamán Poma de Ayala, *Nueva corónica y buen gobierno*, 1:218–20 and 1:370–71. See also 1:219–220 and 2:26–28. Only in the context of the last of these images, in which a man is lashed by a priest for suspected robbery, does

Guamán Poma make an explicit reference to the use of nakedness as part of the punishment:

> . . . I say that a father [priest] in the *repartimiento* of Andamarca Indians . . . was so brutish and haughty that he would take the Indians for guilty [of robbery], male or female, by seeing them well groomed, or wearing new clothes, then he would have them stripped *en cueros* [completely naked] like they came into the world, until he saw their shamefulness, then he would give them many lashes and burn them with lit-up maguey, tied to four poles from the four parts, feet and hands, and punished them until blood would run down their body. . . .

For images of the *chunchus*, see ibid., 1:119–28 and 1:229–35.

40. Orlove, "Sticks and Stones."
41. Ibid, 151–52, 160 n. 8. Orlove's assessment implies that the sense of shame produced by forced stripping (as punishment) in the West stems from an ingrained prudery, from "rendering visible the parts of the body that are ordinarily kept covered." He notes, however, that metaphors such as "a cutting glance" suggest that the gaze itself is often physicalized and that uncovering and looking can therefore also constitute a kind of physical injury.
42. In an interview with González, the woman supposedly depicted in this *tabla* stated that her punishers had left her bottom underwear on.
43. *Caretas*, "La Ley de Fuente Ovejuna."
44. De Soto, *El otro sendero*; Revilla and Price, *Administración de la justicia informal.*
45. Macera and Forns, *Nueva Crónica del Perú del Siglo* XX, 484–85.
46. Ardener, "Nudity, Vulgarity, and Protest," 704. See also "Sexual Insult and Female Militancy" and "A Note on Gender Iconography."
47. Ardener, "A Note on Gender Iconography," 113.
48. Chuchryk, "Subversive Mothers"; Kaplan, "Community and Resistance"; Kaplan et al., "Women and the Politics of Spectacle"; and Schirmer, "'Those Who Die for Life'" and "The Seeking of Truth."
49. Kaplan, "Community and Resistance," 260.
50. Chuchryk, "Subversive Mothers" (author's emphasis). In *Disappearing Acts*, Diana Taylor notes in relation to the Madres de la Plaza de Mayo that in their identities as mothers they were already the product of political representation, even if this defines motherhood as apolitical; she examines Evita Perón's efforts to "extend political visibility and representation" to women by compelling them to "accept their domestic 'destiny' and 'mission.'" Taylor, *Disappearing Acts,* 186.
51. Ardener, "Sexual Insult and Female Militancy," 432.
52. Ardener says that the vagina is sometimes used as a condensed symbol to cover all the "secret" areas of women and that it provides "a unitary counterpart or symbolic inversion" of the penis. The female breasts, which are

also used for symbolic pairing with the penis, Ardener speculates, have attributes that are parallel (rather than contrary) to the penis. "A Note on Gender Iconography," 135.

53. Ibid., 118.
54. Ardener, "Sexual Insult and Female Militancy," 430–31.
55. For Latin America, see Kaplan, "Community and Resistance"; and Chuchryk, "Subversive Mothers."
56. Turner and Brownhill, "Why Women Are at War with Chevron."
57. Wipper, "Riot and Rebellion among African Women"; and "Kikuyu Women and the Harry Thuku Disturbances."
58. Wipper, "Riot and Rebellion among African Women," 66–67.
59. Schirmer, "'Those Who Die for Life,'" 27.
60. Taylor, *Disappearing Acts*, 185, 192.
61. Bataille, *Accursed Share*, 3:93.
62. Ibid., 3:197–211.

CHAPTER EIGHT

1. Arguedas, *El zorro de arriba*.
2. Ibid., 20–21.
3. Foucault, "Preface to Transgression," 35.
4. Arguedas, *El zorro de arriba*, 24.

Bibliography

Acosta de Arias Schreiber, R. M. *Fiestas coloniales urbanas. Lima, Cuzco, Potosí.* Lima: Otorongo Producciones, 1977.

Adorno, T. *Hegel, Three Studies.* Translated by S. W. Nicholsen, with an introduction by S. W. Nicholsen and J. J. Shapiro. Cambridge, MA: MIT Press, 1993.

———. *Negative Dialectics.* Translated by E. B. Ashton. New York: Continuum, 1983.

Andrade, A. "Prólogo." In *La Ciudad Posible. Lima, Patrimonio Cultural de la Humanidad*, edited by J. Ruiz de Somocurcio, 11–14. Lima: Municipalidad Metropolitana de Lima, 1999.

Andrien, K. *Crisis and Decline. The Viceroyalty of Peru in the Seventeenth Century.* Albuquerque: University of New Mexico Press, 1985.

Ardener, S. "A Note on Gender Iconography: The Vagina." In *The Cultural Construction of Sexuality*, edited by P. Caplan, 113–42. London: Tavistock, 1987.

———. "Nudity, Vulgarity, and Protest." *New Society* 27 (1974): 704–5.

———. "Sexual Insult and Female Militancy." *Man*, n.s., 8, no. 3 (1973): 422–40.

Arguedas, J. M. "The Novel and the Problem of Literary Expresión in Peru." In *Yawar Fiesta*. Translated by F. Horning Barraclough. Austin: University of Texas Press, 1985.

———. *Los ríos profundos.* Madrid: Ediciones Cátedra, 2000.

———. *El zorro de arriba y el zorro de abajo.* Buenos Aires: Editorial Losada, 1971.

Ariès, P. *Western Attitudes toward Death: From the Middle Ages to the Present.* Baltimore: Johns Hopkins University Press, 1974.

Arrom, J. J. "Criollo: Definición y matices de un concepto." *Hispania* 34, no. 2 (1951): 172–76.

Barriga Calle, I. "La experiencia de la muerte en Lima. Siglo XVII." *Apuntes* 31 (1992): 81–102.

Barrós Arana, D. "El entierro de los muertos." In *Obras Completas*, vol. 10, 227–53. Santiago de Chile: Imprenta Cervantes, 1911.

Basadre, J. *El Conde de Lemos y su tiempo. Bosquejo de una evocación y una interpretación del Perú a fines del siglo XVII.* Lima: Editorial Huascarán, 1948.

Bataille, G. *The Accursed Share.* Vols. 2 and 3. Translated by R. Hurley. New York: Zone Books, 1993.

———. "Attraction and Repulsion I: Tropisms, Sexuality, Laughter and Tears." In *The College of Sociology (1937–39)*, edited by D. Hollier, translated by B. Wing, 103–12. Minneapolis: University of Minnesota Press, 1988.

———. "Attraction and Repulsion II: Social Structure." In *The College of Sociology (1937–39)*, edited by D. Hollier, translated by B. Wing, 113–36. Minneapolis: University of Minnesota Press, 1988.

———. "The College of Sociology." In *The College of Sociology (1937–39)*, edited by D. Hollier, translated by B. Wing, 333–41. Minneapolis: University of Minnesota Press, 1988.

———. *Erotism. Death and Sensuality.* Translated by M. Dalwood. San Francisco: City Lights Books, 1986.

———. "Georges Bataille: Writings on Laughter, Sacrifice, Nietzsche, Un-Knowing." Special issue, *October* 36 (Spring 1986).

———. "The Notion of Expenditure." In *Visions of Excess: Selected Writings, 1927–39*, edited and with an introduction by A. Stoekl, translated by A. Stoekl, with C. R. Lovitt and D. M. Leslie, Jr., 116–29. Minneapolis: University of Minnesota Press, 1985.

———. "The Psychological Structure of Fascism." In *Visions of Excess: Selected Writings, 1927–39*, edited and with an introduction by A. Stoekl, translated by A. Stoekl, with C. R. Lovitt and D. M. Leslie, Jr., 137–60. Minneapolis: University of Minnesota Press, 1985.

———. *Theory of Religion.* Translated by R. Hurley. New York: Zone Books, 1992.

Bataille, G., and R. Caillois "Sacred Sociology and the Relationship between 'Society,' 'Organism,' and 'Being.'" In *The College of Sociology (1937–39)*, edited by D. Hollier, translated by B. Wing, 73–84. Minneapolis: University of Minnesota Press, 1988.

———. "Sacred Sociology of the Contemporary World." In *The College of Sociology (1937–39)*, edited by D. Hollier, translated by B. Wing, 157–58. Minneapolis: University of Minnesota Press, 1988.

Bataille, G., et al. "Note on the Foundation of a College of Sociology." In *The College of Sociology (1937–39)*, edited by D. Hollier, translated by B. Wing, 3–5. Minneapolis: University of Minnesota Press, 1988.

Benjamin, W. *The Origin of German Tragic Drama.* Translated by J. Osborne. New York: Verso, 1977.

Beverly, J. "Las dos caras del barroco." In *Una modernidad obsoleta: Estudios sobre el barroco*, 13–27. Los Teques: Fondo Editorial ALEM, 1997.

de Beauvoir, S. *The Second Sex*. Translated and edited by H. M. Parshley, with an introduction by D. Bair. New York: Vintage Books, 1989.

Bonet Correa, A. "La fiesta barroca como práctica del poder." In *El arte efímero en el mundo hispánico*, 78–81. Mexico, D.F.: Universidad Nacional Autónoma de Mexico, Instituto de Investigaciones Esteticas 1983.

Bradbury, M. *Representations of Death: A Social Psychological Perspective*. London: Routledge, 1999.

Brandt, H-J. *Justicia popular. Nativos campesinos*. Lima: Fundación Friedrich Naumann, 1987.

The Bratton Group LLC. "Plan de Acción para la Ciudad de Lima." http://www .seguridadidl.org.pe/infodocs/planbratton.doc.

Burke, E. *A Philosophical Enquiry into the Origin of Our Ideas of the Sublime and the Beautiful*. Edited and with an introduction by A. Phillips. Oxford: Oxford University Press, 1990.

Caillois, R. "Festival." In *The College of Sociology (1937–39)*, edited by D. Hollier, translated by B. Wing, 279–303. Minneapolis: University of Minnesota Press, 1988.

Canavesi de Sahonero, L. de *El traje de la chola paceña*. La Paz: Editorial Los Amigos del Libro, 1987.

Caretas (Lima). "La Ley de Fuente Ovejuna," February 14, 2002.

———. "La ruta del terror," September 9, 1999.

———. "Limpias intenciones," July 18, 1996.

———. "No da más Lima," February 1, 1996.

———. "Por qué ganó," April 12, 1995.

———. "Prensa y monitoreo. Habla Segisfredo Luza," February 11, 1999.

Carpentier, A. *Razón de ser: conferencias*. Caracas: Universidad Central de Venezuela, Ediciones del Rectorado, 1976.

Casalino Sen, C. "Higiene pública y piedad ilustrada: La cultura de la muerte bajo los Borbones." In *El Perú en el siglo XVIII. La Era Borbónica*, edited by S. O'Phelan, 325–44. Lima: Instituto Riva Agüero, Pontificia Universidad Católica del Perú, 1999.

Castañeda León, L. *Vestido tradicional del Perú*. Lima: Museo Nacional de la Cultura Peruana and OAS, 1981.

Cavero, R. *Los dioses vencidos. Una lectura antropológica de Taki Onqoy*. Huamanga: Universidad Nacional de San Cristóbal de Huamanga, Centro de Pesquisa em Etnologia Indigena, Brasil.

Chuchryk, P. "Subversive Mothers: The Women's Opposition to the Military Regime in Chile." In *Women, the State, and Development*, edited by E. Charlton, 130–51. Albany: SUNY Press, 1989.

Cipolla, C. *Miasmas and Disease: Public Health and the Environment in the Pre-Industrial Age*. Translated by E. Potter. New Haven: Yale University Press, 1992.

Clement, J-P. "El nacimiento de la higiene urbana en la América Española del siglo XVIII." *Revista de Indias* 43, no. 171 (1983): 77–95.

Cobo, B. *Historia del Nuevo Mundo*. Vol. 2. Madrid: Biblioteca de Autores Españoles. Ediciones Atlas, 1956.

———. "Historia de la fundación de Lima." In *Monografías históricas sobre la ciudad de Lima*. Lima: Librería e Imprenta Gil, 1935.

Comaroff, J. "The Empire's Old Clothes. Fashioning the Colonial Subject." In *Situated Lives: Gender and Culture in Everyday Life*, edited by L. Lamphere, H. Ragone, and P. Zavella, 400–19. New York: Routledge, 1997.

El Comercio (Lima). "Contra agresiones del SITRAMUN," June 24, 1999.

Coordinadora Nacional de Derechos Humanos. "Dossier Fujimori." http://www.cnddhh.org.pe.

Corbin, A. *The Foul and the Fragrant. Odor and the French Social Imagination*. Translated by M. Kochan. Cambridge, MA: Harvard University Press, 1986.

The Daily Nation (Nairobi). "Angry Mothers Strip as Police Charge," March 4, 1992.

———. "Mothers Vow to Continue Strike," March 5, 1992.

———. "MYWO (Maendeleo Ya Wanawake Organization) Criticises Women Strippers," March 10, 1992.

———. "Nude Demonstration Supported by Elders," February 13, 2001.

Degregori, C. I. *La década de la antipolítica. Auge y huída de Alberto Fujimori y Vladimiro Montesinos*. Lima: Instituto de Estudios Peruanos, 2000.

Degregori, C. I., C. Blondet, and N. Lynch. *Conquistadores de un nuevo mundo. De invasores a ciudadanos en San Martín de Porres*. Lima: Instituto de Estudios Peruanos, 1986.

De la Cadena, M. *Indigenous Mestizos: The Politics of Race and Culture in Cuzco, Peru, 1919–91*. Durham, NC: Duke University Press, 2000.

———. "Women Are More Indian." In *Ethnicity, Markets, and Migration in the Andes: At the Crossroads of History and Anthropology*, edited by B. Larson, O. Harris, and E. Tandeter, 329–48. Durham, NC: Duke University Press, 1995.

Derrida, J. "From Restricted to General Economy: A Hegelianism without Reserve." In *Writing and Difference*. Translated by A. Bass. Chicago: University of Chicago Press, 1978.

De Soto, H. *El otro sendero. La revolución informal*. Lima: Editorial El Barranco, 1986.

Douglas, M. "Pollution." In *International Encyclopedia of the Social Sciences*, vol. 12, 336–42. New York: Macmillan, 1968.

———. *Purity and Danger: An Analysis of Concepts of Pollution and Taboo*. New York: Praeger, 1966.

Driant, J-C. *Las barriadas de Lima: Historia e interpretación*. Lima: DESCO and Instituto Francés de Estudios Andinos, 1991.

Durán Montero, Ma. A. "Lima en 1613. Aspectos Urbanos." In *Anuario de Estudios Americanos*, XLIX. Sevilla: Escuela de Estudios Hispanoamericanos, 1992.

———. *Lima en el siglo XVII: Arquitectura, urbanismo y vida cotidiana*. Sevilla: Diputación Provincial de Sevilla, 1994.

Durkheim, E. *The Elementary Forms of Religious Life*. Translated by K. E. Fields. New York: Free Press, 1995 [1912].

Eames, E. "Ìjà Obìrin Ondó/The Ondo Women's War: The Politics of Women's Wealth in a Yorùbá Town." PhD diss., Department of Anthropology, Harvard University, 1992.

Echeverría, B. *La modernidad de lo barroco*. Mexico, D.F.: Ediciones Era, 1998.

———, ed. *Modernidad, mestizaje cultural, ethos barroco*. Mexico, D.F.: Universidad Nacional Autónoma de Mexico, 1994.

Elias, N. *The Civilizing Process*. Malden, MA: Blackwell, 2000.

Evans-Pritchard, E. E. "Some Collective Expressions of Obscenity in Africa." *Journal of the Royal Anthropological Institute* 59 (1929): 311–31.

Expreso (Lima). "Andrade mentiroso cumple con la ley!" June 24, 1999.

Foucault, M. "Preface to Transgression." In *Language, Counter-memory, Practice*, edited by D. F. Bouchard, translated by D. F. Bouchard and S. Simon. Ithaca, NY: Cornell University Press, 1977.

Fraser, V. *The Architecture of Conquest: Building in the Viceroyalty of Peru, 1535–1635*. Cambridge: Cambridge University Press, 1990.

Frazer, J. G. "Taboo." In *Encyclopedia Britannica*. 9th ed. 1898.

Freud, S. *Totem and Taboo*. London: Routledge, 2001.

Geertz, C. "Thick Description." In *The Interpretation of Culture*, 3–30. New York: Basic Books, 1973.

Glave, L. M. "El virreinato peruano y la llamada 'crisis general' del siglo XVII." Cuadernos de Historia 2. Lima: Departamento Académico de Ciencias Humanas, Universidad de Lima, 1986.

González Cueva, E. "Ciudades paralelas: imaginarios urbanos en Lima." Tesis de Licenciatura en Sociología, Departamento de Ciencias Sociales. Lima: Pontificia Universidad Católica del Perú, 1994.

———. "Ciudades paralelas: una investigación sobre el imaginario urbano." In *Ciudad de jóvenes. Imágenes y cultura*, edited by E. González, R. Mendoza, and M. Santos, 11–39. Colección Temas en Sociología 5. Lima: Pontificia Universidad Católica, 1995.

Grompone, R. "Perú: La vertiginosa irrupción de Fujimori. Buscando las razones de un sorprendente resultado electoral." *Revista Mexicana de Sociología* 52, no. 4 (1990): 177–203.

Guamán Poma de Ayala, F. *Nueva corónica y buen gobierno*. 2 vols. Caracas, Venezuela: Biblioteca Ayacucho, 1980.

Günther Doering, J., and G. Lohmann Villena. *Lima*. Lima: Colecciones MAPFRE, 1992.

Hall, J. *Dictionary of Subjects and Symbols in Art*. London: Murray, 1975.

Hart, K. "Informal Income Opportunities and Urban Employment in Ghana." *The Journal of Modern African Studies* 11, no. 1 (1973): 61–89.

Hemming, J. *The Conquest of the Incas*. New York: Harcourt Brace Jovanovitch, 1970.

Hertz, R. *Death and the Right Hand*. Translated by Rodney and Claudia Needham, with an introduction by E. E. Evans-Pritchard. Glencoe, IL: Free Press, 1960.

Hesperiophilo, *El Mercurio Peruano*, February 13, 1791. Folio 121.

Hollier, D. *Against Architecture. The Writings of Georges Bataille*. Cambridge, MA: MIT Press, 1989.

———, ed. *The College of Sociology (1937–39)*. Translated by B. Wing. Minneapolis: University of Minnesota Press, 1988.

Howard, C. *Architecture and the After-Life*. New Haven: Yale University Press, 1991.

Instituto Nacional de Estadística e Informática, Censos Nacionales 1940, 1961, 1972, 1993. http://www.inei.gob.pe.

Isbell, B. J. *To Defend Ourselves: Ecology and Ritual in an Andean Village*. Austin: University of Texas Press, 1978.

Iwasaki, F. "Toros y sociedad en Lima colonial." *Anuario de Estudios Americanos* 49 (1992): 311–33.

Kagan, R. "Piety and Polity." *Urban Images of the Hispanic World, 1493–1793*. New Haven: Yale University Press, 2000.

Kaplan, T. "Community and Resistance in Women's Political Cultures." *Dialectical Anthropology* 15 (1990): 259–67.

Kaplan, T., M. Agosin, and T. Valdez. "Women and the Politics of Spectacle in Chile." *The Barnard Occasional Papers on Women's Issues* 3, no. 2 (1988): 2–9.

Jochamowitz, L. *Ciudadano Fujimori. La construcción de un político*. Lima: Peisa, 1994.

———. "La morgue." In *Mundos interiores*, edited by A. Panfichi and F. Portocarrero, 431–41. Lima: Universidad del Pacífico, Centro de Investigación, 1995.

Jupp, P., and Howarth, G., eds. *The Changing Face of Death: Historical Accounts of Death and Disposal*. New York: St. Martin's Press, 1997.

Lavorería, D., ed. *Prontuario de Legislación Sanitaria del Perú. Recopilación de las leyes, decretos i demás disposiciones relativas a cuestiones sanitarias*. Vol. 1 (1870–1920). Lima: Imp. La Equitativa, 1928.

Lechner, J. "El concepto de 'policía' y su presencia en la obra de los primeros historiadores de Indias." *Revista de Indias* 41 (1981): 165–66.

Leiris, M. *La literatura considerada como una tauromaquia*. Series los heterodoxos, 18. Madrid: Tusquets Editor, ca. 1946.

Lévi-Strauss, C. *The Elementary Structures of Kinship*. Boston: Beacon Press, 1969.

Lohmann Villena, G. *El Conde de Lemos, Virrey del Perú*. Madrid: Escuela de Estudios Hispano-Americanos de la Universidad de Sevilla, 1946.

———. "La memorable crisis monetaria de mediados del siglo XVII y sus repercusiones en el Virreinato del Perú." In *Anuario de Estudios Americanos* 33 (1976): 579–639.

Lynch, N. "Negación y regreso de la política en el Perú." In *Política y antipolítica en el Perú*. Lima: DESCO, 2000.

Macera, P., and S. Forns. *Nueva Crónica del Perú del Siglo XX*. Illustrated by Miguel Vidal. Lima: Fondo Editorial del Congreso del Perú, 2000.

Maine, H. S. *Ancient Law; Its Connection with the Early History of Society and Its Relation to Modern Ideas*. London: Murray, 1924.

Maravall, J. A. *Culture of the Baroque: Analysis of a Historical Structure*. Minneapolis: University of Minnesota Press, 1986.

Matienzo, J. de *Gobierno del Perú*. Paris and Lima: Institut Francais d'etudes andines, 1967.

Matos Mar, J. *Las barriadas de Lima, 1957*. Lima: Instituto de Estudios Peruanos, 1977.

———. *Desborde popular y crisis del estado*. Series Perú Problema, 21. Lima: Instituto de Estudios Peruanos, 1984.

Mauss, M. "Techniques of the Body." *Economy and Society* 2 (1973): 70–88.

McManners, J. *Death and the Enlightenment: Changing Attitudes to Death among Christians and Unbelievers in Eighteenth-Century France*. Oxford: Clarendon, 1981.

Mehlman, J. *Revolution and Repetition: Marx/Hugo/Balzac*. Berkeley: University of California Press, 1977.

Mejías Álvarez, M. J. "Muerte regia en cuatro ciudades peruanas del barroco." *Anuario de Estudios Americanos* 49 (1992): 189–205.

Melville, H. *Moby Dick, or, The Whale*. New York: Penguin Books, 1992.

Memoria del Honorable Consejo Provincial de Lima, 1886–87. Alcalde de Lima, General César Canevaro, 1887.

El Mercurio Peruano (Lima), February 17, 1791. Folio 130.

Michelson, A. "Heterology and the Critique of Instrumental Reason." *October* 36 (1984): 111–27.

Moreyra y Paz Soldán, M., and G. Céspedes del Castillo, eds. *Virrreinato peruano. Documentos para su historia. Colección de cartas de Virreyes: Conde de la Monclava*. Vol. 1. Lima: Lumen, 1954.

Mumford, L. *The City in History: Its Origins, Its Transformations, and Its Prospects*. San Diego: Harcourt Brace Jovanovich, 1989.

Municipalidad Metropolitana de Lima. *La Ciudad Posible: Lima, Patrimonio Cultural de la Humanidad*. Edited by J. Ruiz de Somocurcio et al. Lima: Municipalidad Metropolitana de Lima, 1999.

———. "Lima... ensueño." Booklet. Lima: Municipalidad Metropolitana de Lima, 1996.

———. *Memoria*. Lima: Municipalidad Metropolitana de Lima, 1996.

———. *Memoria*. Lima: Municipalidad Metropolitana de Lima, 1997.

Murra, J. V. "La función del tejido en varios contextos sociales y políticos." In *Formaciones económicas y políticas del mundo andino*. Lima: Instituto de Estudios Peruanos, 1975.

Musgrave, E. "Memento Mori: The Function and Meaning of Breton Ossuaries 1450–50." In *The Changing Face of Death: Historical Accounts of Death and Disposal*, edited by P. Jupp and G. Howarth, 62–75. New York: St. Martin's Press, 1997.

The Nando Times. "Women in Nigerian Oil Standoff Threaten Nudity," July 14, 2002.

Oliart, P. "Alberto Fujimori: 'The Man Peru Needed?'" In *Shining and Other Paths*, edited by S. Stern, 411–25. Durham, NC: Duke University Press, 1998.

O'Phelan, S. *La gran rebelión en los Andes: De Túpac Amaru a Túpac Catari*. Cuzco: Centro de Estudios Regionales Andinos "Bartolomé de las Casas," 1995.

Orlove, B. "Sticks and Stones: Ritual Battles and Play in the Southern Peruvian Andes." In *Unruly Order: Violence, Power, and Cultural Identity in the High Provinces of Southern Peru*, edited by D. Poole, 133–64. Boulder, CO: Westview Press, 1994.

Ortega y Gasset, J. *Sobre la caza, los toros, y el toreo*. Madrid: Revista de Occidente en Alianza Editorial, 1986.

Ortiz de Zevallos, A., ed. *Lima a los 450 años*. Lima: Centro de Investigación de la Universidad del Pacífico, 1986.

Ortner, S. "Is Female to Male as Nature is to Culture?" *Feminist Studies* 1, no. 2 (1972): 5–31.

Osorio, A. "Inventing Lima: The Making of an Early Modern Colonial Capital, ca. 1540–ca. 1640." PhD diss., Department of History, SUNY Stony Brook, 2001.

Otero, G. A. *La vida social en el coloniaje. Esquema de la Historia del Alto Perú hoy Bolivia, de los siglos XVI, XVII, XVIII*. La Paz: Editorial Juventud, 1958.

Pacheco Vélez, C. "Esplendor barroco, larga decadencia y posible salvación de Lima." In *Lima a los 450 años*, edited by A. Ortiz de Zevallos, 137–81. Lima: Centro de Investigación de la Universidad del Pacífico, 1986.

———. *Memoria y utopía de la vieja Lima*. Lima: Centro de Investigación de la Universidad del Pacífico, 1985.

Patiño, V. M. *Vestidos, adornos, y vida social: Historia de la cultura material en la América equinoccial*. Vol. 4. Bogotá: Instituto Caro y Cuervo, 1992.

Phillips, A. "Introduction." In *A Philosophical Enquiry into the Origin of Our Ideas of the Sublime and the Beautiful*, by E. Burke. Oxford: Oxford University Press, 1990.

Picón Salas, M. *A Cultural History of Spanish America: From Conquest to Independence*. Berkeley: University of California Press, 1966.

"Plan Maestro Centro de Lima. Ordenanza No. 201." *Diario Oficial El Peruano* (Lima). Normas Legales, April 12, 1999.

Poole, D. *Vision, Race, and Modernity: A Visual Economy of the Andean Image World* Princeton, NJ: Princeton University Press, 1997.

Portocarrero, G. "Ajuste de cuentas. Las clases medias en el trabajo de TEMPO." In *Las clases medias: entre la pretensión y la incertidumbre*, edited by Portocarrero, G., 13–34. Lima: Taller de estudios de las mentalidades populares (TEMPO), Sur Casa de estudios del socialismo, and OXFAM, 1998.

———. "Los fantasmas de la clase media." *Hueso Húmero* 20 (1985): 65–88.

Povinelli, E. "Radical Worlds: The Anthropology of Incommensurability and Inconceivability." *Annual Review of Anthropology* 30 (2001): 319–34.

Protzel, J. "El paradigma del príncipe: El líder, la razón de Estado y los medios electrónicos." *Contratexto* 7 (1994): 203–23.

Pulgar Vidal, J. *Geografía del Perú: Las ocho regiones naturales del Perú*. Lima: Editorial Universo S.A.

Radcliffe-Brown, A. R. *Structure and Function in Primitive Society: Essays and Addresses*. New York: Free Press, 1965.

Rama, A. *The Lettered City*. Edited and translated by J. C. Chasteen. Durham, NC: Duke University Press, 1996.

Ramón, G. "Urbe y orden: Evidencias del reformismo borbónico en el tejido limeño." In *El Perú en el siglo XVIII: La Era Borbónica*, edited by S. O'Phelan, 295–324. Lima: Instituto Riva Agüero, Pontificia Universidad Católica del Perú, 1999.

Read, K. E. *The High Valley*. New York: Columbia University Press, 1965.

La República (Lima). "Ex-dirigentes politizados rompen el diálogo con la municipalidad y reinician violencia contra la ciudad y los vecinos," June 19, 1999.

———. "Madres obreras protestan desnudas en defensa de su estabilidad laboral," June 20, 1996.

———. "Piden que Congreso se pronuncie sobre liquidación de ESMLL," July 5, 1996.

———. "Protesta a lo Cicciolina," June 20, 1996.

Revilla, A. T., and J. Price. *La administración de la justicia informal: Posibilidades de integración*. Lima: Fundación M. J. Bustamante de la Fuente, 1992.

Ricketts, M., ed. *Lima, paseos por la ciudad y su historia*. Lima: Adobe Editores, 1999.

Riel-Salvatore, J., and G. Clark. "Grave Markers: Middle and Early Upper Paleolithic Burials and the Use of Chronotypology in Contemporary Paleolithic Research." *Current Anthropology* 42, no. 4 (2001): 449–79.

Rincón, C. "El universo neobarroco." In *Modernidad, mestizaje cultural, ethos barroco*, edited by B. Echeverría, 349–88. Mexico, D.F.: Universidad Nacional Autónoma de Mexico, 1994.

Riofrío, G. "Barriada y ciudad: Crisis de crecimiento y crisis actual." In *Lima a los 450 años*, 211-221. Lima: Centro de Investigación de la Universidad del Pacífico, 1986.

Ritzenthaler, R. "Anlu: A Women's Uprising in the British Cameroons." *African Studies* 19, no. 3 (1960): 151–56.

Roberts, H., ed. *Encyclopedia of Comparative Iconography*. Chicago: Fitzroy Dearborn, 1998.

Ronda, S. "Estrategias de legitimaciones y discursos: La utilización de las políticas de rehabilitación de los centros históricos." In *Desarrollo cultural y gestión en centros históricos*, edited by F. Carrión, 85–103. Quito: Facultad Latinoamericana de Ciencias Sociales, 2000.

Rospigliosi, F. *Montesinos y las fuerzas armadas: Cómo controló durante una década las instituciones militares*. Lima: Instituto de Estudios Peruanos, 2000.

———. "Un Presidente Combi." *Caretas* (Lima), October 26, 1995.

Rowe, Ann P., ed. *Costume and Identity in Highland Ecuador*. Seattle: University of Washington Press; Washington, DC: Textile Museum, 1998.

Rubin, G. "Traffic in Women: Notes on the 'Political Economy' of Sex." In *Toward an Anthropology of Women*, edited by R. Reiter, 157–210. New York: Monthly Review Press, 1975.

Salazar Bondy, S. *Lima la horrible*. Mexico: Ediciones Era, S.A., 1964.

Sarduy, S. *Barroco*. Buenos Aires: Editorial Sudamericana, 1974.

"Sentencia expedida por el visitador general del reino José Antonio Areche contra José Gabriel Túpac Amaru" In *Colección Documental del Bicentenario de la Revolución Emancipadora de Túpac Amaru*, vol. 3, edited by L. Durand Florez. Lima: Comisión Nacional del Bicentenario de la Rebelión Emancipadora de Túpac Amaru, 1981.

Simmons, O. "The Criollo Outlook in the Mestizo Culture of Coastal Peru." *American Anthropologist* 57, no. 1 (1955): 107–17.

Smith, W. R. *Lectures on the Religion of the Semites: The Fundamental Institutions*. New York: Macmillan, 1927.

Stein, W. *Dance in the Cemetery: José Carlos Mariátegui and the Lima Scandal of 1917*. With a foreword by G. Portocarrero. Lanham, MD: University Press of America, 1997.

Szeminski, J. "Why Kill the Spaniard? New Perspectives on Andean Insurrectionary Ideology in the 18th Century." In *Resistance, Rebellion, and Consciousness in the Andean Peasant World*, edited by S. Stern, 166–92. Madison: University of Wisconsin, 1987.

Tamayo Herrera, J. *La muerte en Lima, 1780–1990: Un ensayo de historia de las mentalidades desde la perspectiva regional*. Cuadernos de historia, XV. Lima: Universidad de Lima, Facultad de Ciencias Humanas, 1992.

Tanaka, M. *La dinámica de los actores regionales y el proceso de descentralización. ¿El despertar del letargo?* Documento de Trabajo 125. Lima: Instituto de Estudios Peruanos, 2002.

Taussig, M. *Defacement: Public Secrecy and the Labor of the Negative*. Stanford, CA: Stanford University Press, 1999.

———. "Transgression." In *Critical Terms for Religious Studies*, edited by M. Taylor, 349–64. Chicago: University of Chicago Press, 1998.

Toledo, F. de *Disposiciones gubernativas para el virreinato del Perú, 1569–1580*. 2 vols. Introduction by G. Lohmann Villena. Sevilla: Escuela de Estudios Hispano-Americanos, 1986.

Tibbets, A. "Mamas Fighting for Freedom in Kenya." *Africa Today* 41, no. 4 (1994): 27–49.

Turner, T. "The Social Skin." In *Not Work Alone*, by J. Cherfas and R. Lewin, 112–140. Beverly Hills, CA: Sage, 1980.

Turner, T. E., and L. S. Brownhill. "Why Women Are at War with Chevron: Nigerian Subsistence Struggles Against the International Oil Industry." Paper presented at the 56th Annual United Nations Department of Public Information/Non-Governmental Organization Conference "Human Security and Dignity: Fulfilling the Promise of the United Nations," New York, September 2003.

Unanue, H. "Discurso sobre el panteón que se está construyendo en el convento grande de San Francisco de esta capital." In *Obras científicas y literarias*, vol. 2. Lima: Consultoría y Equipamientos Médicos S.A. CEM, 1975.

———. "Idea general del reino del Perú y su sistema de gobierno." In *Obras científicas y literarias*, vol. 3. Lima: Consultoría y Equipamientos Médicos S.A. CEM, 1975.

United Nations Second Conference on Human Settlements (Habitat II). "The Habitat Agenda." Istanbul, 1996.

Velarde, H. "El neo-barroco en Lima." In *El barroco: Arte de conquista* Lima: Universidad de Lima, 1980.

Villarán, F. "El fenómeno Fujimori o la crisis de las ideas convencionales." *Revista Quehacer* 64 (1990): 30–35.

Wipper, A. "Kikuyu Women and the Harry Thuku Disturbances." *Africa: Journal of the International African Institute* 59, no. 3 (1989): 300–37.

———. "Riot and Rebellion among African Women: Three Examples of Women's Political Clout." In *Perspectives on Power: Women in Africa, Asia, and Latin America*, edited by J. F. O'Barr, 50–72. Durham, NC: Duke University Press Center for International Studies, 1982.

Wolfflin, H. *Renaissance and Baroque*. Ithaca, NY: Cornell University Press, 1964.

Wuffarden, L. E. "La ciudad y sus emblemas: imágenes del criollismo en el virreinato del Perú." In *Los siglos de oro en los virreinatos de América: 1550–1700*, 59–77. Madrid: Sociedad Estatal Para la Conmemoración de los Centenarios de Felipe II y Carlos V, 1999.

Zapata, A. "Notas para la historia de la muerte en el Perú. El debate sobre los cementerios en las páginas del Mercurio Peruano, 1792." In *Pretextos*, 97–102. Lima: DESCO, 1991.

Zolezzi Chocano, M. "El Centro de Lima. Sus vecinos y ocupantes actuales." In *Lima a los 450 años*, 197–210. Lima: Centro de Investigación de la Universidad del Pacífico, 1986.

Acknowledgments

Shortly after I arrived in Lima in the winter of 2006, I placed a call to two of my main research interlocutors in Lima, who appear in this book as Señora Roberta and Mr. Gómez. I called them on the same numbers I had used for years to contact them, eager to follow up on their labor claims against the city, which I knew had now reached the Inter-American Human Rights Court in Costa Rica. Both phone numbers, Señora Roberta's neighbor's and Mr. Gómez's cell phone, were no longer in service. That Señora Roberta's neighbor no longer had a working line wasn't a surprise since in Lima this is one of the first things one sacrifices when money is tight. But I briefly wondered if Mr. Gómez's phone being shut down signaled changes in his leadership role among the laid-off city workers that he represented or in their now ten-year-old labor struggle.

I showed up unannounced at Señora Roberta's home in Villa El Salvador, and her granddaughter said that she was, incidentally, at the funeral of one of her former coworkers who had just died of TB. A few days later when we met, we sat on her sofa and Señora Roberta spoke with urgency in her voice: "Remember Mr. Gómez?" Of course I did, I said, adding that I hadn't been able to reach him on his phone. "He's gone, señorita," she said. "He's left us." It took me a moment to realize this did not mean that Mr. Gómez had left for a better position elsewhere, perhaps betraying the workers in some way. Mr. Gómez had died. Coming home from a late night out with friends, he had fallen and hit his head on the front stairs of his home; at the public hospital emergency room, he had been left waiting his turn, and there in the hospital hallway, Señora Roberta said with tears collecting in her eyes, he passed away. *"Nos ha dejado mal, señorita,"* Señora Roberta said, before explaining that of all the leadership at her former union, it was Mr. Gómez whom she and her former coworkers most trusted. He was one of the few who believed that the workers who had cashed the severance packages offered by the city—like Señora Roberta had— still had a case. This showed the degree to which Señora Roberta had relied on Mr. Gómez, whose quiet, understated ways could occasionally be interpreted as aloofness. Señora Roberta's hopes were now pinned on a relatively expensive lawyer representing the workers who had not cashed their severance, the *"no cobradas,"* in Señora Roberta's parlance.

I was distraught to learn about Mr. Gómez's death at such a young age and in such inexcusable circumstances. Unfortunately, his wasn't the only death that had taken place since I began work on the project that is the basis of this book. In 2003–4, the lawyer and big-game hunter who appears in this book as Alfonso Forga and his wife of many years experienced sudden illness and died within months of each other. Ours was initially a chance encounter through a mutual friend, but for my research they generously opened their homes—both their house and, after they moved, their apartment in San Isidro—and made themselves available for long and fruitful conversations about hunting and religiosity, which were sparked by the numerous animal head trophies that they had so deliberately arranged on their living-room walls.

There is a unique dimension to the experience of loss brought about by the death of individuals who we meet and rely upon during fieldwork. Without their knowledge, they become a steady presence, an unrelenting company throughout the long, sometimes pleasurable, sometimes tortuous writing process. We revisit their words, over and over again, as we write and rewrite, edit and proofread the different versions of the narrative that finally becomes a book, often wondering, perhaps with some anxiety but also with anticipation, what they will think of our particular rendering of events. If there is any flicker of hope that we might one day be able to reciprocate their kindness, sharing with them the work they helped create is an important component of that hope and their death makes this impossible. I nevertheless begin these acknowledgments by thanking Orlando Estrada, Enrique Normand, and Rosa María Fort de Normand for their immense generosity, even though I am aware that with their deaths the circle of the gift has been broken. My sadness about their passing is compounded by the sense of loss and regret that usually accompanies an unreciprocated gift.

When we met in that winter of 2006, Señora Roberta was facing not just the loss of a good friend and of years of hard work in her efforts to claim justice for herself, but also the daunting task of reinvesting trust, resources, and hope in the new leadership and of rebuilding her case. I was pleased to find her, however, as strong and optimistic as ever despite the gigantic challenges she has to overcome every day as the still-unemployed head of a large household. In the early 1970s, she was one of the first occupants of the newly formed shantytown of Villa El Salvador after she and her children had been homeless for some time. As a single mother, she tried her hand at several kinds of employment, including domestic service, before she landed a relatively well-paid job as a street sweeper at the city-run cleaning agency in charge of sanitation in downtown Lima. Having already experienced several devastating turns of fate in her life, it wasn't until the mixed blessing of steady employment, however, that she experienced real anguish as her late-night shift forced her to spend the nights away from her young children, who stayed alone at home doing their best to look after one another. She would put them to bed and, mortified, leave the house to travel from one end of the city to the other, where she swept streets, avenues, and bridges until dawn, when she returned home to find them, to her relief, playing quietly on the floor and waiting for breakfast. Learning about Señora Roberta's life through my conversations with her taught me more about Lima's past and present history than a book like this could ever contain, and I will always be grateful to her for this.

If what I learned about Lima from Señora Roberta's stories offered perspectives that were radically different from my experience of the city, in important ways I rediscovered my old Lima through the eyes of the man I have in this book called Manolo Santillana. Manolo and I had been living abroad and were having a somewhat painful reencounter with our city when we met in 1999; some of our shared experiences that year made me realize that writing the story I wanted to tell about Lima would be an intellectual and emotional challenge since this would be an ethnography of my own home, a place about which I felt deep ambivalence. As an artist, writer, and fellow émigré, Manolo became a sort of alter ego, someone in whom I saw, with a strange mixture of familiarity and detachment, the same confusion I felt about the growing realization that, despite being physically back, no true return home was possible. In Manolo, I also saw a genuine desire to reconstitute the terms in which he would, from then on, relate to the city; and while I didn't know it then, the open, raw quality of his experiences in Lima that year became a kind of conduit for reflection on my own attempts at redefining my place there. I leave Señora Roberta's and Manolo's real names undisclosed, trusting that they will recognize themselves in these pages and hoping that they will accept my gratitude.

Many other people in Lima facilitated the work that has materialized in this book. Many thanks to Luis Poma and Hernán Valdez at *La República* for procurement of the photographs of ESMLL's protests and for their insightful views on the protests' meaning; to Luis Ordinola at Lima's municipal library for his help navigating the library and for the newspaper material he made available to me; to Rosa María Palacios for the written documents about Lima's "recuperation" campaign that she generously provided me; to my good friends Patricia Oliart and Chela Ubí, mines of ideas, resources, and information, which defined, in various ways, the direction that some of the interwoven stories took; to Philippe Gruenberg and Pablo Hare, the photographers who created the fantastic image on the cover of this book and generously gave me permission to use it; and to my immediate family—Salvador Gandolfo, Marcia López de Romaña, Carlos Gandolfo, Flavia Gandolfo, Christopher Parkman, and Ignacio Parkman Gandolfo—to whom I dedicate this book.

In the United States, I am indebted to Michael Taussig, my dissertation adviser and mentor at Columbia University. The ideas in this book, shaped over years of exchanges, were profoundly influenced by him, as were my passion for anthropology and my love for writing, which I learned from him is a labor of discipline as much as of creativity. Also at Columbia, I am grateful to my friend Todd Ramón Ochoa. Todd and I wrote our dissertations in tandem; in countless *almuerzos ejecutivos*, we hashed out problems and solutions for our texts in brief but productive exchanges that would set us up for another long afternoon of writing. He read every single page in my dissertation and provided insight about the content until the very end of the process of turning it into a book. My dissertation committee members—Rosalind Morris, Neni Panourgiá, Deborah Poole, and Anna Blume—were challenging and immensely insightful about my project in its different stages, understanding it, I sometimes felt, better than I did.

My heartfelt thanks also to Olga González Castañeda, Richard Kernaghan, Dora King, Juan Obarrio, Valeria Procupez, Carlos de la Puente, Karina Rosenborg, and Lisa Stefanoff, in whose brilliance and breadth of knowledge I always find inspiration for my work. The following friends were, at different times during the writing of this book, also important interlocutors: Jon Carter, Deirdre de la Cruz, Alejandra Leal, Stuart McLean, Paul Mendelsohn, Lisa Mitchell, Zoë Reiter, Emilio Spadola, and Drew Walker; my thanks to each of them for their intellectual generosity and support. To my colleagues at Wesleyan University—Besty Traube, Gina Ulysse, Anu Sharma, Doug Charles, Kehaulani Kauanui, Akos Ostor, Linc Keiser, Sarah Croucher, and Mary Jane Rubenstein—for so much sound advice, support, and encouragement as I began teaching full time at Wesleyan and, simultaneously, finished work on this book and tried my hand at motherhood. To Alexa Jay and Jessica French Smith, both students at Wesleyan who assisted me with the copyediting process; I thank them for their intelligent observations and wonderful eye for all the ways I have learned to misuse English prepositions. To Omolola Kuye, also a student at Wesleyan, for being a fantastic research assistant in the summer of 2007. To Kathleen Stewart and the other, anonymous reviewer of my manuscript for comments that were at once generous, encouraging, challenging, and clear, all of which I greatly appreciated. Finally, I am deeply grateful to my editors at the University of Chicago Press, T. David Brent, Laura J. Avey, and Erin C. DeWitt for supporting my book project wholeheartedly and for their endless willingness to assist me at every phase of the publication process, as well as to Lisa Wehrle and Bonny McLaughlin for their good work and immense patience in the copyediting and indexing of the book.

Illustration Credits

Photo of Lima boardwalk, 2007, by Flavia Gandolfo. 32

Photo of ESMLL protest in Lima, 1996, by Hernán Valdez, © Diario La Républica. 37

Photos of ESMLL protest in Lima, 1996, by Hernán Valdez, © Diario La Républica. 54

Engraved map of Lima, based on a plan by Juan Ramón Koninick and an engraving by Pedro Nolasco, first published in 1688 by Francisco de Echave y Assu. 74

Map of Amsterdam, from Lewis Mumford's *The City in History*. 74

Detail of map of El Cercado, Lima, 1970s, artist unknown. © Ediciones Peisa / Guía Inca de Lima Metropolitana. 98

Drawing, "Of the Inca. Punishment for (female) Adulterers," early 1600s, by Felipe Guamán Poma de Ayala. 203

Drawing, "*Corregidor* confronts the mayor for two eggs that he did not receive from *mitayo*," early 1600s, by Felipe Guamán Poma de Ayala. 203

Painting, *Castigo a los Soplones*, 1991, ADAPS (Asociación de Artistas Populares de Sarhua), from the Collection of Con/Vida—Popular Arts of the Americas, courtesy of Barbara Cervenka. Photo by Beatrice Kuenzi, courtesy of Olga González. 206

Drawing, "Lynching," 2000, by Miguel Vidal. © Fondo Editorial del Congreso de la República. 207

Index

Coliseo de Gallos, 139–40

"Colonial Arcadia," Sebastián Salazar Bondy on, 87–88, 217

COMACA (Comandantes, Mayores, Capitanes), 18

Co-Madres (El Salvador), 59

Comedores Populares, women's activism in Lima and, 60

El Comercio, 25, 27, 43, 144, 145

Communications Decency Act, U.S., 229n7

conos de Lima, 8

Constitutional Tribunal, and ESMLL, 115

Coordinadora Nacional de Viudas (CONAVIGUA) (Guatemala), 59

Corbin, Alain, 137–38

corpses in church burials. *See* Lima (city), relationship to the dead

corralones, and Lima's original grid plan, 87

corruption in church burials. *See* Lima (city), relationship to the dead

Corte de Policía (1786), 139

Costa Verde (Lima), 6, 7, 154; freeway, 155

Counterreformation: and the baroque, 69–70; and death, 134–35

criollo: class and desire for separation, 33–34; class and exodus from city center, xi, 8; class and "recuperation" of the city, 33–34; culture as essence of *lo limeño*, 69, 83; defined, 221n2, 222n3; tradition, 33, 63; women, representations of, 19. *See also* middle class

Cristóbal de Molina, 196

crying virgins, in Carmen de la Legua, 106

CUT (Central Única de Trabajadores) protest, 171–72

Cuzco (city), 7; rivalry with Lima, 72, 76; women, rank by clothing style, 198

Daily Nation (Nairobi), and protests by Kikuyu women, 56, 57

damero, 71

Damero de Pizarro, xi, 71

danse macabre, 135; 1917 at the Cementerio General, 129

dead, respect for the: Georges Bataille and, 38, 132–33; Lewis Mumford and, 132; Robert Hertz and, 93

death: and the aesthetic experience, 79; and *Anlu*, 58, 58; and baroque culture, 129, 131, 134–36; and bullfighting, 163–64; cemetery burials, 130–32; church

burials, 130–31, 135, 136–37, 230n5; early modern scientific attitudes toward, 130, 136; and Georges Bataille's notion of continuity, 133; and history of Lima's morgue, 143–45; José Tamayo and the secularization of, 145–46; nakedness and, 55–56, 58, 208, 210; Philippe Ariès and European attitudes toward, 129, 230n5; romantic attitudes toward, 129; as "social fact," 134, 140; and sovereignty, 174; state management of, 142, 143, 144; and taboo, 13, 93, 125, 133. *See also* Lima (city), relationship to the dead

de Beauvoir, Simone: on Hegel's dialectic of master and slave, 179, 180, 212; *The Second Sex*, 179

decency: Marisol de la Cadena and, 225n5; as marker of social class, 34; as marker of "whiteness," 225n5

de la Cadena, Marisol, 197, 198–99, 225n5

"desborde popular," José Matos Mar and, 8–9

Desborde popular y crisis del Estado (José Matos Mar), 113

Diallo, Amadou, 26

diary writing: and Arguedas, 215; and Malinowski, 216; and performance, xiv–xv, 220

Díaz, Suzy (Peruvian Cicciolina), 36

Diderot, Denis: *Encyclopédie*, 136

DINCOTE (Dirección Contra el Terrorismo), 22

Dirección de Salubridad Pública (1903), 144

Durán Montero, María Antonia, 218; and Lima's city wall, 227n17; study of 1613 census of "Indians," 86–87; study of Lima's *Libros de Cabildo*, 86

Durkheim, Émile: on the ambiguity of the sacred, 12; *The Elementary Forms of Religious Life*, 12, 192; on the gaze as contact, 192; and sacred/profane distinction, 11–13; and taboo and transgression in ritual, 13

Eames, Elizabeth: and Nigeria's Women's War (Ìjà Obìrin), 57, 177–78

Echave y Assú, Francisco: *La estrella de Lima convertida en Sol sobre sus tres coronas*, 227n18

Palacio de Justicia, 84, 99–100
Palacio Municipal, 84. *See also*
  Municipalidad de Lima building
Palma, Ricardo: *Tradiciones peruanas*, 84
Parado de Bellido, María, 186
Parque Salazar, reconstruction as Larco Mar
  mall, 47–48
Parque Universitario, 41
Pasaje Santa Rosa, 40
Paseo Colón, 99
Paseo de Aguas, 140
Paseo de la República, 99, 100
Paseo Militar, 140
Patiño, V. M.: and magical properties of
  Spanish clothing, 234n13
Peña Horadada, 7, 222n1
Peralta y Barnuevo, Pedro, 136
Père Lachaise Cemetery (Paris), 131
Perón, Evita, 236n50
Peru: 1980s and early 1990s economic and
  political crisis, 60, 156, 218, 224n38;
  1990s economic recovery, 1–2; state
  policies directed at women or family in
  1970s and 1980s, 60. *See also under*
  Fujimori, Alberto
El Peruano, Diario Oficial (Lima), 42
Peruvian Cicciolina (Suzy Díaz), 36
Philip II (king), 71, 77, 228n30
Phillips, Adam: on power and the sublime
  in Burke, 79–80
Picón Salas, Mariano, 70, 84, 227n21
pirañitas, 40
Plan Maestro, 29, 42, 69, 81
Plaza de Armas. *See* main square (Lima)
Plaza Mayor. *See* main square (Lima)
Plaza San Martín, 11, 14, 100–101
Plazoleta del Àngel de la Resurrección, 181
PNP (Peruvian National Police), 26, 150,
  157; and Andrade, 65; Emergency
  Squadron, 27
policía, 76–78; *baja*, 143; Cobo and, 77–78;
  Corte de Policía, under Viceroy Amat y
  Juniet, 139; definition of, 228n30; in
  Historia del Nuevo Mundo, 77–78; *Nuevo
  Reglamento de Policía* (1785), 138; and
  reducciones, 76; *Reglamento de Policía*
  (1769), 138; in Unanue's *Idea general del
  reino del Perú*, 139
pollera, 197, 199
Poole, Deborah, 198
Portal de Maravillas, 130

Portocarrero, Gonzalo: on desire for
  distance of middle class, 33, 34, 35; and
  "Fantasmas de la clase media," 223n12
Potosí, silver mine of, 86
Povinelli, Elizabeth: on "practice of
  commensuration," 82
Presidential Palace. *See* Palacio de Gobierno
  (Presidential Palace)
Price, J.: on "informal justice," 205
Priestly, Joseph, 231n28
prohibition. *See* taboo; transgression
public hygiene: in Latin America, 231n28.
  See also Lima (city), and public hygiene
pueblos jóvenes, 3. See also *barriadas*
La Punta (El Callao), 6, 7

qala, 200–201
qalakuna, 200, 201
querencia, 218–19
quincha, 149, 165

Radcliffe-Brown, A. R., 140
Rama, Ángel, 75
"recuperation" of Lima. *See under* Andrade,
  Alberto
reducciones, 76, 77, 192, 193
Reglamento de Policía (1769), 138
Reglamento General de Sanidad (1887), 143
relaciones de fiestas, 73
Relima: and ESMLL workers, 44, 168;
  working conditions at, 41
repartimientos, 234n15
La República (Lima), ix, 25, 46, 51, 178;
  Andrade's ad criticizing SITRAMUN in,
  43–44; report on street sweepers' protest,
  xii, 36–37, 101
retablo ayacuchano, 186
Revilla, A. T.: on "informal justice," 205
Ribeyro, Julio Ramón: "Los gallinazos sin
  plumas," 22, 23, 38
Rilke, Rainer Maria: *Duino Elegies*, 67
El Rímac (district of Lima), 156
Rímac River, 3, 7, 156
Rímac River boardwalk, 11
Rímac River valley, 2, 8
Riva Agüero, José de la: and Lima's baroque
  period, 84–85
rondas campesinas, 202, 235n38
Rospigliosi, Fernando, 19
Rouskaya, Norka, 129
Rowe, Ann P., 233n5